Cannon's Guide to Freshwater Fishing with Downriggers

by Tom Huggler

Cannon/S & K Products, Inc.
Muskegon, Michigan
Division of Armstrong International, Inc.

Library of Congress Cataloging in Publication Data

Huggler, Tom
    Cannon's Guide to Freshwater Fishing with Downriggers

ISBN 0-9616991-0-8

Copyright ©1986 by Cannon/S & K Products, Inc.
Division of Armstrong International, Inc.
All rights reserved.

Production of this publication was directed and
coordinated on behalf of
Cannon/S&K Products, Inc., by
Century Group, Inc., Traverse City, Michigan:

Project Director: Charles Janis
Editor: Daniel Rebant
Art Director: Daniel Hansel
Production Director: Donald McGlashen
Calligrapher: Mark Hawkins

Assisting Century Group was Thomas McConnell
Associates, also of Traverse City, Michigan:

Designer: Sandra Carden
Illustrator: Thomas McConnell
Production Assistant: Janet Mortensen

Other contributors included:

Color Separations: Alitho Graphics,
Traverse City, Michigan
Typesetting: North Country Typesetting,
Traverse City, Michigan
Printing & Binding: R.R. Donnelley & Sons Co.,
Chicago, Illinois
Cover Illustration by Don Ray, Springfield, Ohio

For several years, we at Cannon have contemplated the idea of publishing a book on downrigger fishing. To do it right, we knew it would take a tremendous amount of time and talent, including the research, the writing, the illustrating, and the many details of production.

Finding the writer was key. He would have to be one with high standards, knowledge of downrigger fishing and the willingness to do a vast amount of research – in short, a rather extraordinary person.

As you know, the writer we found was Tom Huggler. Once you read the book, I think you will agree that he met our requirements completely, and then some. The Tom Huggler byline is familiar to anyone who reads the better outdoor publications. He is the author of six books and hundreds of magazine articles. Tom is himself a skilled angler as well as a long-time advocate of downrigger fishing.

Tom's work on *Cannon's Guide to Freshwater Fishing with Downriggers* involved personal contact with nearly 100 expert downrigger fishermen throughout the United States and Canada. The effort entailed much travel, countless phone calls and meetings, and extensive photographic work, since many of the photos in the Guide are his, too. The project turned out to be most of a year's hard work for Tom; but we at Cannon find the finished product one that provides hours of pleasurable, informative reading. We think you will agree with our findings.

Another major contributor to the Guide is outdoor illustrator Don Ray, who supplied the cover illustration for the work. Don's true-to-life art has also adorned the covers of major fishing publications. We looked for the best illustrator we could find because we wanted the cover to reflect the contents. In other words, the quality you see on the outside reflects the quality you will find on the inside. (We might add that Don's commitment to accuracy involved personal underwater research and photography to render the king salmon on the cover as realistic as possible.)

Once you begin reading our Guide, you will notice that it is not all facts and how-to's. It is also filled with anecdotes out of the author's own experience or from that of the experts he consulted. As you read, you will no doubt find yourself informed and entertained at the same time. Many excellent photographs and drawings contribute to the book's educational and aesthetic value. In fact, we believe that Cannon's Guide will become *the* downrigger fishing manual for years to come.

Although this book is worthy of enshrinement on your shelf or coffee table, we prefer that it be used . . . over and over. That's why it's packed with useful information for beginners and seasoned charter-boat captains, and everyone in between. And that's why it discusses downriggers in the context of a total trolling system – rods and reels, lines and lures, electronics, temperature and even species of fish.

Yes, we're proud to have published the First Edition of *Cannon's Guide to Freshwater Fishing with Downriggers*. It is the finest, most authoritative work yet on downrigger fishing. Of course, we recognize that fishing techniques and downrigger products are subject to change (Cannon is in the forefront of such change); therefore, no book like this can stand "complete" or as "the ultimate reference" for long. For now, however, it's the best there is. It's a book to be learned from . . . to be enjoyed . . . but, most of all, to be *used*!

Ed Sutton
Vice President/Sales & Marketing

Mike Harris
Director of Promotion & Public Relations
Cannon/ S & K Products, Inc.
Division of Armstrong International, Inc.

Contents

Downriggers		10
Rods and Reels		20
Lures		28
Rigging		40
Temperature		60
Electronics		66
Trout		82
Salmon		98
Walleye and Bass		112
Pike and Muskie		126
Cooking		134

Downriggers

"The invention of the downrigger is no less important a discovery to sport fishing as the moldboard plow was to farming or the wheel was to transportation."

Evolution of the downrigger has resulted in a handsome, low-profile tool that is easy to use, safe, and deadly effective at putting lures in the strike zone and keeping them there.

The big lake is unsettled and fish are scattered. Large, post-storm rollers with creamy heads run over on each other. They cuff the boat bow with a wet smack. You've been on the lake since dawn, searching for salmon, but have yet to get that all-important first strike. Your electronic eye, the paper-driven graph, scratches out a sterile reading, as it has for miles. So far your trolling score is like a yawn-producing baseball game: no runs, no hits, no errors.

Maybe the seagulls know where the salmon are. Etched white against the blue sky, they hover nearby on the summer wind. A couple pinwheel to the heaving sea. Suddenly, you notice a bowed rod-tip jiggle, then snap-to like an uppercut punch. "Fish on!" someone yells. But when you get to the sprung rod, the line is disappointingly slack.

Check the graph. Magnum hooks show king salmon at 40 to 45 feet! Your lines are not there...yet. One buddy flips a portside downrigger switch. In seconds the lure drops from 20 feet to 42 feet. The other pal hits the switch on the starboard-side downrigger to raise the cannonball from 60 feet to 40 feet. While this is happening, you reset the tripped line and spear it back to 45 feet.

It's halfway there when the portside rod leaps to. Your buddy, right on top of the action, grabs this rod, now bucking like a rodeo bronc with a bur under the saddle. His yelp is answered by one to your right. Both friends are now swapping muscle with summer-charged king salmon.

It is your turn. You touch the electric switch to drop the lure a foot, then touch it again to raise it a little. The tantalizing flutter this action imparts to your orange spoon is too much for a king salmon that has been bird-dogging it. His savage strike releases the rod from its downrigger shackle, and the fight is on. Once, twice, three times, the line sizzles from your reel. You begin to gain some back just when the spool is showing bare.

Over the next 20 minutes you and your partners complain of aching arms from fighting these powerful salmon. Your stomach is sore from a rod butt jammed into it. Yet, one by one, the chrome-bright battlers come aboard. 18 pounds. 21 pounds. Then your brute, a 24-pounder who knows how to breakdance across the boat floor. You subdue

Why a Downrigger?

the trio, cooler them on ice, and prepare to trim the lines again.

There is no better feeling than fish in the box. Maybe the seagulls had something to do with this after all; you send them a two-fingered salute.

But did the seagulls actually cause that flurry of action? No. Was luck responsible? Although no true fishermen will ever rule out luck completely, probably not. What then? Answer: The correct lure at the right depth at an opportune time. To catch any kind of fish – Great Lakes salmon, West Coast river steelhead, Deep South reservoir striped bass, New York Finger Lakes lake trout, inland lake bass or pike – you have to put lures on the money.

Downriggers do the job. Quickly, efficiently, without fail. For generations fishermen have experimented with ways to get their lures to certain depths where they believed fish to be. They have used, and still use, every gimmick available – sinkers in all shapes, weights and sizes; lead-core and wire line; big-lipped crankbaits and other lures that dig down. These tactics work fairly well, but there are usually built-in problems. First, heavy weights and stiff lines can dampen the fighting action of your fish. Second, unless you are bumping bottom and know how deep bottom is, you may not have a clue where your lures are running.

Doesn't it make sense to have a device that will take lures to any depth you want – two feet or 200 feet – then hold them there? Wouldn't it be a tremendous advantage to always know where your lures are running?

Now comes the downrigger – one of the simplest, yet most effective tools ever discovered for fishermen *everywhere*. Through the use of heavy weights, downriggers take your lures to any depth of your choosing, then hold them there. A striking fish releases your monofilament from the weight and you play the fish on a "free" line, just as though there were no weight at all.

Imagine that! Now you can send lures to the bottom of that deep and remote Canadian lake where the big lakers lie. Now you can drop those big muskie plugs right under the boat in the prop boil where those St. Lawrence River giants want them. When largemouths are socking lures trolled just over the weedline at eight feet deep, a downrigger can put your bait on target. The same is true for stripers that haunt brush piles, for smallmouths that lie along a drowned riverbank at 23 feet, for northern pike just outside the river-mouth current at eight-feet deep, even for crappies moving over a five-foot-deep gravel bar to feed.

Downrigger fishing. It started in the Great Lakes only 20 years ago, yet today has changed the way hundreds of thousands of sportsmen fish from coast to coast. The invention of the downrigger is no less important a discovery to sport fishing as the moldboard plow was to farming or the wheel was to transportation.

Like the early myths that surrounded those inventions, misconceptions have attached themselves to downrigger fishing. One myth says that they are for deep-water angling only. Not true. Downriggers are effective for any depth *you choose*. In fact, no other fishing aid allows anglers to fish at a prescribed depth hour after hour, day after day.

Another myth says downriggers are for trolling only. False again. In slick-running rivers of the West Coast, as well as in the Great Lakes, some drift-boat fishermen are relying on downriggers to keep lures down in the fast current while they hover over steelhead lies. Walleye anglers backtrolling in powerful rivers below hydroelectric dams rely on downriggers for the same purpose. Innovative ice fishermen are even using downriggers to jig for whitefish and lake trout!

A third myth says downriggers are only for Great Lakes trout and salmon, that they have little or no value elsewhere. True, downriggers get top billing on the five Great Lakes, but primitive methods were used to run wires deep on the East Coast in the 1930s; and West Coast commercial fishermen have relied for years on a pulley-type system called the *hurdy-gurdy*, a crude form of the downrigger. Between the pages of this book, you will see that fishermen across the country are dispelling the myth that downriggers are only for big-water trout and salmon. The fact is, downriggers can be used to catch just about any kind of freshwater fish species, from largemouths to lake trout, from small-

Pinpoint-depth trolling allowed these fishermen to put their lures on the money. The result is a fine Lake Michigan Chinook salmon.

Cannon's new Digi-Troll II is the state-of-the-art downrigger for freshwater fishing.

mouths to steelhead, from river shad to Chinook salmon. The truth is, their value is limited only to an angler's imagination.

A fourth myth suggests that downriggers are useful only on big boats. As we have already seen – and as you will learn from this book – there is a downrigger for every size and type of boat. In fact, smaller boats often have the advantage of getting into tight or shallow areas to fish with downriggers where larger boats don't dare go.

Perhaps the biggest myth of all contends that downriggers are mechanical monsters, difficult to learn how to use. It is hard to imagine something simpler than a downrigger. A reel that may be four inches to 10 inches wide holds up to 600 feet of wire cable. Mounted to a bracket – which, in turn, is mounted to the side or back of a boat – the reel lies along the same plane as a boom or arm. The boom extends over the boat for a distance of 12 inches to several feet. It carries the cable to the end of the boom where a small pulley feeds it to the lake or river.

At the end of the cable is a weight of three to 15 pounds. Usually the weight is shaped like a cannonball, but it might look like a foot-long submarine or even resemble the crude outline of a fish. The weight is attached to the cable by way of a heavy-duty swivel and snap. Somewhere on the weight itself or attached to the cable just above is a line release. It may be a pinch-pad type, doughnut-shaped or other pressure-type device that holds the fishing line until a strike breaks it free. The angler's lure trails behind the release at any distance he or she desires – one foot to 100 or more feet.

A hand crank on the reel itself (or mounting bracket) allows the fisherman to reel in or to release more cable. Such models are usually called "manual" downriggers, and they are not very expensive. Cannon's *Easi-Troll* is a popular compact manual that retails for about $120. An even lighter-weight manual is the *Econo-Rigger*, selling for around $100. Both downriggers can be fitted with an optional C-clamp for temporary mounting to your canoe, johnboat, rowboat or rental boat. When you're done fishing, put the downrigger back in the car trunk or the backpack. Some fishermen permanently mount downriggers to their boats (we'll explain how in the next chapter). Others like the portability of these exciting fishing aids.

Two full-sized manuals are offered by Cannon for larger boats and more permanent use. These are the *Uni-Troll 6 II* and *UT Marlin*, retailing at about $180 and $190 respectively.

Fishermen who spend a lot of time on the water often choose Cannon "electric" downriggers. They operate just as simply as manual downriggers but eliminate hand cranking and save time when changing lures. Cannon makes a compact unit, the *Mini-Mag*, and two full-sized units, the *Magnum 10A II* and the *Digi-Troll II Marlin*. Prices here range from about $180 for the *Mini-Mag* to around $480 for the top-of-the-line computerized *Digi-Troll II Marlin*. Various boom lengths are available for all Cannon downriggers.

Cannon has been in the business of making downriggers only since 1980, yet already Cannon downriggers are the number one seller among a dozen manufacturers. The reason is twofold: Besides offering a superior product line of dependable, durable downriggers, Cannon is in the forefront of product innovation. Cannon makes the world's only electric downrigger with computerized control. The *Digi-Troll*, *Digi-Troll II* and now the *Digi-Troll II Marlin* automatically raise and lower lures at timed intervals; Digi-Troll downriggers also have a built-in memory. If you caught a fish at 57 feet deep, for example, the Digi-Troll will return your lure to that exact depth within seconds. Just push the keypad button.

Cannon's new Marlin Series downriggers, although designed for saltwater fishermen who demand anti-corrosion features, are fast catching on with freshwater anglers, too. The company even makes a kit that allows Marlin and Mag 10A owners to add Digi-Troll options.

Other fishing innovations will continue to come from Cannon. Just now making their debut are new temperature and trolling-speed indicators that measure these variables at the downrigger weight. Cannon's new surface agitator, the *Excitor*, makes flatline trolling come alive by imparting new action to lures. In the future, look for downriggers and weights to take on new shapes and styles.

Why a Downrigger?

Power options other than muscle power and batteries are forthcoming as are a host of new fishing aids.

But why the downrigger, you ask? Well, catching fish adds to fishing fun, and downriggers are no longer a luxury – indeed, they have become standard to the sport of freshwater fishing.

Are downriggers for you, then, even though the tried-and-true tactics may still work?

Yes, but only if you want to become an even better fisherman.

How to Mount Downriggers

A built-in rod holder comes with all Cannon downriggers. It is especially handy on portable units, which can be fished from canoes, johnboats and cartoppers.

Working and living space. In our daily lives we confront it and grapple with it. Somehow, we learn to work around and live within its limitations. From the office desk to the kitchen cupboard, from the sock drawer in the upstairs bedroom to the cockpit of our automobile, we are always trying to make efficient use of working and living space.

Nowhere is the wise use of a limited amount of space more critical than in a fishing boat. You may spend up to hundreds of hours per angling season in an area within an arm's reach of your steering wheel. Even if your fishing time is reduced to the annual family vacation at Lake Wherever, you will appreciate having a place for rods, lures, gas can, depth finder, net, cooler and downriggers. No one has a patent on how to squeeze the maximum amount of efficiency from the space on your fishing boat (after all, every boat has its own special design). Even so, throughout this publication, we will offer plenty of suggestions for you to consider.

Let's start with downriggers and their placement. In a recent survey of nearly 100 veteran freshwater fishermen throughout the United States and Canada, I asked the question: "What special information should a book on freshwater fishing with downriggers include?" "Explaining to readers where to place downriggers on their boats" was the response mentioned most often.

It is easy to see why. Buying a downrigger is more than a dollar investment. It is a commitment to a new and exciting way to fish. What better way to realize the full value of that investment than making sure you have mounted these innovative tools at the right spots on your boat? And where are the right spots? Consider these five points in your decision:

1. Easy access to rods, reels and downriggers for you and other anglers aboard your boat.
2. The creation of key pockets or "open" areas between downriggers for landing fish.
3. Location in relation to engine housing and propeller as well as lower inboard units.
4. Your complete rigging program. In other words, how can you best place downriggers so that they don't tangle with themselves and other lines?
5. Safety and ease of operation.

Because there are nearly as many ways to mount downriggers as there are boats, most manufacturers offer a host of mounting options. There is not a fishing boat made that cannot accept a downrigger. The key to proper placement is knowing all the options available, then choosing the downriggers that suit your own fishing program and make the best use of your boat's design.

Small Boats: One or Two Downriggers

The simplest form of mount is the C-clamp or portable mount. It may be permanently attached to the downrigger itself, or it can be a special aluminum sliding mount with a plastic knob and heavy-duty coarse-thread screw. Such is Cannon's *Clamp Mount,* designed for use with its Econo-Rigger, Easi-Troll and Mini-Mag models. Simply screw the mount anywhere you please on your boat, then slide the downrigger unit into the mount. You can leave the mount permanently on your boat or remove it, along with the downrigger, with a twist of the knob.

The Clamp Mount is popular with fishermen using small boats, such as cartoppers, johnboats and canoes. It comes in handy when you must rent a boat, and it is light enough and small enough to carry on an airplane or in a backpack for those remote fishing trips to wilderness lakes.

The ideal place to temporarily mount such a small unit is on the side of the boat, where you're likely to sit while running the motor. The standard 18-inch boom on Cannon manual downriggers is long enough to extend the cable and weight away from the boat – far enough to avoid tangling with a second line, perhaps off the stern, and with the propeller itself. Be careful, however, not to mount the downrigger too far forward from the boat rear since a sharp turn could catch the cable in the propeller. As a general rule-of-thumb, locate side-mount downriggers (also called "out-downriggers" or "out-downs" when thus mounted to the boat side) no farther than one-fourth the length of the boat from the stern.

In other words, on a 16-foot boat, the downrigger should be no farther than four feet from the stern. Beam width on the boat

Downrigger Placement

Forward placement from stern not to exceed ¼ of boat length

Long boom widens trolling alley, plus spreads lure to reduce tangle

Swivel mount recommended for outdowns

and boom length on the downrigger, however, can increase or decrease this suggested distance.

When I began fishing with downriggers from a 16-foot aluminum boat about 10 years ago, most of today's varied mounting options hadn't yet made it to the drawing board. So my friends and I simply bolted our downriggers to the ends of a 2-inch x 8-inch board, which we then C-clamped or bolted to the gunnels of our boats. The practice is still popular today because it is inexpensive and allows for quick removal if you want to use the boat for water skiing or other purposes besides fishing. Another suggestion is to screw lag bolts through the board, then drop them into the oarlocks. When choosing a mounting board, select wolmanized lumber or coat an untreated board with a good marine varnish. Best locations to place the board include across the stern or in front of the driver's seat.

You can mount your downriggers to the board with either a Clamp Mount or an *Econo Base Plate* (same mount without the set screw – simply bolt it to the wood). For stern-end mounting, consider positioning your downriggers at right angles to the board so that they can be run directly off the stern. When mounting in front of the driver's seat, you will have to mount the downriggers so that they can be run off the boat sides.

Be careful, though, not to extend them too far from the boat or they may collide with docks, gasoline pumps, and anything else that gets in the way. To avoid such problems, one option is to use Cannon's *Uni-Swivel Mount.* Its five-point locking feature lets you return the boom to the boat when the downrigger is not in use.

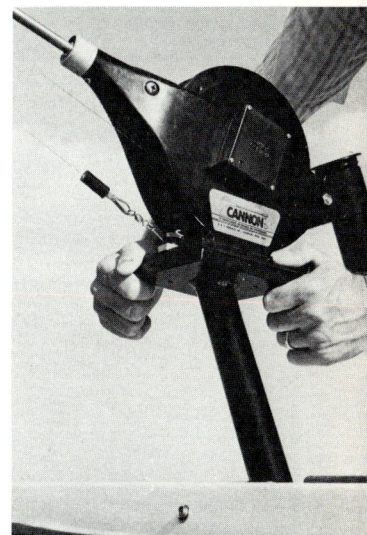

Cannon's Gimbal Mount allows for quick, easy placement of downriggers in recessed rod holders.

How to Mount Downriggers

Medium-Sized Boats: Two to Four Downriggers

Cannon's Clamp Mount base makes three low-cost models (Econo-Rigger, Easi-Troll and Mini-Mag) truly portable. A plastic knob and set screw allows quick mounting to gunnel or transom of your boat. When the fishing day is over, simply slide the downrigger from the base or remove the base, too, with a twist of the knob.

There are many mounting options available for boats from 16 to 24 feet long. Again, keep in mind the five points outlined earlier. Remember, too, that most stern-mounted downriggers feature short booms (18 inches) while corner and out-down models usually have booms of 42 inches or 66 inches. Not only do the longer booms reduce the chance for tangle with other downriggers set closer to the boat, but they also increase the width of the overall trolling alley. More fish are then likely to see your lure offerings, and that can result in more tails sticking out of your cooler. (Detailed rigging tips are offered throughout this publication.)

To repeat, one of the simplest ways to mount up to four downriggers is with a 2-inch x 8-inch mounting board across the stern. Simply bolt the board to the deck on your boat. If the boat has a guard rail, then use U-brackets to clamp the board to the rail. A good tip is to add Cannon's *Universal Deck Plates* to the board at each downrigger location. The Universal Deck Plate is drilled and tapped to fit most major downriggers. Made from a solid block of aluminum, it is especially recommended for safely securing downriggers with long booms.

Most trollers like to mount and operate their downriggers from a waist-high position. On low-profile bass boats or other craft with high railings, you've got a real problem. The answer lies in securing downriggers to a raised platform such as a plank of wood. Cannon makes pedestals in three heights — 4-3/4 inches, 6 inches, and 12 inches — to position the platform at a comfortable level. By installing a mounting plate for each pedestal, you can quickly add or remove the pedestals with the use of four locking screws.

The pedestals are ideal for flat stern decks. For curved ones, you may have to add support blocks of wood at each end. Whether or not you rely on pedestals or permanently mount the board to your boat, you will need three-point support – at each end plus in the middle – by way of screws, bolts or fasteners.

An alternative to the board itself is Cannon's *Rigger-Mount*, a handsome, all-aluminum mounting board that is 90 inches long and that comes complete with four deck plates. An attractive feature of the Rigger-Mount is that you can slide the deck plates to any location you wish, then lock them into place with permanent bolts or set screws (sets of 16 each come with the Rigger-Mount System). You can then attach either a stationary *Base* or *Swivel Base*. If the aluminum board is too long, you can cut it to desired length with a hacksaw or saber saw with hacksaw blade. Be sure to smooth the finished cut with a file or sanding disk on your electric drill.

Stern-end mounting boards, whether aluminum or wood, allow you to place two, three or even four downriggers. Swivel Base mounts, along with varying boom lengths, permit a wide range of stern- and out-downrigger mounting options. Just remember to keep your work area uncluttered and plan for pockets to net fish. Know, too, that when choosing downriggers with 42-inch or longer booms, Swivel Bases are most helpful for swinging booms away from potential objects of collision. For safety's sake, do not allow the mounting board to extend beyond the side of your boat.

Two other mounting options deserve mention. Many boats feature rod holders recessed into gunnel or transom decks. Cannon's *Gimbal Mount*, a 12-inch long aluminum tube mounted to a *Cannon Deck Plate*, is ideal for making full use of those rod holders. Simply add a downrigger to the mount and drop the tube into the available rod holder. Since all Cannon downriggers feature built-in rod holders, you're ready for action in seconds. The other mounting option is the *Rail/Side Mount*. It allows you to fit a downrigger to a side rail on your boat when mounting to the gunnel is not practical.

Some fishermen opt for permanent mounting of downriggers to boat decks, using a standard stationary Base or Swivel Base – both fit all full-sized Cannon downriggers. Mounting options are keyed to the thickness of the deck itself. For those that are 1/4-inch, use four Cannon 1/4-20 x 4-inch Trus Head Bolts and Wellnuts. Simply use the Base as a template to mark location, then drill four 1/2-inch holes. Tighten bolts so Wellnuts are firmly compressed.

To avoid deflection when decks are thinner than 1/4-inch, first mount a Cannon Deck Plate to the boat deck, then attach the

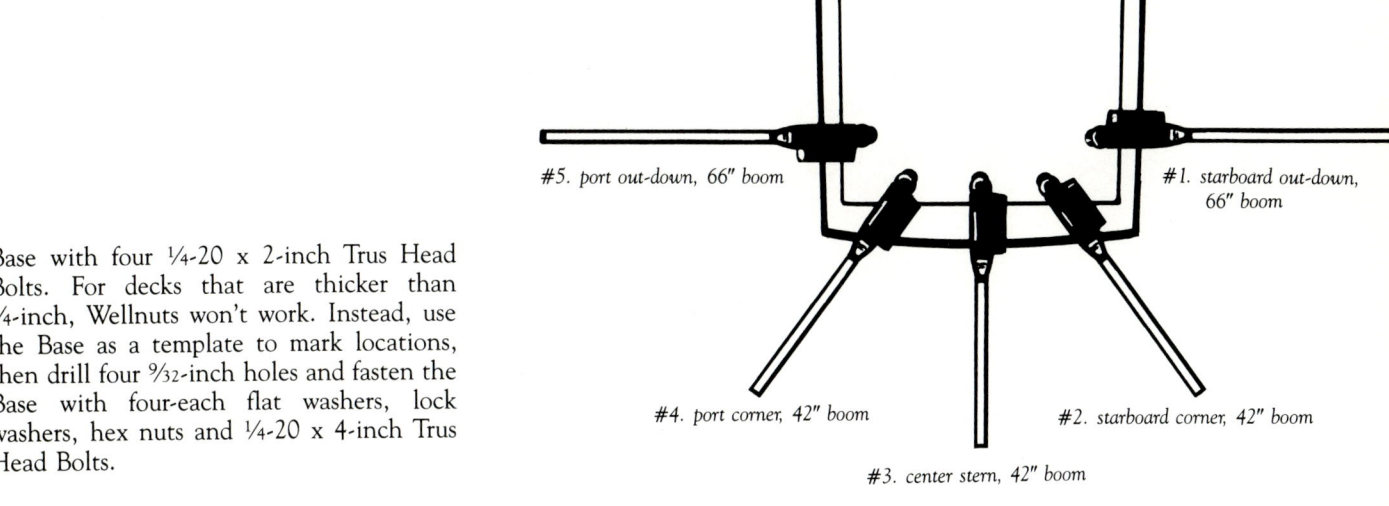

#5. port out-down, 66" boom

#1. starboard out-down, 66" boom

#4. port corner, 42" boom

#2. starboard corner, 42" boom

#3. center stern, 42" boom

Downrigger placement on Jim Beyer's boat

Base with four ¼-20 x 2-inch Trus Head Bolts. For decks that are thicker than ¼-inch, Wellnuts won't work. Instead, use the Base as a template to mark locations, then drill four 9/32-inch holes and fasten the Base with four-each flat washers, lock washers, hex nuts and ¼-20 x 4-inch Trus Head Bolts.

Large Boats: Five or More Downriggers

You can fine-tune a trolling program on a boat that is 24 feet or longer to accommodate five or six downriggers. Boats with beams of 10 or 12 feet usually offer plenty of working space and mounting options. Some trollers mate two Cannon Rigger-Mount boards, then cut one to length. Others make use of Gimbal or Rail/Side mounts to maximize sidewall space. Coupled with other trolling options such as stacking systems, outriggers, planer boards and flatlines, it is possible to run a dozen or more lines – when the number of fishermen aboard make such rigging legal.

Most trollers who rely on multiple downriggers number their units from left to right when standing in the boat and facing the stern. Thus, a starboard (left side from this position) out-downrigger would be Number One. The starboard corner unit would be Number Two; stern-end models, Three and Four; the port-side corner downrigger, Number 5; and the port-side out-down, Number 6. When running two rods off the same downrigger (a system called "stacking"), a good tip is to number the rods themselves in a corresponding fashion.

Besides the number of rods, exact placement of downriggers also depends upon the trolling tactics you expect to use and the species of fish you are seeking. (Later in this publication, we will cover special tactics for all freshwater gamefish.) One point to keep in mind early on, however, is that when trolling for Great Lakes trout and salmon, corner downriggers often outfish those placed elsewhere. Many big-water fishermen have therefore learned to mount stern-end downriggers as closely as possible to corner units.

Jim Beyers, a Cannon field tester and charter-boat captain from New Baltimore, Michigan, is one such veteran. Beyers skippers a 27-foot Sportcraft on Lakes Erie, Huron and St. Clair. Years ago, he custom-fitted a downrigger mounting board of tube iron to go across the 10-foot-wide stern of his boat, *Fishin' Machine*. Jim runs five Cannon Digi-Troll downriggers. Number 1 and 5 are corner-set out-down models with 66-inch booms. Numbers 2 and 4 are mounted on the inside corners, and the 42-inch booms angle to the outside at a 45-degree position. The Number 3 downrigger also features a 42-inch boom, but it extends straight out over the inboard/outboard lower unit.

When I fished with Beyers for Lake Erie walleyes, typical rigging involved shallow-depth settings on the out-downs, and moderate depths on the two inside corner setups. The center stern unit was the deepest. Beyers' placement of his downriggers and corresponding V-shaped rigging method (see Chapter 4 for a diagram) gives him an effective, tangle-free trolling program.

Wise use of available space on your boat begins with thoughtful mounting of the downriggers. Common sense often dictates where everything else goes. A cooler, for example, might double as a seat, or perhaps it can go over the boat stern via special mounting brackets. The likely place for electronics is on or around the dashboard, although some downrigger fishermen like to have trolling speed indicators, pH meters and temperature gauges near the stern-end work area. A good place for your net is in an unused rod holder. Lures can be categorized according to size, color or use. In upcoming chapters, we'll have plenty of suggestions for storing them and all other equipment.

Working and living space. On a trolling boat, maximum usage adds to fishing fun. It can also help catch more fish.

Numbering downriggers and/or rod holders is a good idea when designing a total rigging program. These Magnum 10A downriggers are mounted to Cannon's Swivel Base, which allows five-point setting plus boom return to boat.

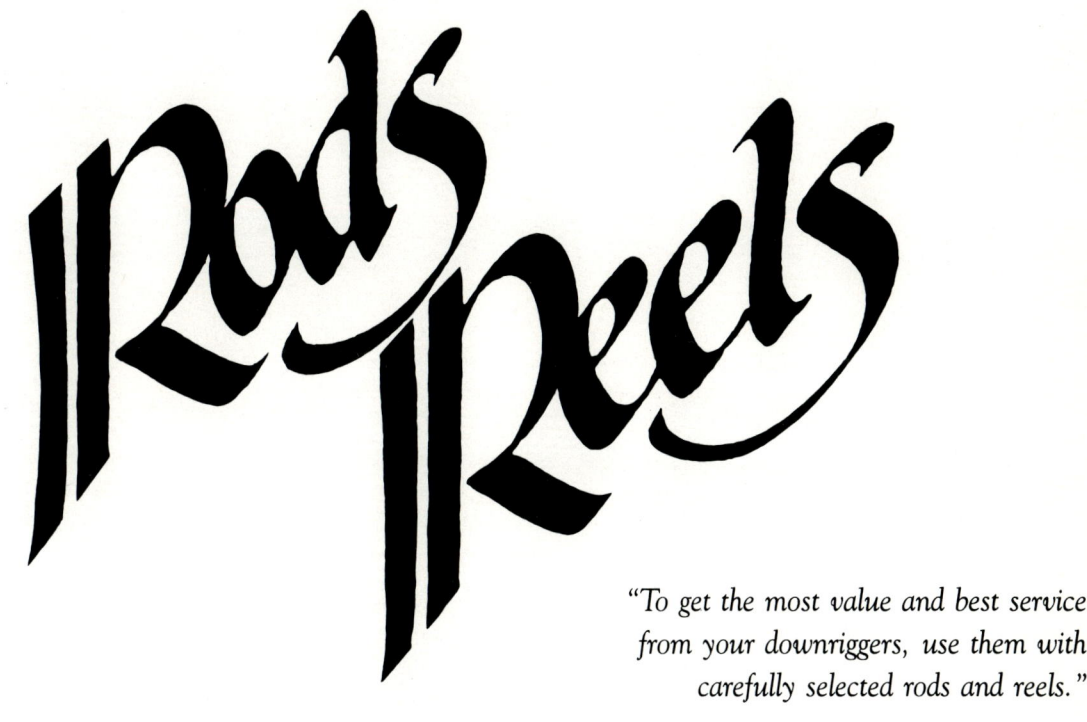

"To get the most value and best service from your downriggers, use them with carefully selected rods and reels."

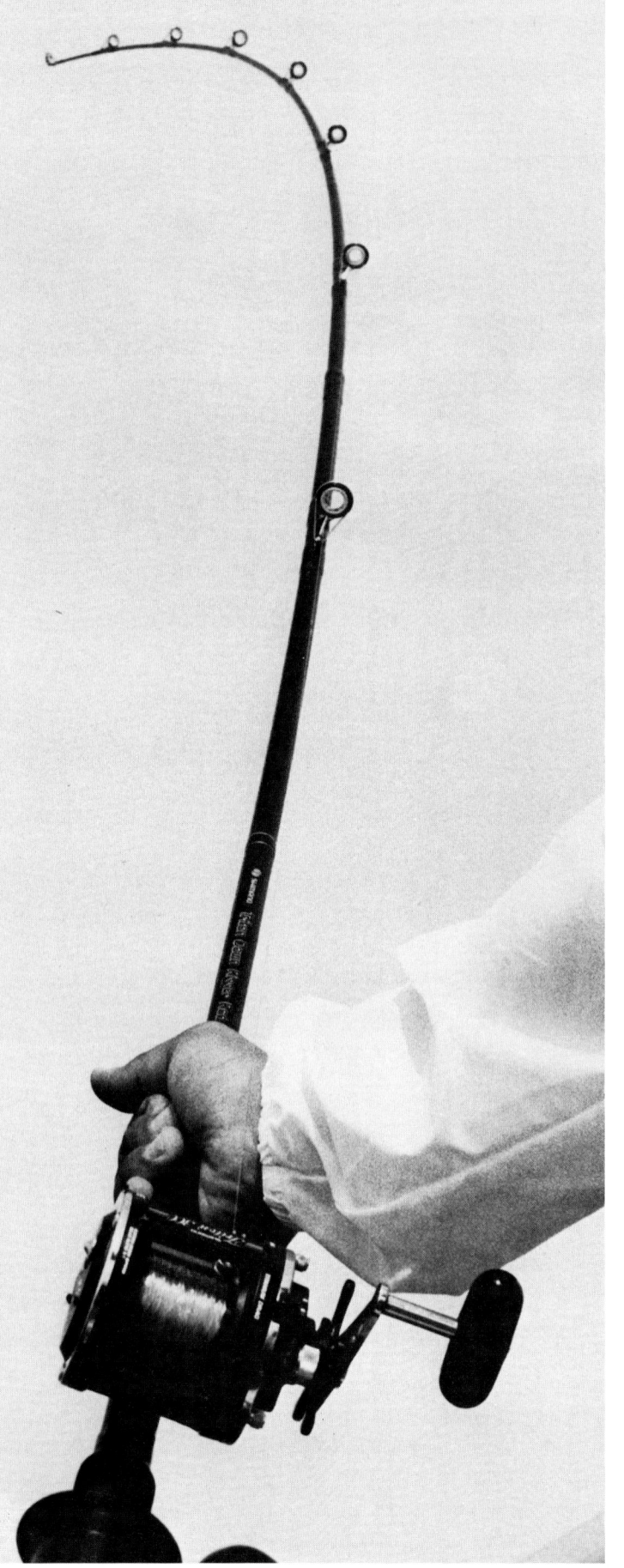

The large number of guides and medium-action of this Shimano rod produce proper bend for downrigger fishing. Note heavy-duty, level-wind reel with star drag, too.

Sometimes technology gets ahead of itself. Twenty years ago, when downriggers were just beginning to make the trolling scene, there were no rods and few reels suitable for the new sport. Fishermen soon learned that their spinning rods were too short or too limber, that they were woefully lacking in the number of guides, and that they wouldn't fit into downrigger rod holders. Reels simply couldn't hold enough line. Rarely did they have anti-reverse features or smooth, strong drags.

Some of the pioneer downrigger fishermen turned to saltwater equipment. But they found the 12-foot surf rods to be too long and the jigging and trolling rods to be stiff as stove pokers. On the other hand, the big level-wind reels used for ocean fishing had merit. Manufacturers began to tailor the reels to Great Lakes fishing purposes, then mated them to specialty rods.

Even so, many of these early attempts at fine-tuning were clumsy at best. I well remember one major manufacturer that brought out its new "Downrigger Rod" amid an avalanche of advertising hype. Apparently no one had harnessed this much-heralded rod to a downrigger because the rod was so stiff that it was impossible to bend into a proper arc. (It would have made a great pool cue, though.) Realizing its mistake, the company brought out a new downrigger rod the next year – a much more limber rod.

It was a fine rod for spring cohos, but the first fall-charged spawning Chinook I hooked with it snapped the rod like an oversized toothpick.

In the continuing evolution of downrigger rods and reels, where are we now? Answer: Much farther down the road with some distance yet to travel. Several manufacturers now produce quality downrigger rods and reels. *Competition* is the best word that consumers can hear because they get to choose among top-flight equipment at an affordable price. Some companies have even begun to offer choices within their own product lines.

Variety – different lengths and weights of rods and sizes of reels – is fast becoming the norm. This is good news, too, for those fishermen who realize that downrigger

What to Look for in a Downrigger Rod

trolling is an exciting way to catch other freshwater species besides trout and salmon.

What to Look for in a Downrigger Rod

The time to find out if you have chosen the right rod is not when you are swapping muscle with a crazed striped bass or Skamania steelhead. When you leave the tackle shop or fishing and boating show – rod tucked under your arm – how can you be reasonably certain that you have bought good equipment?

"The most important feature to look for in a downrigger rod is the action," said Mike Harris, director of Cannon field test operations. Harris should know. He has over 20 years of experience fishing the Great Lakes and holds captain's licenses in Michigan and Ohio waters. Further, he has fished with downriggers throughout the U.S.

"A medium-action rod is best overall," Harris explained, "because it will handle most fighting fish. A medium-light action rod might be fine for king salmon in spring, but when those fish come back to spawn in fall, they will have doubled in weight. Then, medium-heavy is more appropriate. But a fisherman buying one rod can cover all the bases if he just sticks to a general medium-action pole."

How can the consumer know what he is buying? "There is no standard in the industry," Harris said, "so fishermen have to go by the manufacturer's recommendations on the rod. Most people shake the rod to see what it will do, but shaking it will teach them nothing about its action."

Instead, Harris suggests that the angler bend the rod to see if it will produce a parabola (a C shape). The best way to do that is with line strung through the guides. A second person can put a load on the rod by pulling the line while you hold the rod. This will also determine if the rod has enough guides. While the rod is in a parabola, if line touches the blank (the rod itself) at any point, there are not enough guides.

Most downrigger rods for trout, salmon and striped bass fishing are 7½ to 9½ feet long and contain from nine to 12 guides. Shorter rods are more popular among fishermen seeking walleye, largemouth and

The Downrigger Rod Buyer's Guide

Mike Harris and I polled the nation's rodmakers to see what was available in terms of downrigger rods. If you are in the market for one, use this table as a guide for comparing features and "ballpark" prices:

Manufacturer/Model No.	Length	Sections	Guides	Line Strength	Price
Childre & Sons TSD-4-286	8'6"	2	8	12-25 lbs.	$30
Childre & Sons TSD-1-29	9'	2		10-20 lbs.	$30
Berkely GF92-76-DR	7'6"	2	9	12-30 lbs.	$50
Berkely GF92-80-DR	8'	2	10	12-30 lbs.	$50
Berkely GF92-86-DR	8'6"	2	11	12-30 lbs.	$50
Berkely GF94-76-DR*	7'6"	2	9	12-30 lbs.	$50
Berkely GF94-80-DR*	8'	2	10	12-30 lbs.	$50
Berkely GF94-86-DR*	8'6"	2	11	12-30 lbs.	$50
Zebco 4365	8'	2	9	8-20 lbs.	$25
Zebco 4394	7'	1		12-30 lbs.	$21
Zebco 4396	7'9"	1		15-40 lbs.	$21
Shimano Triton TDR-1802	8'	2	10	8-17 lbs.	$20
Shimano Triton TDR-1803	8'	2		12-25 lbs.	$20
Shimano Triton TDR-2802*	8'	2		8-17 lbs.	$20
Shimano Triton TDR-2803*	8'	2		12-25 lbs.	$20
Fenwick (Graphite Riggerstik) MFS86*	8'6"			8-20 lbs.	$90
Fenwick MFS86-C	8'6"			8-20 lbs.	$90
Fenwick MDR90*	9'			10-25 lbs.	$90
Fenwick MDR90-C	9'			10-25 lbs.	$90
Fenwick (Fiberglass Riggerstik) DR76*	7'6"			6-17 lbs.	$80
Fenwick DR76-C	7'6"			6-17 lbs.	$80
Fenwick DR82*	8'2"			8-20 lbs.	$80
Fenwick DR82-C	8'2"			8-20 lbs.	$80
Eagle Claw SF400	8'6"	2	9	12-20 lbs.	$31
Eagle Claw PL 501	7'6"	2	7	15-30 lbs.	$28
Eagle Claw DG502	8'6"	2	8	12-20 lbs.	$42
Browning 932983	8'3"	2	9	6-15 lbs.	
Browning G12960	6'	1	7	8-17 lbs.	$40
Browning G12965	6'6"	2	7	8-17 lbs.	$40
Browning G12970	7'	2	7	8-17 lbs.	$40
Browning M12960	6'	1	7	8-17 lbs.	$30
Browning M12965	6'6"	1	7	8-17 lbs.	$30
Browning M12970	7'	1	7	8-17 lbs.	$30
Ryobi C983M	8'3"	2			$35
Daiwa KG784	7'6"	2	10	12-20 lbs.	$40
Daiwa KG785	8'	2	11	12-20 lbs.	$40
Daiwa KG786	8'6"	2	11	12-20 lbs.	$40
Daiwa SK784	7'6"	2	8	12-20 lbs.	$30
Daiwa SK785	8'	2	9	12-20 lbs.	$30
Daiwa SK786	8'6"	2	10	12-20 lbs.	$30
Shakespeare BWB1101	9'	2	10		
Shakespeare BWD1101	8'3"	2	10		
Shakespeare BWD1120	7'	2			$45
Shakespeare BWD1131	7'	1			$45
Shakespeare BWD2200	8'	2		12-30 lbs.	
Shakespeare CA1350	8'6"	2			$45
Shakespeare CA1350	9'	2			$45
Kunnan 6380ML	8'	2			$25
Kunnan 6380SML	8'	2			$25
Kunnan 6386ML	8'6"	2			$49
Kunnan 6386SML	9'6"	2			$49
Garcia XC86M 12360	8'6"	2		10-25 lbs.	
Garcia XS86M 13392	8'6"	2		10-25 lbs.	

*Indicates a spinning rod

smallmouth bass, and other warmwater species. Because downrigger rods are not designed for casting, flipping or jigging, rod length is a personal choice. So are weight and rod composition. An all-graphite rod, for example, will have a smaller diameter than one made of fiberglass, plus graphite tends to have a tighter action than glass. The trade-off for these features, if you like graphite, is price. Graphite costs more than a fiberglass or composite rod.

What else besides action and number of guides should the wise rod buyer look for? Proper butt-length or handle, according to Harris, is also important. The butt length should be long enough so that the reel will not bottom out when the rod is placed in a holder. Yet it should not be so long that it is uncomfortable to hold – that it jams tightly into the stomach – when the angler has to fight a big fish for 20 minutes or more. The foregrip (the tapered handle ahead of the reel) should be comfortable, too.

Most rod makers produce handles of cork, Hypalon or other synthetic material. Although cork is the most comfortable to hold, Harris does not recommend it for day-in, day-out use. "Cork will wear itself out," he cautioned. "In time, the rod holder can actually eat a ring around the cork handle."

Another important tip, according to the expert, is to make sure that locking rings for the reel-seat screw from the top down rather than from the bottom up. "When they seat from the bottom up, the reel can come loose in the excitement of fighting a fish," Harris said. "I've seen customers (on his fishing charters) end up with the rod in one hand and the reel in another."

Some anglers store their rods above the cabin in special rod holders. Handles of downrigger rods should fit nicely into rod holders, as these do, without bottoming out.

Making Your Own Rods

Making Your Own Rods

Some fishermen, like Jim Smith of Lake Orion, Michigan, like to make their own downrigger rods. Smith, 57, began building his own rods a few years ago when he couldn't find what he wanted to buy. "The companies are doing much better today," he said, "because they're trying harder. But I still get much satisfaction from making my own rods."

Smith's rods are more than exacting tools of the trade. They are also works of art, each bearing an original design and special serial number. Skillfully wrapping a 10- to 12-inch section ahead of the foregrip can involve 2,600 yards of fine thread. That process, for which Smith wears special jeweler's glasses, and the rod building itself can take up to 40 hours. Here's how he does it:

First, he lays out on paper his specifications – type and length of rod, handle, foregrip, art design and reel seat. The entire rod is therefore planned, step by step, before actual work begins.

Next, Jim selects a blank and inspects it for defects. "You can get defective blanks just like you can buy a pair of pants that aren't sewn in the right places," he said. He also determines which side of the blank is the most flexible, since all rods have a spline or stiff spot that separates the weak side from the strong or stiff side.

Once he has determined the dimensions of the butt grip, foregrip and reel seat, Smith sands the corresponding portions of the blank by hand so that when these components are glued to the blank, they won't slip. Then he uses a slow-cure (24-hour) epoxy to secure the butt grip, composed of up to a dozen cork "rings." He usually doesn't rely on preformed handles, preferring to build them according to hand size and blank diameter. Each ring is then fitted to that portion of the rod to which it will be glued.

When the handle is dry, Smith next glues the reel seat and foregrip, again letting the components dry for 24 hours. He then tapes the reel seat to keep it from getting marred while sanding the butt grip into an attractive and comfortable contour and the foregrip into a progressive taper. That job done, Smith glues on the butt cap.

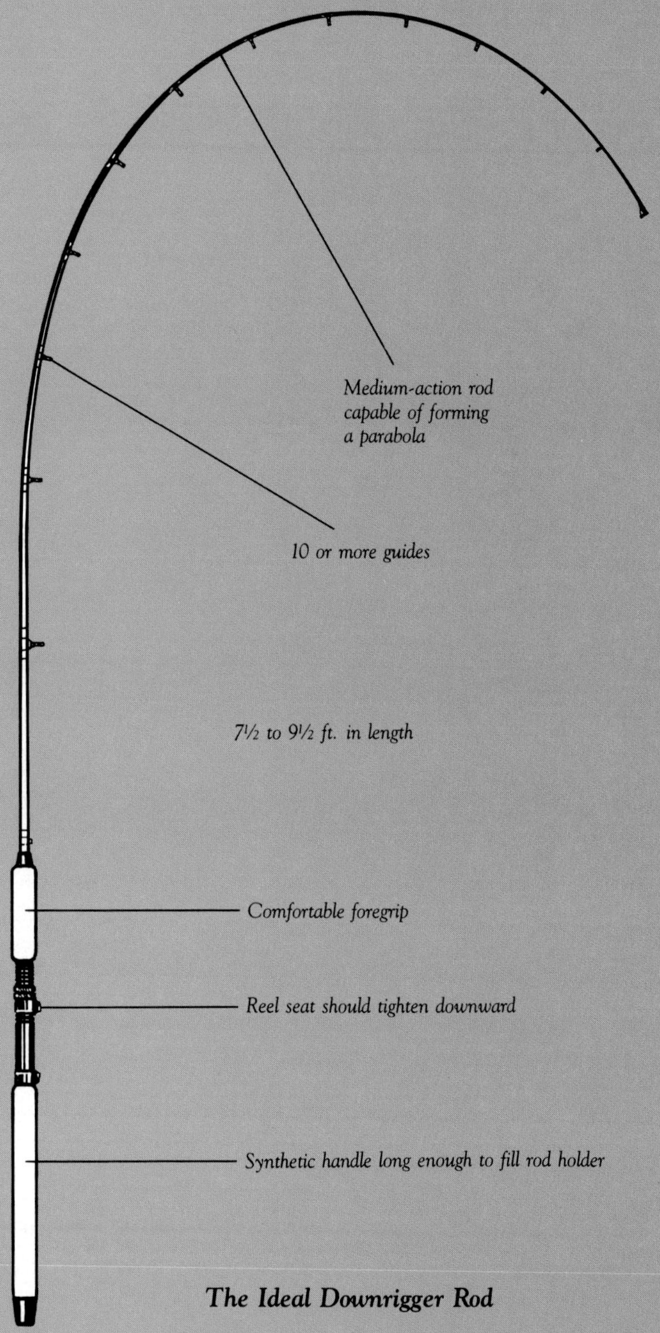

The Ideal Downrigger Rod

- Medium-action rod capable of forming a parabola
- 10 or more guides
- 7½ to 9½ ft. in length
- Comfortable foregrip
- Reel seat should tighten downward
- Synthetic handle long enough to fill rod holder

Making Your Own Rods

A spinning outfit can successfully double as a downrigger rod and reel.

Wrapping the area ahead of the foregrip is the next step. He uses pattern ideas from Dale P. Clemen's books, plus has designed his own styles. "The art of wrapping lies in changing or improving designs, not just in taking them from a book," he said. He will weave as many as seven colors, thread by thread, into intricate diamond, chevron, tarman, thunderbird, fish, Maltese cross and other patterns.

Smith's rods feature extra touches such as a hook keeper, which he builds into the wrapped portion. The hook keeper eliminates the need to attach hooks to guides, thus preventing abuse, plus it puts a lure or bait hook within easy reach. Then Smith adds three or four coats of color preserver over the wrap. In addition to stopping color fade, the preserver protects the artwork from dirt or marks while Jim works on the rest of the rod.

The next step is to tape the guides and a tip top to the rod. Adding a reel, Smith runs line through the guides, then puts stress on the blank to be sure that the line follows the contour of the rod and that line spacing from the rod to each guide is equal. Satisfied that the line doesn't touch the rod blank at any point, Smith then wraps the guides to secure them. The final step is to add Flex Coat, a polymer sealer. After a 36-hour drying time, the rod is ready to use.

Rodmaking requires long hours of patience, but the reward, according to Jim Smith, is that you could end up with a work of art that is also highly functional. Several rod companies, including Shakespeare and Fenwick, make blanks for do-it-yourselfers. You can buy them, along with Dynaflex, Lamiglas or Loomis blanks, from catalogs put out by fishing-tackle craft distributors. Three good ones include *Cabela's* (812 13th Ave., Sidney, NE 69106), *Bass Pro Shop* (P.O. Box 4046, Springfield, MO 65808-4046), and *L.L. Bean* (Casco St., Freeport, ME 04033).

The companies also carry good books on the subject of rodbuilding. Your local library is another source. Further, many of the off-season fishing and boating shows and some progressive fishing tackle retailers feature rodmaking seminars.

Cannon Field-test Director Mike Harris looks for special features in downrigger rods and reels. One is that they can handle powerful fish like this Chinook salmon that Harris is netting for Ed Sutton, Cannon Vice President of Sales and Marketing.

What to Look for in a Downrigger Reel

Reels for downrigger fishing are as specialized as the rods. They should have free-spooling features that allow line to go out at a controlled rate and a spool click that prevents the line from overrunning as the weight is lowered. When reels are so equipped, the fisherman will not have to thumb the spool. An anti-reverse feature that prevents line slip is important. So is a strong, smooth drag that can handle long runs by big fish.

Level-wind reels have long been the choice of downrigger fishermen. However, some of the newer baitcasting and spincasting reels are fine, provided they do not have lower pushbutton features that can be triggered by a rod-holder lip and provided they hold enough line. Personal choice dictates right- or left-hand handle (when available), reel size, and gear ratio (as ratios increase, retrieval speed also increases but power decreases accordingly).

How much line and what test you will need depend on the type of fish you are seeking. Other factors involving line choice include trolling depth, lure action desired, and water clarity. Line manufacturers are as competitive as rod and reel makers, so there is a wide variety with a corresponding spectrum of prices from which to choose. For best results, also select a premium-quality line and check it periodically for nicks and fray, replacing it when it becomes weak or worn.

The following list of reels have all the features necessary to provide the angler trouble-free performance when using downriggers.

To get the most value and best service from your downriggers, use them with carefully selected rods and reels. If you're not sure of what to buy, look at what successful anglers are using and ask their advice. Also, you will find that manufacturers' representatives, usually available at in-store promotions and special fishing seminars, are most knowledgeable when it comes to choosing the right rod and reel. This is especially true if their company makes downrigger trolling equipment.

Manufacturer/Model Number	Gear Ratio	Line Capacity	Price
Daiwa 27H Sealine	3.8 to 1	230 yd / 14 lb.	$38
Daiwa 47H Sealine	3.8 to 1	380 yd / 14 lb.	$43
Daiwa 47SH Sealine	5.1 to 1	380 yd / 14 lb.	
Daiwa 30H Sealine	3.8 to 1	380 yd / 14 lb.	
Daiwa 30Sh Sealine	5.1 to 1	380 yd / 14 lb.	
Daiwa SL175H Sportline	4.2 to 1	380 yd / 14 lb.	$33
Daiwa SL250H Sportline	5.1 to 1	380 yd / 25 lb.	$38
Shakespeare Sigma 245			$30
Shakespeare Sigma 250			$30
Ryobi V-Mag 5	5.3 to 1	120 yd / 12 lb.	
Ryobi V-Mag 40	5.0 to 1	120 yd / 10 lb.	
Ryobi V-Mag 50	5.3 to 1	135 yd / 12 lb.	
Shimano Triton 100GT			$35
Shimano Triton 200GT			$38
Shimano 300			$50
Shimano Bantam Mag 50			$70
Penn 209	3 to 1	350 yd / 20 lb.	$32
Penn 210	4 to 1	350 yd / 20 lb.	$35
Zebco Quantum QD310	5.1 to 1	160 yd / 12 lb.	
Zebco Quantum QD420	5.1 to 1	250 yd / 12 lb.	
Garcia Ambassadeur 5500C	4.7 to 1	195 yd / 12 lb.	
Garcia Ambassadeur 6500C	4.7 to 1	300 yd / 12 lb.	
Garcia Ambassadeur 5000	4.7 to 1	195 yd / 12 lb.	
Garcia Ambassadeur 6000	4.7 to 1	300 yd / 12 lb.	
Garcia Ambassadeur 7000	4.0 to 1	325 yd / 14 lb.	

Lures

"At least 10 common denominators apply to all lures, no matter how or for what they are fished."

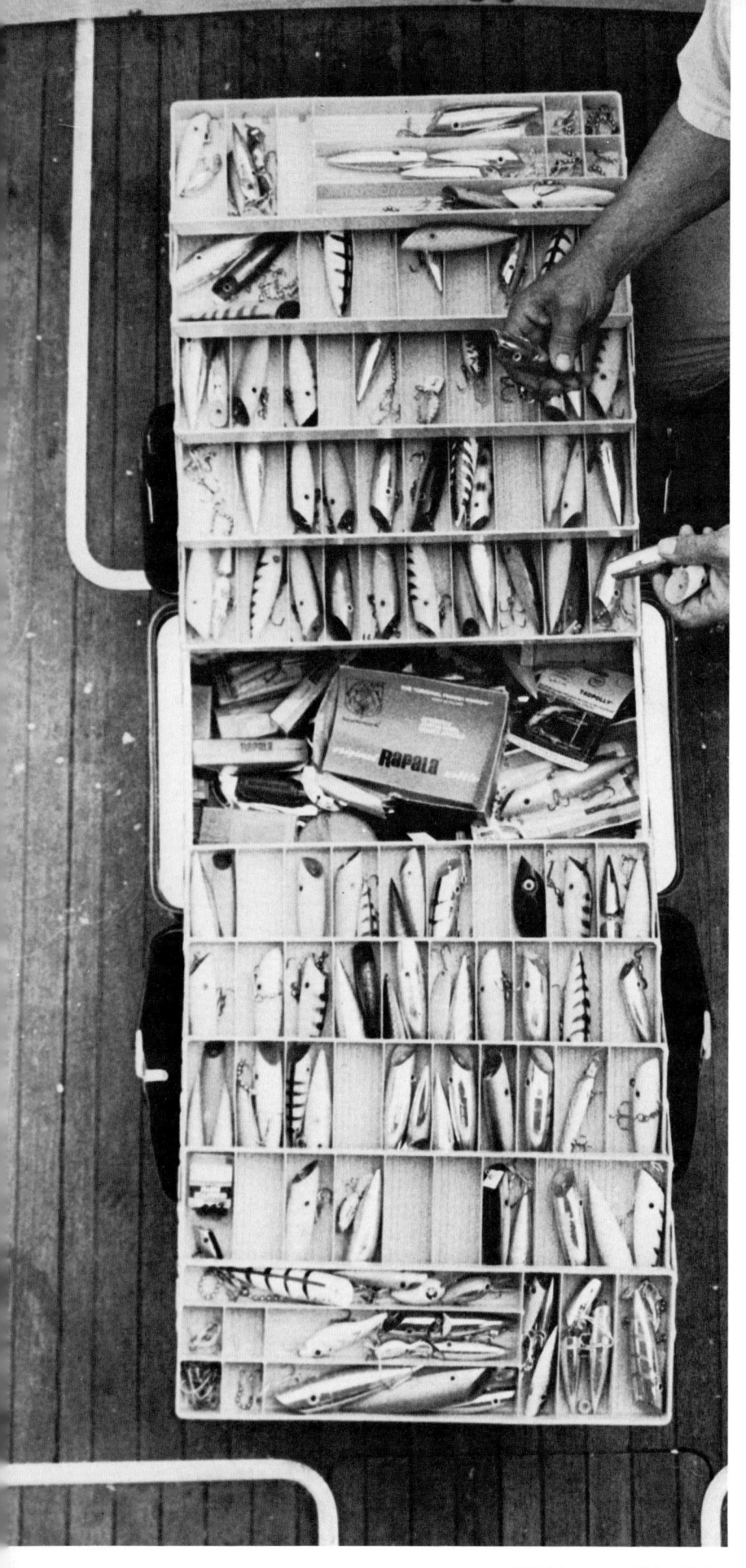

Which lures to use? This tackle box has a broad selection of J-Plugs.

You won't find "lurology" in your dictionary. But that doesn't mean there is no such word. To the contrary, lurology is alive and growing among the nation's fishermen.

Lurology is the never-ending search for the right color, size and action of lure that will trigger a certain type of fish into striking. *Any fish* will do when all efforts of the lurologists fail, and it is amazing what some of these sophisticated, modern fishermen will do to get fish to strike. I have seen grown men make wishes before pitching pennies off the back end of trolling boats. To kill human odor when making a lure change, one fellow I knew years ago used to dunk everything – hands, lures, even cannonballs – into a bucket of anise-flavored water. Another veteran angler used to carry the odor thing a bit further – he mopped his lures in a mixture of sardines and Alpo dog food.

Both were top-notch fishermen who must have known what they were doing. Today, years later, a dozen or more manufacturers produce oils, sprays, dips, scents and tablets aimed at creating lures that are supposed to taste good, too – at least to fish.

Lurology is as old as fishing itself. It goes back to the first time man baited a hook and patiently waited for something to strike it. I am fascinated by lurology, but I'm not at all sure I understand what makes a fish strike a certain color, size and wiggle of lure one minute, then snub it the next. I do know that lurology can be exciting and fun. Superstition and a little mumbo-jumbo black magic get added to the memories and accurate log books kept by most serious students of lurology.

"Last year just about this time of day," a fisherman will relate, I was trolling this reef and picked up a 24-pound king salmon on a clown-colored Flutter Chuck. I wonder if that lure will do the job again today." Then he mutters something about the color of shirt he was wearing that day, and you wonder if the guy has been bouncing with the waves too long.

To understand lurology as it applies to downrigger fishing, begin by understanding the types of lures that can be fished with downriggers. Such lures fall into four broad classes: spoons, plugs, spinners and flies. All

Types of Lures

Eppinger Flutter Chucks are popular spoons with trout and salmon downrigger fishermen on the Great Lakes.

are supposed to represent something to eat.

Spoons are oblong-shaped pieces of metal featuring a split ring or hole on one end for securing line and a hook at the other end. Shape and weight determine how spoons flutter, wiggle or wobble. Plugs are usually made from balsa or plastic. When plugs are minnow-shaped, they are sometimes called "body baits." Rapalas, Rebel Fastracs and Long A Bombers are examples. Plugs such as J-Plugs and their many imitations resemble cut bait. Those with large lips – crankbaits – wiggle violently and work their way down into deep water when trolled. Spinners feature a blade attached to a clevis so that it may rotate around the body of the lure – often a bead or two with a treble that is skirted with squirrel hair or plastic. Trolling flies are made from feathers, plastic or hair. They receive their action when pulled behind attractors such as Cowbells or Dodgers.

Details on how to fish these types of lures are presented in the chapter on rigging and in the chapters describing downrigger trolling tactics for the various freshwater species. At least 10 common denominators, however, apply to all lures, no matter how or for what they are fished. Considering the 10 can help you become a better fisherman plus gain the full value of your equipment investment.

1. *Lure Color.* Many fishermen rely on the standard saying: "Dark day, dark lures; bright day, bright lures." That seems to work, but – except for the fact that more trollers than not adopt the method – I cannot explain why. In fact, you might expect the opposite to be true. In other words, on a dark day, a bright-colored lure should show up better – when viewed from underneath – against a dark sky. Conversely, on a bright day, you would think that a dark lure might stand out better.

I am convinced that much remains to be learned about lure color. One giant step forward, however, has occurred with the recent introduction of the Color-C-Lektor. The battery-operated Color-C-Lektor is a light meter that answers the question, "What lure can fish most easily see under present fishing conditions? The angler determines the water clarity by a simple test, then drops the probe to desired depth. A needle stops at the color that can be most easily seen at that depth under those conditions.

We have used Color-C-Lektor with varying degrees of success while trolling for Great Lakes trout and salmon. Now that the manufacturer has increased cord length from 50 to 150 feet, it is a simple matter to tie the probe to your downrigger weight and send it down for a test.

2. *Other Local Conditions.* Water temperature, oxygen level, and pH and atmospheric pressure can dictate how fish will react to lures. As a general rule, troll slowly when the water is cold (under 45 degrees F.) or hot (over 70 degrees F.) as fish will be sluggish. A high-pressure system (bright, clear sky; high wind) can put fish deep and give them lockjaw. Then, slow-trolled lures in easy-to-see colors and presented right on the mark may produce strikes.

Low oxygen levels may send fish to a wave-pounded shore where oxygen is more available. Then, lures run just under the surface could score. Some fish, such as bass, often lie along pH breaks, and that can determine just how deep your lures should run.

No wave action might mean that running an attractor ahead of your lure could impart enough flash to interest even turned-off fish.

Local conditions also affect traffic volume. Especially along Great Lakes harbor mouths, when steering your boat requires all the skills of a Pac-Man wizard, it might be a good idea to choose lures that produce good action when close-set to downrigger weights.

3. *Species of Fish.* The type of fish you are after will, no doubt, dictate the best lures. Knowing your fish, along with their habitat and food preferences, can help you choose lures that resemble the food they seek and in the places where they expect to find that food. For example, small plug-bodied lures, such as Wobble-Glos, that resemble sculpin, are popular for lake trout trolling along Lake Huron reefs where both sculpin and lakers live.

4. *Trolling Speed.* No two types of lures track exactly the same when trolled, and that is why it is important to fine-tune and test your lures. Keep in mind, too, that each lure has an optimum trolling speed at which it imparts the best action. Many fishermen like

to mix different rigging tactics, which is fine, except that lures chosen may not run in harness with each other. A lure that constantly bellies up, fouls on weeds, or wanders off on its own adventures to tangle with other lines can cost valuable fishing time.

You can often avoid these problems by testing lures alongside the boat before cannonballing them. Merely hold the rod tip underwater or attach the lure to the downrigger release and send it down a couple of feet. The test, however, may not be 100 percent accurate because waves and currents can produce a different speed at the boat from that spot where the lure will be actually run. That is why sophisticated electronics that measure both boat speed and lure speed have become popular.

5. *Lure Size.* One day fish will pound large lures, then ignore them the next day for smaller offerings. Variables such as lure action, visibility and temperature are probable reasons. Consider, too, food preferences and availability. A reduced forage base in Lake Michigan, for example, has resulted in salmon and trout picking off small alewives. Trollers have found that by downsizing their lures to approximate the smaller baitfish, their luck has improved.

Stream trout fishermen have known for years the importance of checking the stomach contents of the day's first fish. They then can duplicate the trout's food preference. Trolling anglers can do the same thing.

6. *Lure Depth.* How deep your lures are running and whether or not you have the strike zone covered are important. Modern electronics to measure temperature, pH and oxygen value can help you to find the preferred depth. A sensitive paper-driven graph, liquid-crystal unit, flasher or video can also help you define bottom and its compositon.

Downrigger fishermen have an advantage over standard trollers in that (1) they always know where their lures are, (2) when using a paper-driven graph, they can usually track the lures because downrigger weights show up on the paper.

7. *Trolling Lane.* Better fishermen know that loops and figure-eight turns cause inside lures to dig deep and outside lures to ride up. Such hesitation or sudden burst of energy from a lure can trigger a predator to strike,

probably because the lure acts like a nervous baitfish. Similarly, zig-zagging, popping the gearshift into *neutral,* or goosing the engine now and then can provide just enough variation to convince a fish to make its move.

When lack of trolling traffic permits it, try running in and out from shore, as well as paralleling the shore. Always keep an eye out for untrolled water, and work the edges of the trolling fleet rather than get caught up in the melee.

8. *Consider Scents.* As with color, much remains to be learned about fish-attracting scents. The olfactory senses of most freshwater species are more highly developed than many people thought, and it is now generally accepted that fish use their ability to smell to help find food. Consequently, the market is quickly being saturated with scents and various ways to apply them to lures. The scents are mostly food-type odors although some products are aimed at masking human scent.

No one scent or method of application is best. In fact, manufacturers must yet perfect a means to keep fish-attracting odor on their artificial lures. But scents are exciting to consider and may well change the way we fish in the near future.

9. *Keep Hooks Sharp.* Some fishermen trust no manufacturer to get hooks pinprick sharp. So, upon removing a lure from its package, the first thing these anglers do is finger-test the barbs, then hone them to a razor's edge.

Also, check hooks to make sure they are strong enough for the gamefish you are targeting. Many of us Great Lakes salmon trollers, for example, have long used crankbaits designed for bass. The reason is simple: crankbaits catch fish but not until we replace small, weak hooks with heavy-duty trebles. We have also learned to add a *stinger hook* when fish slap at lures without securely hooking themselves. The stinger hook is a small trailing treble hook that is tied an inch or so behind the main gang.

10. *Believe in Your Lures.* Two successful Lake Michigan charter-boat captains I know approach the solution to a common problem – which lures to run – from opposing philosphies. For 10 years the first skipper has relied on a mere handful of lure types and colors.

Minnow-imitating lures, also called "body baits" or "stick baits," are excellent for spring salmon.

Types of Lures

"I'm not against experimenting," he says. "I just don't have to. These work fine."

The other fellow has literally thousands of lures. Spend a day on his boat and you will see him change his mind more often than a kid at an ice cream shop. His reasoning is simple: "I catch more fish by changing things around. The minute I lose confidence in a lure, I change it."

Confidence in a lure. Successful fishing is as much a game of confidence as anything else. Why else are my two acquaintances among the most sought-after guides?

The nation's lure makers do not seem to be running out of ideas these days. New shapes, models and colors come on the market each year. Most go the way of the Edsel car, but every so often a new lure takes off in a big way. The Eppinger Dardevle, Luhr Jensen J-Plug, Normark Rapala and Helin Flatfish were all lures that someone no doubt laughed at a long time ago. What makes one lure successful over another is a combination of many ingredients, not the least of which are luck and promotion.

Lurology. Always changing, along with being frustrating, fun, exciting and *so, so* necessary.

This 12-pound lake trout fell for a Wobble-Glo pulled behind a string of attractors.

Lure Holders

Bill Muirhead uses nook-and-cranny space for storing his favorite lures. He added this piece of styrofoam to an out-of-the-way spot that at the same time is handy for quick retrieval.

We were casting for bass after dark behind my partner's home on Lake Orion in southern Michigan. The inky night had settled in around us, and, except for mercury lights from the backyards of Joe's neighbors, there was nothing to look at. There was nothing to see with either, since I had lost my flashlight somewhere in the junk piles in my car. A big bass had just given Joe a good scrap before breaking his line. Now my partner needed a new lure.

"Open my tackle box of surface plugs," he said. "It's under the seat you're using."

I drew out what must have been a hard plastic case, then fumbled with the latch until it opened. "Now what?" I wondered.

"Run your hand along the outside until you feel the upper left-hand corner," Joe instructed. There's a large container there, right?"

"Right."

"Okay, one more pocket to the right of that container is a black Hula Popper. Careful. Don't get a hook in your finger."

I found the lure and gingerly handed it to my partner, closed the box, and slid it back under the seat. "How did you know exactly where that black Hula Popper was?" I asked.

"I know *exactly* where all my lures are," Joe said. There was a touch of sarcasm to his voice and that was because Joe had fished with me out of my boat a few times. Since I'm a pile maker, my boat looks like Sanford and Son's backyard – lures, rods, and other paraphernalia are scattered helter-skelter. I envy Joe, who has the pickup habits of a surgical nurse.

"You see," he explained, "that top tray contains my dark-colored surface lures, starting with black at the top and working down to dull orange. I also arrange lures according to size. In that big corner container are my black Jitter Bugs."

"I see," I said, knowing full well what was coming.

"*Better* fishermen always know where everything is on their boat, but especially their lures."

That was years ago, and yet I can still imagine the big smile on my partner's face. And more than ever, today I know that he was right, too. That is because over the years I have fished on dozens of boats with scores of anglers. The ones who catch the most fish are usually the fussiest fishermen.

Doesn't it make sense? If you tend to be orderly, you will probably run a fine-tuned fishing operation. Picky anglers don't lose prize fish to tight drags, dull hooks or line nicks. The fisherman with a filing-cabinet mind knows where everything is – especially lures – and that helps him to fish with determination and confidence. I won't soon forget the day another friend and I bemoaned the fact that he had left his Lightning Lures at home. Lightning Lures were the spoons-of-choice that day on Lake Michigan. No matter what we substituted for them, nothing worked as well. So imagine our frustration when we cleaned out the boat at day's end and found a stack of Lightning Lures under a pile of life jackets.

Another morning while trolling with guide Bob Bingle out of Oscoda, Michigan, on Lake Huron, I saw him lay out four complete changes of J-Plugs before we left the dock.

"What are you doing?" I wondered.

"Getting ready," Bob explained. "I start with dark colors off the pierheads, then lighten up by degrees as daylight comes on. By the time the sun is up, I'll be fishing mostly silver plugs. You have to be able to change lures fast. I can't do that if I don't know where they are."

No matter what species of fish you're trying for, the simplest way to arrange your lures is according to some scheme. Suggestions include separating small lures from big ones, bright colors from dull ones, hot fish-takers from mediocre offerings, spring lures from fall lures, and spoons from plugs from spinners from flies. The truth is, there are probably as many ways to separate lures as there are fishermen; and so each angler should consider his own fishing methods and amount of available space on his boat. Besides having a place for each type, color and size of lure, the sorting-out process is an excellent off-season project and is a good time to sharpen hooks and check for weak trebles and screw eyes.

Many of the bigger fishing boats feature cabinets and drawer space which can be

Jon Nissen relies on several clear-plastic sleeves for holding the many lures and attractors he uses. The plastic sleeves snap to boat walls near his downriggers so lures are always available.

utilized for storing lures. And fishermen with smaller boats might want to consider commercially made tackle boxes as there have been tremendous improvements in recent years. Gone, for example, are the days of the metal boxes and cheap plastic containers. Years ago, fishermen never knew what to expect when they opened their tackle boxes. Sometimes hooks would be rusted, and sometimes strange chemical reactions would have melted plastic skirts on lures. Unidentified odors might have been strong enough to curl crankbait lips. Plano and Kennedy are among several manufacturers now offering innovative products. The Plano Company, for example, makes tackle boxes keyed to Color-C-Lektor placement of lures.

As nice as the new manufactured tackle boxes are, they are not cheap, and so many fishermen have come up with creative ways to store lures at low cost. Some buy five-inch by 12-inch plastic boxes for as low as a buck each. They use a magic marker to label each box, then secure several boxes – according to spoons, plugs, etc. – with rubber bands.

Another neat trick is to hang lures from styrofoam. Large plugs, such as those used for muskies or northern pike, can be hung from the inside of a small $1.95 cooler, which is ideal for keeping those nasty gangs of hooks out of the way. Several innovative fishermen I know glue a piece of one-inch thick styrofoam – the kind used for insulation – to cabin walls on their boat. Lures can be easily added or removed from the styrofoam.

Jon Nissen of Toledo, Ohio, uses hundreds of lures each trolling season while chartering for Lake Erie walleyes and Lake Michigan trout and salmon. Nissen relies on lure jackets made of plastic for holding Dodgers and flashers. The holders can be purchased commercially or made at home from cloth stitched on a sewing machine. A grommet-and-snap arrangement makes for flexible location anywhere on his boat, the *E-Z Ketch*.

Lures such as Spin-N-Glos, P-Nuts, L'il Guys and Burke Soft Touch plugs are often rigged with detachable treble hooks on short leaders. Because these lures easily tangle, they can be difficult to store. The Plano Company makes a special cabinet with spring-loaded holders for securing such lures. Fishermen handy with tools can make their own, too, from plywood or masonite tacked to two pieces of one-by-two inch stripping. Cut the stripping in the shape of a rectangle, each 15 inches wide by 30 inches long. On the inside, a piece of styrofoam at one end holds hooks. The angler then pulls the leader tight and ties the end to a nail (small springs which can be purchased at a hardware store also do the job nicely). Lures fill up the space in between. Be sure to hinge sides of the box in the middle so that it will close like a book, then add a clasp and a handle outside.

Imaginative anglers with small boats can make wise use of nook-and-cranny space for holding lures. My friend Joe described at the beginning of this section, no longer has the little bass boat which we used for midnight fishing trips behind his home. Now he owns a 17-foot Sea Nymph complete with four Cannon downriggers, magnum cooler, CB and marine radio, and enough rods, reels and lures to open a tackle shop. True to form, he has a place for everything. Joe carries lures in small plastic boxes, according to plugs, spoons and attractor/flies. Then, boxes of the same lure type go into color-coded plastic milk-carton containers, which Joe picked up from some dairy that went out of business.

Another neat idea he has added to his boat is a long, narrow box he made from a piece of paneling trimmed with chrome – the type used to edge kitchen counters. The box is about six inches wide, four inches high, and six feet long. Joe bolted it to the transom of his boat, right in front of his downriggers. The box is ideal for holding stackers, pliers, swivels, favorite lures and other items frequently used when downrigger trolling.

Having a place for everything is the key to successful trolling. That is especially true for lures, the nuts-and-bolts of the sport itself.

Larger boats often contain cabinet space which can be utilized for lure storage.

Largemouth bass like weeds. The weeds attract plenty of things to eat, and they help the predatory bass to hide in ambush. Such a predator, a *big* largemouth bass, was lying just inside a bed of thick-matted milfoil in a southern reservoir. Shafts of light from the early rising sun were beginning to penetrate our lunker's dark lair. He watched a school of minnows, their sides winking silver with the new light, scoot by. A smaller bass gave chase, and the minnows scattered like cars before a highway patrolman with his siren screaming.

Except for continuing to slowly fan his pectorals, the giant bass did not budge. True, he had seen the chase and could easily have caught the baitfish. His stomach held room for more food, too. The reason he did not attack the prey was that the trigger finger – those electrical impulses that stimulate the "attack center" somewhere in a brain fold – was down. The bass, of course, knew nothing about attack centers, electrical impulses and brain folds. He had simply identified the baitfish as food. That and the fact that they were catchable were reinforced by the smaller bass. But the bigger bass had not responded. End of story.

Almost. A moment later the bass noticed faint vibrations that steadily grew stronger. Soon a shadow passed overhead. It created a stream of bubbles just under the reservoir surface and a widening V-shaped wake on the surface itself. The bass was not alarmed; often he had seen the fishing boats, and there was no reason to flee or to sink deeper into the milfoil. Before the boat had passed beyond his picture window though, the bass noticed a twinkling object that seemed to follow a black ball about 10 feet in front of it. Farther above was a second ball with trailing lure; then another wiggled by within 10 feet of his lair. Unknown to the bass, the trigger finger on his attack center was tightening. Seconds later, when a lure with maddening action rumbled just over the weeds, the bass hit it with the fury of an NFL All-Pro nose guard.

Sharp steel hooks drove deeply into the bass's lower jaw. A young man hollered, stood up in the boat, and was fast locked in battle with the biggest largemouth of his life. A half-hour later he and his father stood

Strike Psychology

admiring nearly 10 pounds of spent fury, safe now in the net at their feet.

"He's got a mouth the size of a two-pound coffee can," the older fisherman said, his eyes wide with amazement. "Bet you could put your fist in there."

"Why did he hit that red-and-white crankbait?" the young man wondered excitedly.

"I don't know, son, but that's a good question."

Why do fish strike? What are the conditions that cause fish to strike? These are questions that began the day Man tipped the first crude fishhook with a worm. Today, we have plenty of theories and no shortage of products – lures, scents, electronics, to name just a few – to help us prove those theories.

When you really think about it, fish strike for two main reasons – hunger or aggression. Some fish, such as yellow perch or catfish, seem to be hungry nearly all the time. Finding a school of ravenous perch is usually the hardest part of catching enough for a meal. The same is true with catfish. Once you put your bait on target, most catfish are quick to respond.

Other species, most notably muskies, are moody, solitary and usually tough to catch. Even the best fishermen spend hours, and sometimes days, trolling or casting to catch a legal muskie. According to the Pennsylvania Fish Commission, a muskie needs only four pounds of food to gain one pound in weight. If the average weight gain of a muskie is only three pounds each year, that means it only has to eat 12 pounds of food annually. Some veteran fishermen, like Ted Eberly of Land O' Lakes, Wisconsin, believe that muskies eat only once or twice every several weeks. They may be right.

On the other hand, while trolling in the Great Lakes, I have caught fat, football-shaped brown trout so crammed with food that they spit minnows all over the boat. How could they possibly be hungry when there is no room to gorge another morsel – perhaps the trigger finger is stronger on a brown trout's brain, but I doubt it. Maybe the answer lies in the fact that browns are a schooling species. When they see others of their kind slashing into a baitfish school, they join the melee out of a predator-pack form of aggression.

Trolling Speed Guide

Here is a handy guide to many of the popular trolling lures used with downriggers. Rely on it as a general reference for choosing lures according to boat speed, local conditions, species and time of year. It can also help you select lures that will be compatible.

Slow-trolled Plugs
Wiggle Wart
Wee Wart
Razorback
Hackleback
Willy's Worm
Flatfish
Kwikfish
Ping-A-T
Tadpolly
Tiny Tad
Clatter Tad
River Runt
Bill Norman Little N
Burke Hunchback
Bagley B Flat II
Geniune Crankbait Bullcat
Bagley Killer B 2
Bagley Mighty Minnow
Beno
Bill Norman Bluefin

Fast-trolled Plugs
J-Plug
Canadian Plug
Dandy-Glo
Tiger Plug
Lucky Louie
Silver Horde
Witch Doctor
Mac Squid
Rebel
Straight Rapala
Jointed Rapala
Long A Bomber
Tomic

Attractors (slow or med.)
Cowbell/Wobble-Glo
Cowbell/sewn minnow
Cowbell/L'il Guy
Cowbell/thin spoon
Cowbell/Clatter Tad
Dodger/squid
Dodger/fly
Dodger/sewn minnow
Flasher/with any of the above

Thin Spoons (slow or med.)
Sagamore Spoon
Sugar Spoon
Salmon Seeker
Williams Salmon Wabler
Acme Looter
Huron Herring
Flutter Spoon
Flutterdevle
G.W. Salmon Slammer
Flutter Chuck
Big Ed Flutter Chuck
Salmon Doctor
Alpena Diamond
Never-Failure
Thumb King
Bishop Spoon
Spring Spoon
Angel Eye
Billie Bait
Sculpin
Finn Spoon
Dr. Hook
Charger
Lucky Lure
Miller Spoon
Sutton Spoon
Andy Reeker
Rattlespoon
Silver Strik-ER
Salmon Seeker
Hookster
Lightning Lure
Northport Nailer
Westport Wobbler
Zipper
Southport Slammer
Thindevle
Red Eye
Manistee Wobbler
Williams Whitefish
Luhr Jensen Silver Plate
Pentwater Long John
Mepps Spoon
Williams Fire Bug

Heavy Spoons (med. or fast)
Hot Shot Wobbler
KO Wobbler
Krocodile
Little Cleo
Little Jewel
Cop-E-Cat Imp
Kush Spoon
Dardevle Imp Klickers
Kastmaster
Mepps Syclops Spoon
Mister J
Loco
Acme Dazzler
Devle Dog
KC Spoon

Medium-trolled Plugs
Countdown Rapala
Fat Rap
Hermans
Hot Shot
Fire Plug
Hot 'N Tot
Thin Fin
Bang-O-Lure
Bomber Speed Shad
Hedd-Hunter
Fish Back
Bug Plug
Rebel Double Deep
Rebel Fastrac
Finnigan's Minnow
Bill Norman's Baltic Minnow
LumaLure

Aggression can certainly be linked to hunger. Witness the vicious attacks of a school of striped bass, silver bass or coho salmon on baitfish unlucky enough to be spotted by the predators. Pure bedlam, with panicked minnows squirting from the water, results. For years, lake trout fishermen have known that slamming lures or bouncing downrigger weights on the bottom can stir lake trout into drilling their hardware. Recently I fished for lakers in the Northwest Territories with portable downriggers. Nearly all the fish we brought to the boat were shadowed by other lake trout, whom I assume were either hungry or curiously aggressive. Maybe both. Walleyes, perch, bluegills and crappies are other species that rarely serve up only one of their kind at any given fishing location.

Aggression can be simply defensive, too. Bluegills, smallmouth bass, salmon and steelhead are species that are territorial, especially during the spawning season. Then, the males in particular will attack rivals of their own kind, as well as other intruders. Anglers who troll or toss hot-colored lures near spawning beds of these protective males usually experience powerful strikes that are lightning fast.

In the first part of this chapter, I discussed 10 factors that fishermen should consider when choosing lures. Variables such as water temperature, trolling speed and lure color are just a few of the factors that figure into the strike psychology of fish. You should also know that downrigger fishermen in particular have advantages going for them that other trolling anglers don't.

Consider *scents*, one of the two hottest fishing developments in the past five years. Fish use their sense of smell (and taste), probably more than most anglers realize. Tests at a southern university prove it. In one experiment, a female bass about to spawn was kept in a five-gallon bucket of water for a short while. Later, the fish was removed and the water added to a large aquarium containing a male bass. He went crazy trying to find the female. In another experiment, unfed bass were kept for a day or two in a large aquarium. When a five-gallon bucket of clean water was added, the bass had no reaction. But when a five-gallon bucket of water that had contained a school of shad for an hour was added, the bass went on the prowl looking for them.

A couple of years ago, Nick Sisley, my friend and fellow outdoor writer, wrote a fascinating article for *Great Lakes Fisherman* on the subject of scents. Nick documented the fact that bass have two sets of nostrils. The ones closest to the fish's lips are called "anterior nodes." Incoming water enters via these anterior nodes, passes over the fish's olfactory organ, and out through the "posterior nodes." The "olfactory organ" is a series of folds, which are actually nerve endings that are capable of detecting scent and passing messages to the brain. Nick says larger and older bass can smell even better because the folds increase in number and size. The same thing is likely true for other fish.

As I mentioned in the last chapter, the problem with manufactured scents is getting them to remain on hard-bodied lures. Lindy-Little Joe has had some success with pelletized scents that can be used with their Pop-Tail lures. Burke Fishing Lures has come out with soft-bodied plugs capable of holding odor longer. Downrigger fishermen, however, now have the ability to add odor attractants to their weights, creating a long-lasting plume of scent that can wash over lures trailing behind the weights themselves. Cannon's new *Stink Pads* feature adhesive behind a paper backing. Simply stick the absorbent pads to either side of your downrigger weights, spray or dab your favorite fish attractant (Cannon does not produce fish scents), and lower the weight to the depth of your choosing.

Specialized rigging is another reason downrigger fishermen have an advantage. Pinpoint-depth trolling allows them to put lures on target and keep them there. Knowing exactly where lures are and how they are working lets fishermen bump bottom with downrigger weights, stack lines to run more offerings and thus cover all the potential strike zones, and set up effective trolling patterns.

For example, downriggers are the ideal way to rig with attractors, such as flashers or strings of blades ahead of lures. The reason is threefold: (1) to put attractors/lures on target without having to add heavy keel sinkers or other weights, (2) to run them close

This whopper northern pike spit the hooks shortly after coming to net in Ontario. Normally solitary fish, pike strike out of hunger and pure, simple aggression.

Strike Psychology

Heading out to the trolling pastures in Lake Michigan. Fine-tuned rigging patterns, along with eliminating variables, helps anglers to score.

together without fear of tangle, and (3) to be able to fight the fish without extra weight. Lots of turning chrome often triggers fish into a striking mood. Consider the fact that, in 1973, researchers off the coast of Washington State caught 1,100 salmon in 43 days using rotating flashers and lures on only four rods.

Further, downriggers permit *pattern fishing*. Savvy fishermen can run a trolling diagram to imitate a school of baitfish. Experimental rigging for color (the second most exciting fishing development in recent years), scent, lure action or size is also possible with downriggers because the fisherman controls the conditions. He can also set up patterns to effectively fish specialized structure, such as an uneven bottom, drowned timber or brush, or sharply inclined river channels.

No one will probably ever fully understand why fish strike lures. But it is no secret that specialized rigging tactics with downriggers is a highly effective way to produce strikes . . . and fish. In the next chapter, we'll lay out those rigging tactics, beginning with the most simple arrangements. Even if you are already fishing with downriggers, we'll suggest some new and exciting ways to troll. And don't forget to check out the sections on the individual fish species later in this publication. We've interviewed dozens of the nation's most respected freshwater fishermen. How they use downriggers to improve their box scores is all here.

Rigging

"Downriggers are at the core of some highly innovative rigging methods – so innovative that beginning anglers are easily confused."

Rigging lines refers to setting up a fishing program. How many lures, for example, will you troll? Then, how deep? How far apart? What methods will you use to stagger them? The answers depend upon which of two rigging philosophies you adopt: (1) concentrate on running only one or two lines, or (2) put out as many lines as possible without breaking the law and without running into tangles.

Downriggers allow you to exercise either philosophy. A lake trout troller in a small boat, for example, might want to nudge bottom with his downrigger weight every few feet, just enough to stir sluggish lakers into a feeding spree. By raising and lowering his weight a few inches every few seconds, the fisherman can put all his efforts into the single-minded operation. On the other hand, many fishing situations call for multiple lines. Fish may be scattered, for example, and in order to catch them, lures must be spread out. Because some Great Lakes fishermen like to cover all the bases, their rigging program might include bottom-running lures for lake trout, mid-depth offerings for suspended salmon, and topwater lures for steelhead. Another example is the boatload of eight trollers who each wants two rods to tend. That means 16 lines must be set, but somebody better know what he's doing or the result could be a huge rat's nest of tangled gear.

Downriggers are at the core of some highly innovative rigging methods — so innovative that beginning anglers are easily confused. Indeed, following *downrigger mounting options*, the second-most offered suggestion by the veteran fishermen I polled for this publication was this: "Explain rigging tactics from most simple to advanced. Emphasize the ABCs but help readers discover that downriggers and their many uses are limited only by a fisherman's imagination."

That's what this section is all about.

To begin, know that the purpose of rigging is threefold: (1) to get lures down, (2) to get lures out to each side of the boat, (3) to get lures back from the boat. To understand how to accomplish any one or all of these objectives, you must first become familiar with the key rigging tactics. It is important to understand them now because in later

How to Rig a Trolling Boat

chapters – both in this section on Rigging and in the section on the individual gamefish species – we will refer to them often.

Flatlines. These are lures trolled on a free line off the stern end of the boat. They are not connected to downriggers but are often used to complement a rigging program involving downriggers. Up to three flatlines may be run at once, although usually one or two is the rule. The boat center is the preferred position, with boat corners or sides the second choice. When long rods are run straight up off the stern or put into rod holders along the sides of a boat cabin or on a fly bridge, they are often called "highlines." Since the object of flatlining is usually to spot lures far from the boat, the practice is sometimes called "longlining." Its goal is to entice hits from shy fish like brown trout or surface-oriented fish like steelhead or coho salmon.

Most flatlines fall between 50 to 150 feet behind the boat, although they can be 300 or more feet. In order to get lures to track straight at such distances, some trollers attach a small bobber 25 feet or so ahead of the lure. Heavy spoons or diving plugs, such as crankbaits, are popular with flatline trollers since such lures dig down from three to 25 feet. Some fishermen rely on keel or rubber-core sinkers to get lures to work a little deeper or to get floating plugs to at least disappear beneath the surface. A few use lead-core or thin-diameter stainless-steel line for the same purpose.

The new Cannon *Excitor* adds a broad dimension to flatline trolling because it automatically sweeps the lure horizontally by 90 degrees. Powered by any 12-volt battery, the Excitor has a three-way switch that sets the continuous back-and-forth motion at two different speeds, plus "off." Further, the length of delay after each sweep can be regulated from 0 to 15 seconds by means of a control knob. A built-in rod holder comes with angle adjustment, and an optional Clamp Mount with C-clamp is also available for quick mounting on boats without standard deck plates.

In heavy boat traffic, flatlining is not always practical since other fishermen might run over your lines. To avoid this problem, some trollers practice a modified form of flat- lining. They attach an alligator-clip or pinch-pad release to a pike leader or foot-long piece of heavy monofilament. Then they secure the other end of the leader to a ski hook on the stern end of their boat. The advantage is twofold: (1) lines enter the water faster, thus shortening the distance the flatline must travel; (2) fish tend to hook themselves solidly since a strike releases the bent-over rod to its upright position.

Downriggers. We have already explained how downriggers work and the mounting options for the many types and sizes of boats. Specialized patterns for fishing with downriggers will be covered later in this section.

Stacking. Stacking refers to the practice of adding rods and/or lures to a working downrigger setup. Stacking can be either fixed-depth or free-sliding. The former occurs when the troller determines exactly how deep he wants his lures to run. For example, if he wants the bottom lure to hold at 45 feet and the stacked lure to stop at 35 feet, he can easily do both by rigging the bottom lure to a release, then lowering the downrigger weight 10 feet. Next, he adds the second lure to a second release and sends the weight down another 35 feet. He could add a third or fourth lure by simply stopping the weight from being lowered at any point. For drawings and further details, see the next section in this chapter.

An alternative to fixed-depth stacking is the use of "sliders" (also called "cheaters"). The angler adds a lure to a strip of monofilament not longer than the rod. The monofilament must have a snap swivel at the opposite end of the lure. The fisherman simply snaps the slider unit to the monofilament of the rod already in place, then pitches the lure overboard. It will "slide" roughly halfway to the depth of the lowest lure; at this point, line bow from the boat's forward progress will hold the slider in place.

Lures chosen to go on the bottom of stacked setups are usually larger or have more digging action than those selected for running higher. For example, bottom-running dodgers and flies can be effectively stacked with spoons above. J-Plugs, Tadpollies or Flatfish are plugs that can accept stacked spoons. Large spoons such as Big Ed Flutter Chucks can be stacked with small spoons like Andy Reekers.

Rigging with downriggers can be as simple as setting a single line while canoeing a small lake, (far left), or as complicated as running several lines when trolling the Great Lakes, (above). Here, Jim Bennett of Onekama, Michigan, prepares to set an outrigger. Note downriggers and a planer board already in use.

A young fisherman aboard the Prime Time, *captained by professional guide Jim Bennett (white shirt) gets his first taste of Great Lakes salmon action.*

There are several advantages to stacking: (1) the fisherman can cover more water depths; (2) he may catch fish that prefer different temperatures and might be suspended at different depths; (3) in waters where anglers are limited to a single rod (such as in Ontario), he can legally double or triple his trolling arsenal.

Outriggers. These are 12- to 24-foot long poles of wood or fiberglass that extend to each side of the boat at a 45-degree angle. Their purpose is to widen the trolling lane to accommodate more lures and to produce strikes from fish that might be spooked by boat shadow, engine noise, or too many lures close to the boat.

Like downriggers, the operation of outriggers is simple. A continuous tether rope of nylon is secured to each end of the pole via small pulleys. On the tether is a fishing line release, usually a pressure snap or clothespin type. The angler tosses his lure overboard, attaches his monofilament to the release, then hand-over-hands the line to the end of the pole. His rod goes into a holder along the gunnel or on the cabin side. A strike pops the line free from the release. To reset the outrigger, the fisherman simply hand-over-hands the release back to the boat.

Popular lures for outrigger fishing include big-lipped crankbaits and heavy spoons. Some fishermen rely on lead-core line or keel or rubber-core sinkers to get lures deep. A few use smooth-cast homemade lead balls that weigh about a pound each. They are attached a few feet ahead of the lure by way of a pressurized sinker release. A strike opens the release, and the weight is then discarded. Outrigger fishermen sometimes stack their lines by adding extra releases along the tether.

Planer boards. Also simply called "planers" or "skis," these are boards that run lures up to 100 feet to boat sides, thanks to a tether rope ususally stored on a large reel mounted to the boat side or to a mast or boom attached to the boat bow. The boards are made of wood, fiberglass or styrofoam and are keel-weighted so that they run on their narrow side. Because they are angle-cut at the forward end, they run away from the boat and take waves head on. Early models featured alligator clips mounted to the boards themselves; newer planers usually rely on pinch-pad releases that slide down the tether via rings. These may be manufactured or homemade from shower-curtain rings or large paper clips. Pinch pads are then soldered or glued to the rings. Stacking with up to four rods is therefore possible, depending upon the length the board is from the boat.

In Lake Superior, where trolling pastures are still largely uncluttered, some innovative fishermen run up to six five-foot-long skis, three to a side, at distances of 300, 150 and 75 feet from the boat. The trolling lane for such rigging, therefore, is 200 yards or the length of two football fields laid end to end! Charter-boat skippers so rigged can legally run up 30 or more lures when they have enough people aboard.

Many trollers make their own planers from single or dual boards that are eight inches to several feet in length. Several companies now make planer boards, too. Cannon's *Dual Plane-R-Board* has been improved by making it collapsible for easier storage. The new design has hinged posts that fold down so that both boards meet flush at either

How to Rig a Trolling Boat

end. Another feature allows for tether line placement at two different points depending on wave conditions.

Most sport fishermen rely on one or two planer boards in spring and fall when easily spooked fish are in shallow water. The same lures that are used for outrigger trolling are effective. Although it is possible to run planer boards with outriggers, few trollers do, at least on the same side of the boat. There are only so many lines you can set without getting into foulups that are time-consuming and expensive to unsnarl.

Diving planers, or what are commonly referred to as "trip divers," are often called a poor man's downrigger. That is because they, too, take lures to a prescribed depth and are inexpensive. A disadvantage, though, is that diving planers do not feature line releases, and so the angler must fight the device as well as his fish. Dipsy Divers and Pink Ladies, both made by Luhr Jensen & Sons, are the most popular of several commercially made models. Dipsy Divers feature a dial which can determine the angle of descent and depth desired. The lure is attached a few feet behind the diving planer. A strike "trips" or releases the gadget, allowing the fisherman to retrieve it and his catch.

Small spoons or plugs work well with trip divers. Besides low cost, their advantage is that they can be run close to the boat to often complement a downrigger trolling program. Evidence of their growing popularity is the fact that some rod manufacturers, such as Wright McGill (makers of Eagle Claw), are now producing special 10-foot "Dipsy Diver" models designed especially for diving planers.

How does a fisherman use downriggers and these associated rigging tactics to best advantage? The answer involves many considerations, including size and type of boat, amount of boat traffic, wind and waves, and target gamefish. Just by itself, the species of gamefish you are after means you should consider time of year, water temperature and depth. These in turn often dictate lure type and color, essential to any successful rigging program. Effective trolling patterns, however, are not as complicated as they may seem. Trial-and-error experimentation, along with common sense and patience, will show

Cannon's Plane-R-Board is ideal for spring trolling in the shallows. Here, a small-boat angler executes a sharp turn.

How to Rig a Trolling Boat

the way. We hope the upcoming sketches and details will help, too.

Besides the specifics of temperature, depth, etc., there are three other considerations to think about when setting up a rigging program. The three are *boat control, trolling etiquette,* and *downrigger weights.*

Boat control means maintaining speed and depth. According to the fishing experts at Mariner Outboards, who published a fact sheet on the subject, four methods are commonly used to control a boat: backtrolling, forward-trolling, drifting and anchoring. Downriggers can be used for each, and combinations of these techniques are also utilized.

Controlled drifting in a lake or reservoir is used to fish points, weed edges and humps. In a river, it involves moving the boat slightly faster (when moving upstream) or slower (when going downstream) than the current. Backtrolling means trolling with motor in reverse so the boat moves backwards, into the wind or current, for maximum control. Forward trolling, of course, is the most popular use of downriggers. Fishing with downriggers while anchored usually involves jigging with lures or bait along bottom or for suspended fish.

When trolling, boat control also means balancing steering tension so that the boat moves easily to left and right. Adjustable trim tabs that come with some motors is one way to accomplish boat control. Some fishermen, like Cannon field tester Jim Beyers of New Baltimore, Michigan, rely on the Sea Anchor, which mounts along one side of the boat via heavy-duty straps. The Sea Anchor acts like an underwater parachute to stabilize boat rock, maintain correct drift, and hold down trolling speed. Other fishermen add an adjustable Beaver-Trol to retard trolling speed when they can't throttle down enough. Additional tactics include the use of small trolling motors instead of the powerful boat engine and tossing a five-gallon bucket tied to boat corners off the stern.

Trolling etiquette determines how you rig, too. As more and more people take up fishing with downriggers, common courtesy grows in importance. When plenty of fishermen are out and boating traffic is heavy, here are five considerations you should keep in mind:

1. Prepare your boat before taking up valuable space at the launch site, and have your fishing tackle and rigging program ready to go before joining the other trollers.

2. Unless you are going to fish far away from the pack, plan to pull lines in close to the boat and to discard side rigging and longlining methods altogether.

3. Figure out the trolling flow, then join it.

4. Give other fishermen plenty of room. Don't troll directly behind another boat, and don't cut other boats off.

5. Don't kill the engine or throw the gearshift into neutral when you have a fish on. To maintain traffic flow, keep on trolling. When you hook a fish, take it to the edge of the pack or outside the pack until you get it into the boat. Similarly, if you observe another boat with a fish on, angle away to give the fishermen some fighting space.

Downrigger weights. Downrigger weights have evolved along with downriggers. Although still called "cannonballs" by many trollers, most weights today no longer really look like the perfectly round balls of the early days. According to Cannon field-test director, Mike Harris, those early cannonballs had a tendency to spin and tangle lines when making turns. They also didn't track straight. Torpedo and fish-shaped weights, which appeared next, went a long way toward solving the problem but still tended to "swim" away from the boat on turns.

Today, downrigger weights come in all shapes and sizes. A survey of Cannon field testers turned up some interesting rigging theories regarding weights. Ron Gusse, a charter-boat captain from Oshkosh, Wisconsin, uses different sizes of weights for different depths while fishing Lake Michigan for salmon and trout and Lake Winnebago for walleyes. In Lake Huron, to depths of 40 feet, Bob Bingle of Fair Haven, Michigan, relies on six-pound weights. From 40 to 80 feet deep, he puts down eight-pound weights, and beyond 80 feet deep, turns to 10-pounders. To bounce bottom while lake-trout fishing in Lake Michigan, Kenneth Voltz of Michigan City, Indiana, uses 13-pound homemade balls and a very slow trolling speed. Hank Peters of Superior, Wisconsin, fishes Lake

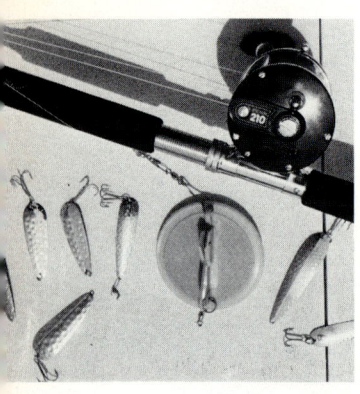

Diving planers such as the Dipsy-Diver by Luhr Jensen & Sons are popular low-cost gadgets that complement downriggers in a rigging program.

Superior depths to 200 or more feet for lake trout. To get his lures on bottom, Peters uses heavy weights made by the Laurvick Company.

Voltz and others caution deep-water fishermen about what is called "cannonball drift" or "blowback." Ideally, you want your weight to be as close to vertical as possible, but underwater currents and the forward motion of the boat can create a bow of sorts in the downrigger cable. Thus, 120 feet of cable released might result in a cannonball at only 100 feet deep. To test for the degree of blowback, drop your weight until it just touches bottom, then compare the foot counter on the downrigger against what your sonar says. You can also "track" downrigger weights on a good graph to see exactly where they are running.

Experimenting fishermen, such as coho anglers in southern Lake Michigan, have found that weights can attract fish to lures. That is why they often paint their weights in bright colors and why some manufacturers (including Cannon) now offer models in various colors. Cannon *Flash Weights*, available in six-, eight-, 10- and 12-pound models, incorporate a flashing prism design for extra lure power. Cannon also offers *Glow Pads* that actually glow in the dark and are ideal for early morning or post-sundown fishing. The pads are designed to adhere to the sides of a trolling-weight fin. Black vinyl coating on Cannon Flash Weights protects your boat from lead marking, and a large keel allows each weight to track true and prevents spinning.

As downrigger trolling increases in popularity among inland lake fishermen, a new problem is that weights can hang up on rocks, drowned timber and other obstructions. The newest design in downrigger weights is Cannon's eight- and 10-pound *Banana* weights. Designed to slide over potential snags while maintaining a true tracking course, the vinyl-coated Banana weights are yellow in color and contain added flash.

There is a downrigger weight for each rigging program, and there is a rigging program for each type of fishing situation and every kind of fish.

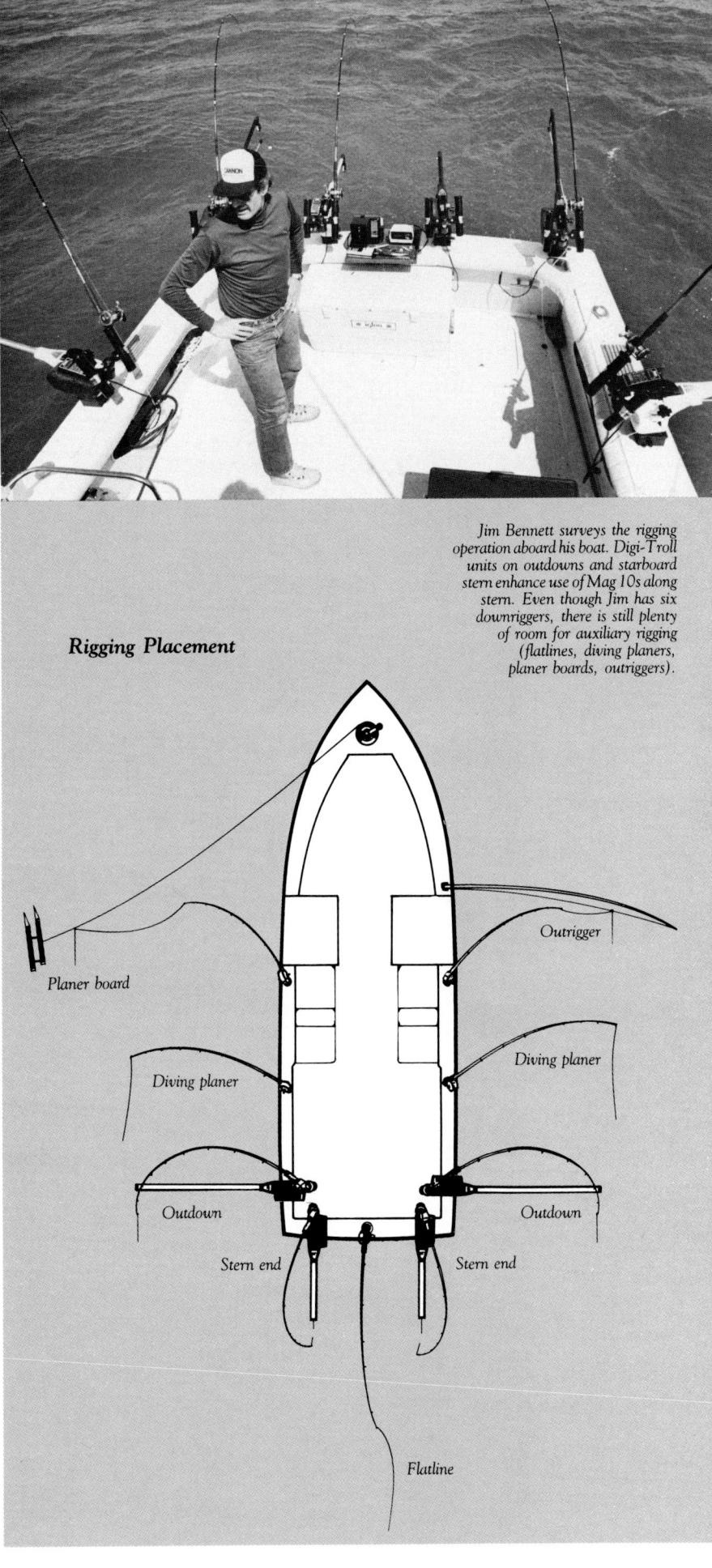

Jim Bennett surveys the rigging operation aboard his boat. Digi-Troll units on outdowns and starboard stern enhance use of Mag 10s along stern. Even though Jim has six downriggers, there is still plenty of room for auxiliary rigging (flatlines, diving planers, planer boards, outriggers).

Rigging Placement

Lure Releases and Stacking Systems

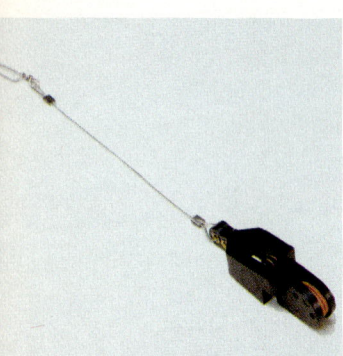

The Offshore Line Release from Cannon features a spring-action clip for fast setting.

Cannon's Quick Release is easy to set and can be adjusted for variable tension.

"It's the little things that count" is an expression we hear often, but nowhere is the saying more true than with downrigger line releases. Some fishermen spend thousands of dollars on their boats, motors and equipment, yet overlook the importance of a $4 release. Paying attention could make them better fishermen.

Good releases are important because they attach the fishing line and lure to the downrigger weight or cable. Most releases are like a trigger or trap in that you set them under pressure. A striking fish sets them off. What happens then is that the fishing line is freed from the shackle of weight or wire cable, and the fisherman can play his catch on a free line.

Good-working releases are one of those little things we take for granted, like sharp hooks. When releases don't work, fish wring off or don't even get hooked in the first place. A release that is too loose may allow line slippage, which makes for lure wandering and incredible tangles. A release that is too tight may cut your line and cost you valuable tackle.

Choosing a downrigger line release is as important as selecting a weight, rod and reel, lure, even a downrigger itself. The release should be simple to set, especially under rough conditions when your boat is pitching and your footing is none too secure. It should be adjustable to accommodate different line weights, sizes and types of lures, rod action, and trolling speed. It should break cleanly under all conditions at all depths.

What is the best release? There are many good ones on the market. Years ago, the Walker Company introduced its popular *Adjustable Line Release*, a tube-type spring-loaded release. Other manufacturers, including Black Marine Products, Wille Products Company, and L.J. Roemer Manufacturing Company, have each devised unique adjustable releases. Cannon's *Quick Release* is a small, easy-to-handle line release with adjustable tension. Also, Cannon recently introduced its *Offshore Line Release*, which features a spring-action clip that opens quickly and easily with finger pressure. When released, tension pads clamp down tightly onto any fishing line, and tension can be increased by inserting line deeper into the pads.

Some fishermen make their own releases from alligator clips, wrapping the teeth with electrician's tape or surgical tubing. Rubber bands are popular as releases, too, with fishermen choosing sizes between No. 12 and 30, according to the amount of tension they want. They secure one end of the rubber band to their fishing line by means of a simple half-hitch. The other end goes into a snap swivel on the downrigger weight or cable.

The advantages of rubber-band releases are low cost, easy rigging and dependability. On the other hand, some trollers with inboard engines complain of getting pieces of the used rubber bands in their bilge pumps. You can buy the rubber bands just about anywhere. Besides its adjustable releases, Cannon makes a rubber-band release, too. Each inexpensive package contains two *Elasti-Clip Line Releases* and 100 *Elasti-Bands*.

Cannon and several other manufacturers also make releases for planer boards, outriggers and stacking systems. As explained in the last chapter, stacking is the practice of adding a rod and/or a lure to a downrigger, outrigger or planer board already working. There are many variations to stacking, and that is why we checked with several Cannon field testers to see how they do it.

When fishing Lake Winnipesaukee for lake trout and landlocked salmon, Pete Grasso of Laconia, New Hampshire, typically rigs his main release off the downrigger weight, then stacks with what he calls a "tail gunner" about 18 inches above the ball. A swivel around the main line attaches the second lure to it, then Grasso adds a rubber band to the downrigger cable for his second release. Such "fixed-depth" stacking can be done at any level. Release lengths (the distance of the lure to the release) vary according to the species he is seeking. Landlocked salmon, for example, need longer releases than lake trout; otherwise, the salmon will come to the net still full of fight.

Ron Yagelski of Michigan City, Indiana, stacks for trout and salmon in southern Lake Michigan. He generally runs heavier baits on bottom and lighter lures on top. To avoid tangles on turns, top-level offerings receive longer release lengths than bottom lures. Jack Jansma of Grand Rapids, Michi-

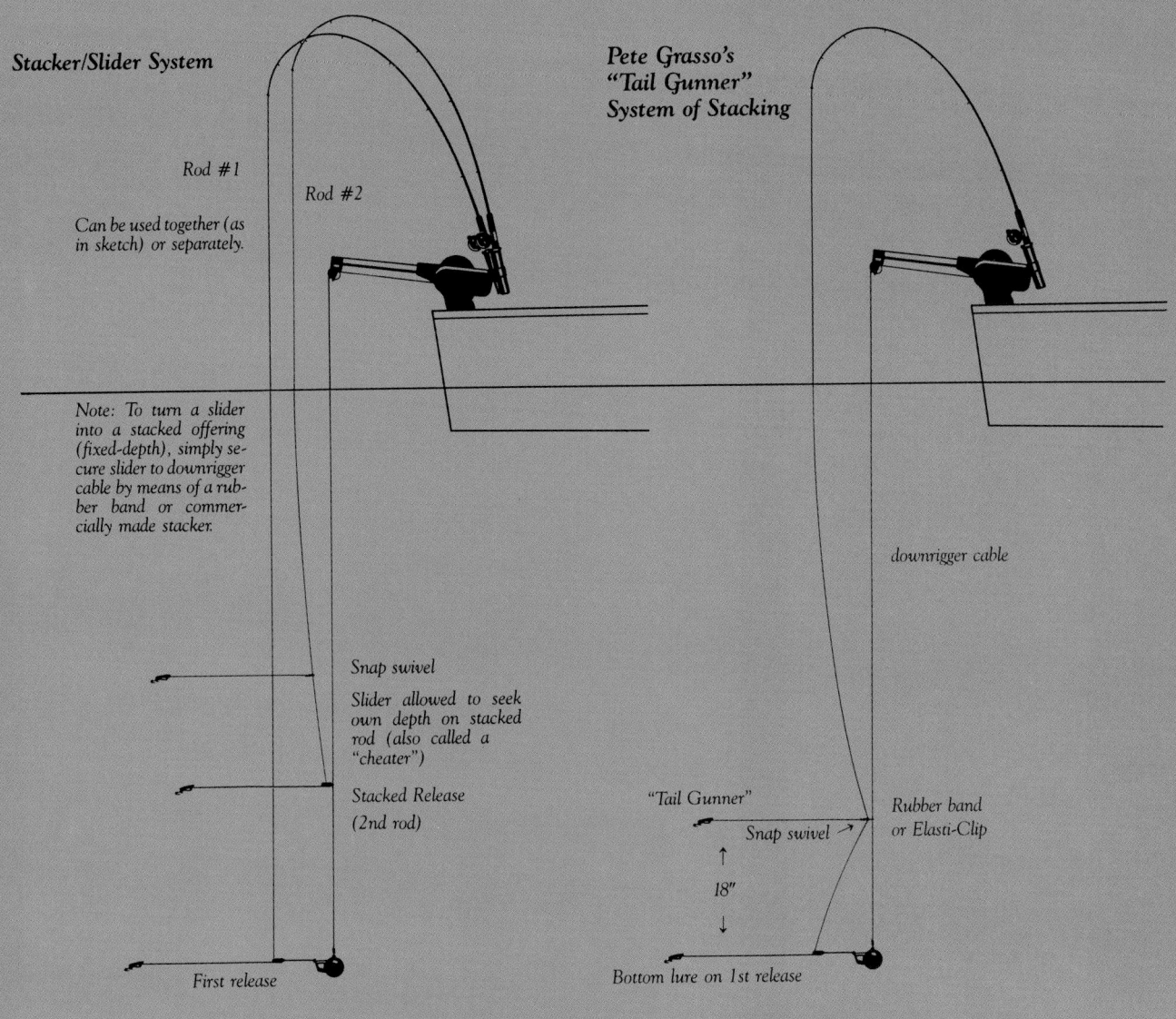

gan, uses the same system but with a twist. On stacked lines Jansma likes to run smaller lures of the same color and type as used on bottom. The result is a "pattern" that might resemble a school of baitfish to a hungry trout or salmon.

When Robert Ribarsky of Port Huron, Michigan, is hunting summer salmon, he often stacks a downrigger about 10 feet above with a similar spoon attached to a separate rod. Then he runs a slider on the extra rod. The result is three baits running at three different levels, all on the same downrigger. Stacking/sliding on just two downriggers is a good way to run a pattern of six lookalike lures to resemble a baitfish school.

Sometimes fishermen have to fine-tune their release system to get them to do what they want. Muskie fishing ace Steve Jones of Mt. Clemens, Michigan, uses downriggers to troll huge muskie plugs and spoons at fast speeds in Lake St. Clair. To keep the violent-action lures in his Offshore Releases, Jones wraps them tightly with rubber bands (Cannon's new *Offshore Saltwater Line Release* features a double-strength spring that may make wrapping the release unnecessary).

George Richey, a trolling-fly manufacturer and lake trout fishing veteran from Honor, Michigan, uses double releases when rigging Dodgers and flies for trolling deep water. At depths of 100 or more feet, too much slack in the line can make hook setting difficult. So Richey secures his fishing line to two Offshore Releases or to an Offshore Stacker which features two releases wired together at different lengths from a snap swivel that is attached to the weight.

Releases are such a small part of the trolling fisherman's program that they are easily overlooked. And that can be a big mistake.

Using downriggers to troll with predetermined patterns can make fair fishermen "good" and good fishermen "great."

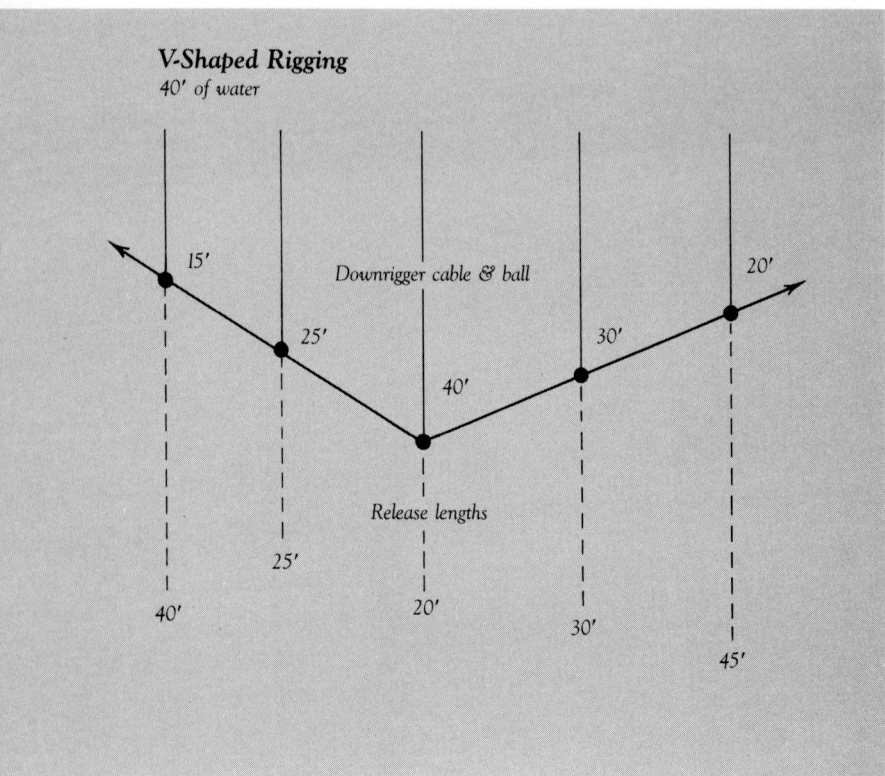

V-Shaped Rigging
40' of water

Fishing waters are as unique as fingerprints. A long time ago, when giant glaciers scoured Canada and the northern states, they left thousands of inland lakes, hundreds of rivers of all shapes and sizes, and five Great Lakes with irregular bottoms. Even man-made reservoirs in the Dakotas and in some southern states feature drowned river banks, gullies, boulder fields, timber. When viewed on sonar, some of these lure-eating structures resemble jagged lunar landscapes. Fishing them can be difficult and, when you lose lures, expensive.

Added to the challenge is the fact that different fish prefer different habitats, which are often keyed to bottom composition, including structure. Some species, such as northern pike, like weed beds. Others, like walleyes or smallmouth bass, prefer a hard bottom of gravel or sand. You can expect some kinds of fish to be suspended between the surface and bottom while others might be found rooted to the bottom itself.

For these reasons, successful freshwater fishing in North America demands the skillful use of specialized tactics. Trolling with downriggers is one of the most effective of all methods, especially when coupled with the use of sensitive electronics. And the best downrigger fishermen are those who rely on trolling patterns.

It makes sense. Trolling patterns offer a blueprint of sorts to help you put the most effective lures at the right places at the right time. Further, they allow you to set up multiple lines and to experiment with little or no fear of tangles. Trolling with predetermined patterns is as much a philosophy as it is a technique. The angler who knows exactly where all his lures are (and how they are working in relation to each other) will outfish the fellow who deep-sixes whatever catches his eye wherever he pleases.

There are many trolling patterns you can try on your favorite lake or river. Adding stackers or sliders to working downrigger setups is one way we have already discussed. Here are some other easy-to-use plans:

When running more than two downriggers, think in terms of rigging them in a general V shape. That is, set inside (stern-end) lines deep and outside (corner or out-down) lines shallower. The reason is that on

Trolling Patterns

turns, outside lures will ride up and inside lures will dig down, whereas those out the back will stay reasonably straight if you have not made leads too long. That's another important point: outside lines can sport longer leads than inside lines. And if you are running attractors, the place to rig them is off the stern.

Thus, *V-shaped rigging* is probably the most popular among trollers with four or more downriggers because it allows them to stagger depths as well as leads with a minimum amount of tangles. Another advantage, of course, is that it allows trollers to cover more water. Here is an illustration of how the pattern works:

Let's say that fish are showing up on the graph at 40 feet deep. Two out-downs are set at 15 and 20 feet respectively. Release lengths (length of lead from release to lure) for these lures are 40 and 45 feet. Corner-set riggers are 25 and 30 feet deep with respective leads of 25 and 30 feet. A single stern-end downrigger is locked at 40 feet deep and features a shorter release of only 20 feet. All the productive depths are therefore covered with varying lead lengths.

V-shaped rigging works very well when fish are either on bottom or suspended or both. A modified form is to keep leads about the same distance and stagger depths only enough to keep lures from tangling. The result is a spread of lures that, to a predator, might resemble a school of baitfish.

Inverted V-shaped rigging, which looks like a caret mark, reverses the order. Now, outside lines are deep (shorter releases) and inside lines are shallow (longer releases). One advantage to this system is that fish are often attracted to outside offerings but end up hitting inside lures. In southern Lake Michigan, for example, coho salmon may be drawn to the propeller boil and brightly painted cannonballs.

According to Dennis Bidigare, a Cannon field tester who lives in St. Clair Shores, Michigan, there is a second advantage to Inverted V-shaped rigging. Dennis first sets up his five downriggers in a typical V-shaped pattern, but if the inside, deeper lines start catching fish, he inverts the V. What happens then is that fish that were hitting the deeper inside lines, now begin striking the

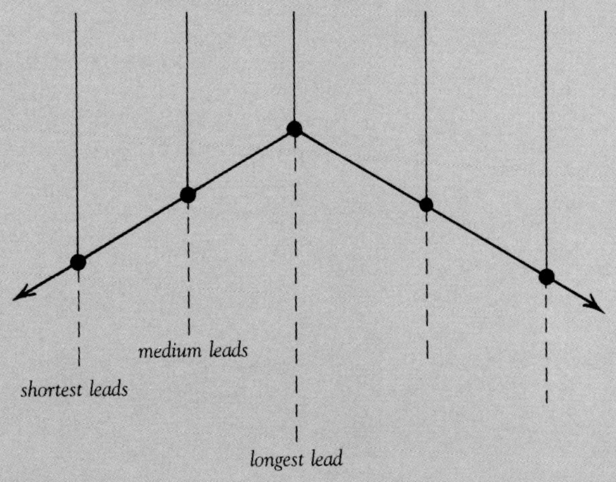

This fisherman mounted his Plane-R-Boom in the center of his small boat for fishing lake shallows in spring.

Inverted V-Shaped Rigging

shortest leads | medium leads | longest lead

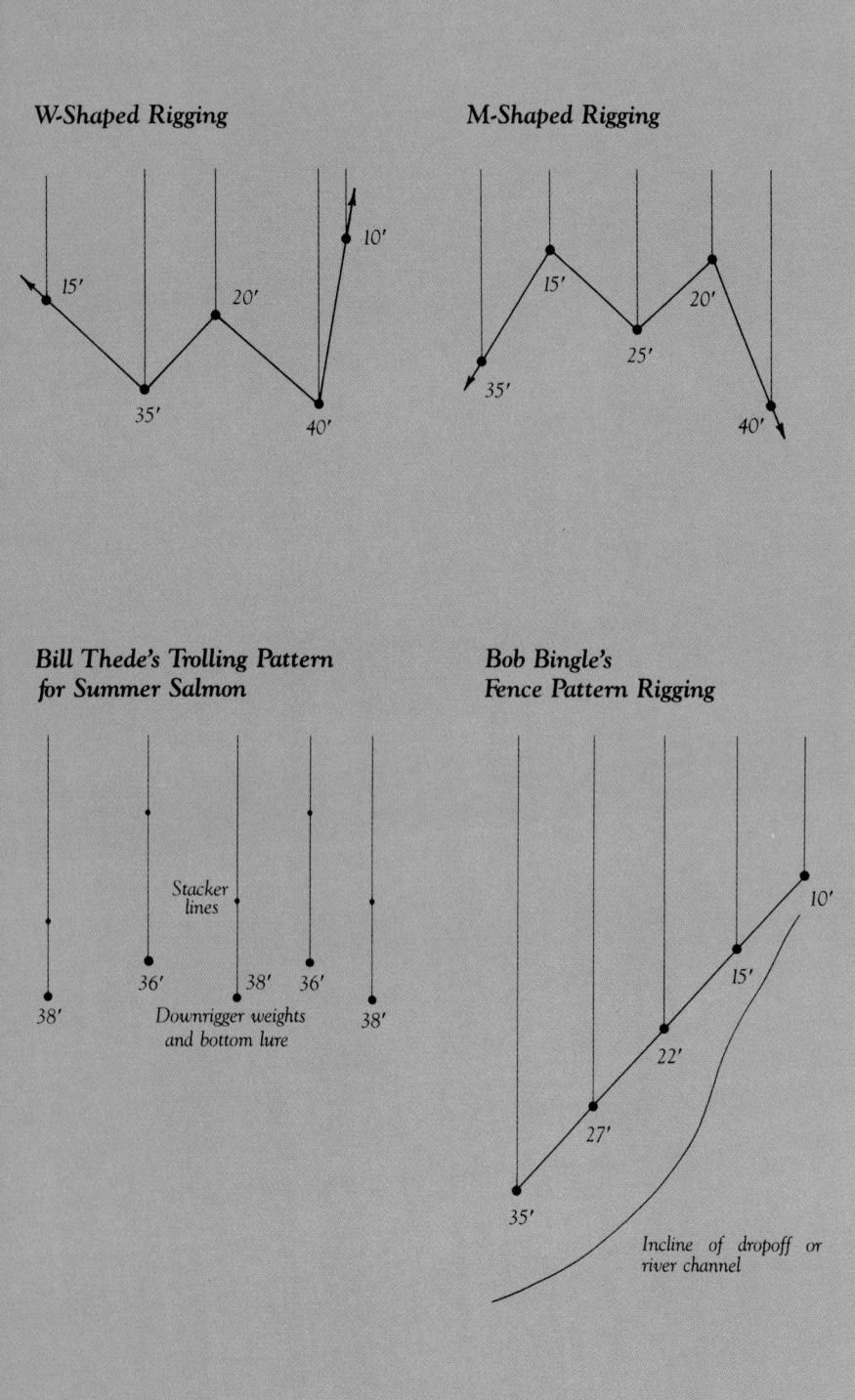

deeper outside lines. Since hooked salmon, brown trout, steelhead and many other species run up and away, the result is fewer tangles.

You can modify these and other rigging patterns to suit your own desires as well as ongoing fishing conditions (waves, boat traffic, etc.). One sunny spring day on Lake Michigan, our party of five were marking fish but could get no takers. On a hunch, I put down a trolling fly behind a big chrome flasher – bright as a welder's flash – on each out-downrigger. Then I lowered three stern-end downriggers, each carrying green-and-chrome Miller Spoons, and locked them in within two feet of each other. Release lengths were all the same, about 100 feet. My theory was that salmon would be drawn to the flashing chrome of the attractor rigs but, because the sun was bright, would back off from striking so close to the boat. Instead, they would snap the smaller, clean-running spoons when they wiggled by a few seconds later.

The theory worked; within five minutes we boated a king salmon and lost another.

One of the slickest ways to set up an imitation of a baitfish school is with *W-shaped* or *M-shaped rigging*. Both patterns tend to spread lures far enough to avoid tangle yet close enough to give a "schooling" effect. Spot lures within a few feet of each other (for example, at depths of 20, 25, 20, 25, and 20 feet for W-shaped rigging or the reverse for M-shaped rigging) and keep leads about the same. To maintain consistent leads, some anglers tie pieces of colored thread or rubber bands to their fishing line. Another method is to count the number of arm pulls as you strip monofilament from the reel. A third is to note the number of line-guide passes across the reel.

Before we leave the subject of schooling effect, consider using the same color and type of lure on all setups. Captain Skip Stafford, a Cannon field tester from New Buffalo, Michigan, practices what he calls "monochromatic" (one-color) fishing when he clusters lookalike lures. Other fishermen, like Bill Muirhead of Milford, Michigan, adopt a limited monochromatic program in which they run lures of the same color close together off one side of the boat, and adopt a different

Trolling Patterns

trolling program on the other side. (The advantage of using two patterns, as I'll explain in detail in a moment, is to give the fisherman options until he sees what will work on that day.) Also, you can practice monochromatic fishing with trolling tactics besides downriggers. As suggested earlier, flatlines, planer boards, outriggers and diving planers can be used with or without downriggers.

And, as we also mentioned, so may stackers be used this way. Bill Thede, a Cannon field tester who guides out of southern Lake Huron ports, makes excellent catches of salmon all season by targeting the 54-degree F. water that kings in particular prefer, then running as many lures as close together as possible within that zone. When wave conditions allow it, Thede typically staggers all five Cannon downriggers on his 25-foot Cherokee at two-foot intervals, then adds stacker lines at five-foot increments.

Once you become familiar with rigging, other trolling patterns of varying depth and release length are possible. You may very well come up with specialized patterns for the area you fish, too. That is what happened to a friend of mine, Bob Bingle, who is a St. Clair River guide from Fair Haven, Michigan. Bingle has always been among the most innovative of Great Lakes anglers. By the time other fishermen learn to copy his tactics, Bob is off on new adventures learning new things. Such experimentation led the way to his "fence pattern."

Spring trolling with downriggers for salmon in the St. Clair River is risky business as fishermen must dodge ice floes and Great Lakes freighter traffic. Besides these hazards, current speed may run as high as eight miles per hour, and so anglers have a tough time keeping lures down in a uniform trolling pattern. Consider, too, that the sharp incline of the river makes it especially hard to keep baits on the money without tangling. The fence pattern is ideal for this situation. It is a formation of gradually deeper lures (with or without corresponding shorter release lengths) from left-to-right or right-to-left, depending on boat direction in relation to shore.

The fence pattern would probably work on Missouri River and Columbia River walleyes and striped bass in Deep South reservoirs as well as other river-channel fishing situations.

Big-boat fishermen with lots of room to set up trolling patterns often rely on automatic pilot features for running the boat while they rig lines. Cannon's *Helmsman* is a unique remote-control steering system that is designed for boats of all sizes and that comes with either a 12-foot cord or wireless one-button hand control that can be carried or clipped to a belt. The Helmsman was designed to allow anglers to fish while steering from anywhere on their boats. Dennis Bidigare mounted his unit at the back of his 25-foot boat, near the stern-center downrigger. His trolling pattern typically involves five stacked downriggers, a pair each of outriggers, Dipsy Divers and flatlines for a total of 16 lines.

"I can't do all that and also steer the boat from inside the cabin," Dennis says. "That's why I use the Helmsman."

You don't need to be a charter-boat captain nor own a big boat to set up an effective trolling pattern. Sport fishermen with only one or two downriggers can be successful, too. Jim Friedel of Fond du Lac, Wisconsin, for example, runs only a pair of lines when fishing Lake Michigan from his 18-foot boat. Friedel's trolling pattern involves short lead-lengths for topwater coho or deepwater kings. When trolling shallow water or when targeting kings near the surface, he increases leads accordingly.

Release lengths should be long enough to produce hits and to clear other lines on turns. According to Pete Grasso of New Hampshire, landlocked salmon and lake trout will both nail lures pulled from six feet to 60 feet behind releases. In midsummer when fish are deep and light conditions are poor, Grasso shortens leads, relying on his weights to act as an attractor. On the other hand, when seeking shy brown trout in shallow water, he might lengthen leads to 200 feet.

The more lures you put out, the more critical release lengths become. Each fisherman will have to adjust his own operation until he gets trolling patterns down the way he wants them. Fine-tuning and a willingness to experiment are reasons that Bill Muirhead is one of the best downrigger fishermen in the business. A look at Muirhead's game plan

The Helmsman handles boat-control chores, freeing an angler to tend to his trolling pattern.

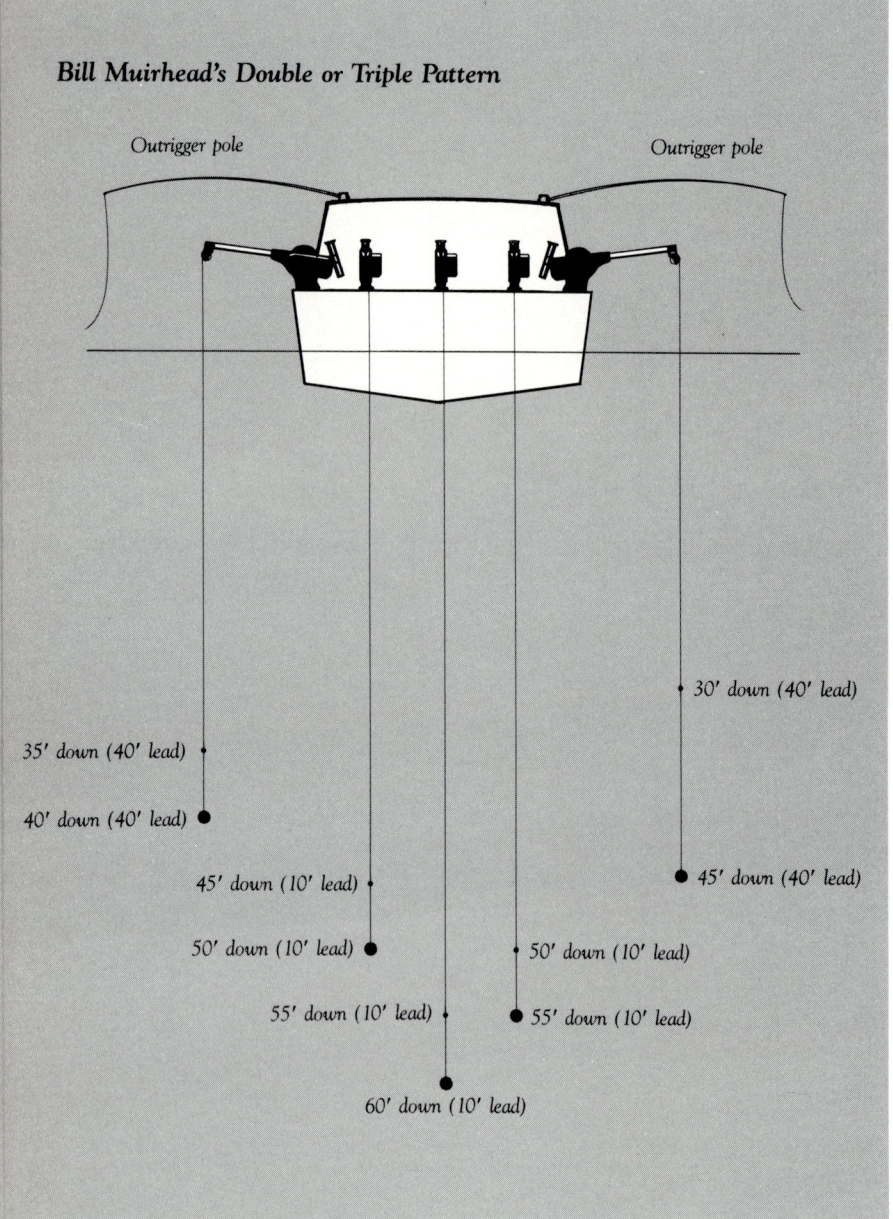

for Great Lakes salmon gives insights into what is possible with downrigger trolling patterns.

Because summertime salmon are often scattered, fishermen must "hunt" them. This means trolling fast with a solid array of lures while keeping an eye on electronics for preferred temperature, baitfish and magnum "hook" marks – the sign of big Chinooks.

On a typical day, Muirhead sets up two trolling patterns with spoons and covers the 30- to 70-foot range of depth while running at about 4½ knots per hour. Heavy, thick spoons such as Locos, Krocodiles and Flutter Chucks go on bottom with somewhat lighter, but still speed-forgiving spoons on top (Lightning Lures with the tail bent up and Flutter Spoons, for example). Bill stacks all five of his downriggers at five-foot increments, but keeps leads at a uniform distance.

"I like to school up my lures," he explained, "and, thanks to downriggers, I can do it in two separate patterns." Out-downriggers, for example, may be set at 40 and 35 feet deep and stacked, respectively, with lures at 35 and 30 feet. Release lengths are all 40 feet. Consequently, the skipper has a "back" pattern of four lures, all 40 feet from the boat, and tiered at five-foot intervals between 30 and 40 deep. Two lures will actually be at 35 feet.

The second pattern involves his three stern-end downriggers. These are set deeper, for example, at 50, 55 and 60 feet (the 60-foot setup is in the middle) and are stacked respectively at 45, 50 and 55 feet. All lures are set at release lengths of 10 feet. Therefore, the second "close" pattern involves six lures, all 10 feet back and at varying depths from 50 to 60 feet. Two lures will actually be at 50 feet and two more will be at 55 feet.

Muirhead's overall rigging pattern of 10 lures is V-shaped; but, as you can see, there are actually two separate patterns within the whole framework. Why two patterns?

"By the time I get two fish in the box, I'll know exactly what is going on," he explained. "In other words, I'll know if fish want deep lures or shallow ones, if they want tight leads or long leads. You can also experiment with lure color and size with the two-pattern system."

Does the skipper switch over com-

Trolling Patterns

pletely to only one program if he starts catching fish? "Not really. But I will make adjustments. For example, if the out-downs produce, rather than raise the stern-end riggers, I might put down a couple of Dipsy Divers to approximate the depth where those strikes occurred. At the same time, if the deeper rigs start producing – rather than drop everything deep, I might just shorten release lengths on one of the out-downs." If stacked offerings interest salmon, Bill may raise a downrigger weight or two or again shorten a couple of release lengths.

Muirhead's two-pattern trolling, then, acts like those research experiments involving both an experimental and control group. When fish start hitting one arrangement, it then becomes the "control pattern." The captain adjusts accordingly without completely ditching what could now be called the "experimental pattern."

Muirhead also runs surface lines such as outriggers, planer boards, flatlines and/or a diving planer or two. This surface arrangement could be thought of as a complement to the two existing patterns or could be considered as a separate third pattern. It largely depends upon what the salmon do. For example, if the flatlines or side-rigged offerings do not produce but other downrigger-trolled lures are working, then Muirhead adjusts the higher lines to copy the successful pattern. For instance, he might add one-pound smooth-cast lead weights to outrigger lures to get them deeper. But if the highlines start producing on their own, Bill removes most of his stacker lines and raises downrigger weights instead.

Each situation is different, but because he knows how and where all his lures are working, Muirhead can adjust his game plan to specific situations. Besides helping to cover all the variables of depth, temperature, lure size, and release length, his overall program also helps him to keep lures in the water and to avoid excessive lure changes.

"I really hate to change lures," he explained, "because it takes too long to re-rig. If I find fish and they won't hit, I'll slow down, even make a couple passes over them in neutral. If that won't work, I try some heavy-duty turns, which tend to speed up those outside-running lures and slow down the inside ones. Sometimes salmon smash lures that rush ahead or hesitate. If that doesn't work, I'll cross fish four ways – upwind, downwind and crosswind – in an effort to get them to go."

If all these tactics fail, the savvy skipper either changes lures or trolls somewhere else. On the other hand, what does he do after the rods have popped, there are fish in the box, and the customers are satisfied?

"I write it all down," Muirhead laughed, "because when circumstances are the same, next time I can go to my log and figure out what will work."

Figuring out what will work involves setting up a predetermined trolling pattern, then fine-tuning it as conditions dictate. Downriggers help make the job easy . . . and fun.

Pair of C-clamped Econo-Riggers on this 16-foot Starcraft boat helps this river fisherman to set up a two-rod trolling pattern.

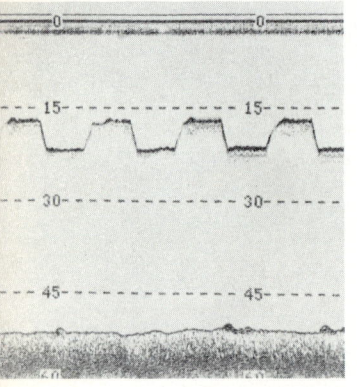

Paper-driven graph can chart a downrigger weight. This is the trolling pattern of a Digi-Troll downrigger set at 5-foot oscillation at 5-second intervals.

In less than 20 years, downriggers changed the way we fish. Now, Cannon's *Digi-Troll* and the new-generation *Digi-Troll II,* the world's first downriggers with computerized control, are changing the way we fish with downriggers.

The Digi-Troll system gives Cannon electric downriggers a memory. Here is what that memory allows fishermen to do:

1. Automatically lower downrigger weights from 5 feet to 699 feet.

2. Store two different depths in memory – then recall either one instantly with a touch of a key.

3. Raise weights automatically while fighting a fish. One touch of the *Auto-Up* key will raise the weight until just before it breaks the water surface. Then it will stop, automatically.

4. Automatically cycle weights up and down in increments of 5, 8, 11, 14 or 17 feet at timed intervals of 5, 10, 15, 30, 45 or 60 seconds. First, the Digi-Troll raises the weight the number of feet you chose. There it pauses for the time interval you selected, then returns to the original depth. The entire cycle repeats continuously until you stop it.

Incredible, isn't it? Computerized downriggers are so new that anglers are continually learning new ways to fish with them. Although primarily designed as a trolling aid, the Digi-Troll is breaking new ground with other fishermen besides trollers. River anglers, for example, can catch trout, salmon, bass, walleyes and pike while cycling their Digi-Trolls as they drift or remain at anchor. The automatic jigging process triggers most fish to hit on the drop as lures flutter down.

Even harder to believe are stories about *ice fishermen* using Digi-Trolls to jig for trout and other fish. But that is what Steve Payne of Post Falls, Idaho, and others do on deep, mountain stream-fed Priest Lake in northern Idaho. The target is huge mackinaw (lake) trout to 35 pounds, which, in winter are usually found on or near bottom in depths to 100 feet. The ice anglers supply electric power to their downriggers by way of portable generators, temporarily mounting the downrigger and generator to a snowmobile or a board across their ice holes. A styrofoam cooler over the generator helps to keep it quiet. After about a half-minute (or until the computer warms up), Payne sets his Digi-Troll pulse-cycle at 3 feet and 5 seconds, then sends down his lure.

The hottest laker-taker is the "Deadly Dick," a one-ounce piece of lead tantalized with a strip of prism tape. Some fishermen add big flashers ahead of the lure to attract the lakers, too. Payne prefers premium-grade, 20-pound-test Ande line, and he keeps release lengths short so as to get a good hook set in the deep water. A battery-powered fish locator is a big help in reading bottom and keeping lures near it.

For years, Great Lakes trollers have known that "fluttering," the practice of popping a release, then putting the rod in a holder and allowing the lure to flutter to the surface, produces strikes. Apparently salmon and trout associate a fluttering lure with an escaping baitfish. The oscillating feature of the Digi-Troll produces a constant fluttering motion to lures. It is especially productive on calm trolling days when there are not waves to lift and drop lures. Cycling the weights also helps lures to cover the upper and lower ranges of a narrow thermocline (the preferred temperature band of water that shows an abrupt change above and below).

No wonder that Great Lakes fishermen report 30 to 80 percent of their catches some days on Digi-Trolls.

Two fishing depths can be stored in memory, even when the power is off. To store the first depth, simply enter the number of feet desired on the easy-touch digit-setting keys. The number will appear on the LED display, temporarily canceling the current depth (000 if you are not fishing). Within four seconds, press *M-1*. Do the same thing for your second depth, only push *M-2.* Within five seconds, the LED display will return to the actual depth you are fishing or 000 if you have not yet set your line. If you forget what depths you have stored, just press *M-1* or *M-2* and the depth currently in that memory will appear on the LED for four seconds.

Think of how easy and fast you can now return a fresh lure or bait to the same spot where you have just caught a fish!

Stacking is a cinch, too, thanks to the Digi-Troll's dual memory bank. For example,

The Digi-Troll System

Great Lakes fishermen report 30 to 80 percent of their catches some days on Digi-Trolls.

Trolling depth is constantly displayed on the Digi-Troll II control so that anglers always know precisely where their lures are running.

let's assume you want one lure to run at 30 feet and another on the same downrigger to stop at 25 feet. Enter 5 feet on *M-1* and 25 feet on *M-2*. Put your bottom lure in the release and press *M-1* followed by *Run*. The weight will drop 5 feet, then stop. Now, stack your second lure and push *M-2* followed by *Run*. Both lures will descend another 25 feet and stop.

Another simple way to set lures with Digi-Troll is to press and hold the *Up* or *Dwn* key. The weight will either rise or fall respectively, changing the LED numbers accordingly, until you remove your finger.

Programming the cycling operation is equally simple. Lower the weight to the depth you desire, then press and hold *C-D*. The LED will show 5, 8, 11, 14, 17 feet and then start over. Choose the amount of oscillation you want (the computer is already programmed for 5 feet, so unless you want a different depth, go to the next step). Now, press and hold *Cyc*. The LED will display the number of pause seconds between movement. It starts with 0 then 5, 10, 15, 30, 45 and 60 before starting over.

Any time you wish to stop the automatic cycle operation, press any of the keys except *Run*, *Cyc* or *C-D* (all conveniently located in the right-hand column).

Besides operational simplicity and adding new and exciting dimensions to fishing tactics, Digi-Trolls have a couple of other nice features going for them. Owners of Cannon *Marlin, Magnum 10A* and *10A II* electric downriggers can upgrade those models (which, incidentally, could have earlier been upgraded from Cannon *Dual Crank 6* or *Uni-Troll 6* manual models) to Digi-Trolls with an optional conversion kit.

Digi-Troll computers are designed for a lifetime of use, too. The entire unit, small enough to fit in your hand, is totally enclosed with epoxy resin so that it will be completely waterproof. In factory tests, a sample unit cycled continuously for 4½ months before the points finally wore out.

Anglers are finding new ways to use Digi-Trolls each season. Soon, we expect to hear success stories from walleye fishermen using them to jig below dam tailraces and from Great Lakes river mouth anglers seeking fall-spawning salmon. Because Digi-Trolls work deep in the ocean to catch grouper on live bait, they will no doubt do the job for live-bait freshwater fishermen, too.

The Digi-Troll. It's sparking a revolution among downrigger fishermen.

With the press of a key, a computerized downrigger will send a lure to one of two depths that can be stored permanently or changed at will.

Damage to booms upon collision with docks and other boats is probably the biggest repair item involving downriggers. Thoughtful placement of out-down units on this boat makes it easy to tow another without danger.

Cannon's Ball Hook allows for a safe storage of downrigger weights while in transit.

There are few things that can go wrong with a downrigger, and they are simple and reasonably safe to use. Even so, since all fishing situations involve potential danger – from baiting hooks to running boat engines – anglers should always be safety-conscious.

Two major problems can crop up when you fish with downriggers. One is that extended booms (or, as discussed earlier, poorly mounted out-downriggers) can collide with docks and other boats. The other main concern is that weights can hang up on underwater structures. Although a good bottom-scanner and the use of Cannon's *Banana* weights can avoid most tangles, sometimes hangups occur without warning. Unmarked commercial fishing nets, for example, can deal downrigger trollers a set of fits. It is a good idea to keep a pair of leather gloves and a wire-cutters handy in case you have to pull a downrigger cable free or cut it off in the event of emergency.

Common sense, such as wearing soft-soled shoes (not leather) and maintaining a healthy respect for the potential dangers of big-water fishing (high waves, marker buoys denoting shipping channels or shallow reefs, boating traffic, etc.) will keep you out of trouble. You should know, too, that Cannon downriggers have been carefully designed with the utmost concern for safety.

There are no holes in the reel, for example, to catch fingers. Indeed, all Cannon reel and clutch systems are enclosed, and all controls are located on the top or side so fishermen don't have to reach to operate them. "The only way to get a finger caught in the cable of a Cannon downrigger is to do it deliberately," said Lou Pomaville, company service manager.

Cannon's *Retro-Ease Weight Retriever* was designed with safety in mind, too. A smooth-rolling nylon pulley fits over the downrigger cable, and a long cord allows you to pull weights to the boat for removal or resetting fishing line releases. The Retro-Ease thus lessens the danger of heavy weights banging into the boat, a particular problem in rough water. A specially designed lock holds the Retro-Ease in place until you release it. When you are done fishing and wish to remove weights, Cannon's *Ball Hook* con-

Safety and Maintenance

veniently and safely lets you stow the weight while in transit.

Likewise, the former safety problem of rising weights banging into the boom is solved with Cannon's *Short Stop* unit. The Short Stop, which is potted in a waterproof epoxy resin, is a tiny insulator that attaches to the downrigger cable just above the weight. The Short Stop sends a small electric current down the cable, and when the insulator breaks the water surface, the rising weight stops automatically. Fishermen can now tend to other matters while their downrigger weights ascend.

The company's new *Switch Guard* is designed to prevent damage to electric switches in handling and to avoid accidental starting of the downrigger motor. Made of a high-impact ABS plastic, the easily installed Switch Guards feature "wings" that protect the toggle switch at the rear of the motor housing.

Downrigger durability has been enhanced with the addition of Lexan polycarbonate, an incredibly tough high-tech resin composite that is lighter than aluminum and acclaimed for its bullet-proof strength. Lexan is now used in *Magnum 10A II* electric and *Uni-Troll 6 II* manual models (in white color), and the black Marlin series, which were primarily designed for saltwater use but are growing in popularity among freshwater fishermen, too. The black Lexan Marlins contain an additive to eliminate fading from ultra violet light.

According to Pomaville, less than one percent of all Cannon downriggers are returned to the factory for repair (bodies and booms carry a lifetime warranty; all other parts are warranted for 90 days). Biggest problems, the service manager says, are broken booms and handles and wrenched swivel-head pulleys from collisions with other boats and docks. Switches may wear out over time, too.

At this writing, Cannon has 36 authorized trained service centers throughout the U.S. and Canada with more being added each year.

Pomaville said that owners can get the most mileage from their downriggers by adopting a simple maintenance program. Once each season, use a multi-purpose grease (not an oil) to relubricate the reel shaft, motor gears and swivel head. Check bearings in *Easi-Troll, Uni-Troll* and all electric models, too. If dirty, soak them in gasoline, then clean and repack with the multi-purpose grease.

Protective switch boots should be replaced periodically. The silicone rubber boots guard the switches from water damage. Replacing worn boots will greatly extend switch life.

Perhaps the most important maintenance consideration is with downrigger cables. That is because the stranded stainless-steel cables become rigid with continued use and eventually lose their strength. Check them periodically with a cotton swab for kinks, curling and broken strands. The lower portion in particular gets the most wear. Since the cable costs less to replace than a downrigger weight, consider changing the cable each year – if your downrigger is an electric model – and every other year if it is a manual unit.

During the cable inspection, pay particular attention to the termination. If there is any sign of wear, reterminate at once. This important job is made easy with Cannon's new *Terminator Kit*. The kit, which contains enough components to reterminate six snap swivels, includes six-each cushion cartridges, stainless-steel collars and snap swivels, along with 50 brass sleeves. Each of the components is neatly contained in separate compartments in a handy see-through plastic case.

Cannon also sells crimping pliers. Pomaville suggests that owners be careful not to overcrush the cable when reterminating. Using the special pliers and crimping with one hand only should make the new crimp as strong as the cable itself.

A downrigger is an investment that should last for many years. To get the most from your investment, follow these simple suggestions on safety and maintenance. Consider, too, adding *Cannon Covers* to your downriggers. Made of tough nylon, the covers snap around all models with single or double rod holders. The covers help protect the downrigger and add to the aesthetics of your trolling operation.

Finally, to guard against theft, you can lock downriggers to their bases with a special Cannon lock that fits above the base.

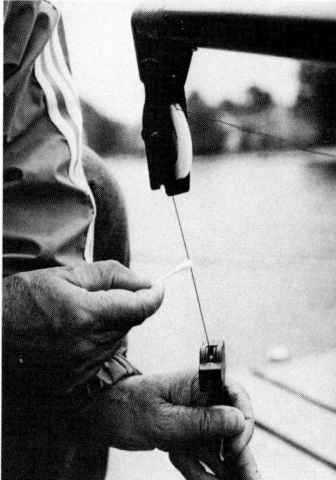

A cotton swab will help check for frayed or nicked cables, especially in the lower portion.

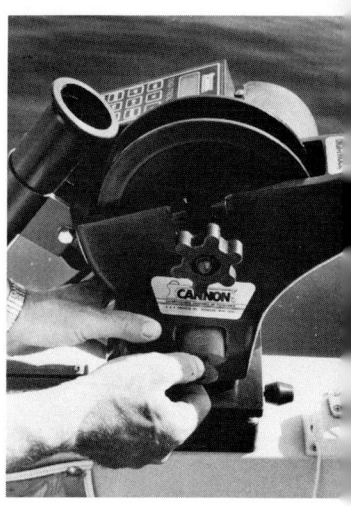

Special locks allow owners to protect their downriggers against theft. Recessed design keeps lock out of the way.

Temperature

"Water temperature is always important, no matter what freshwater species you are seeking or where you are fishing; yet many anglers never even think to consider it."

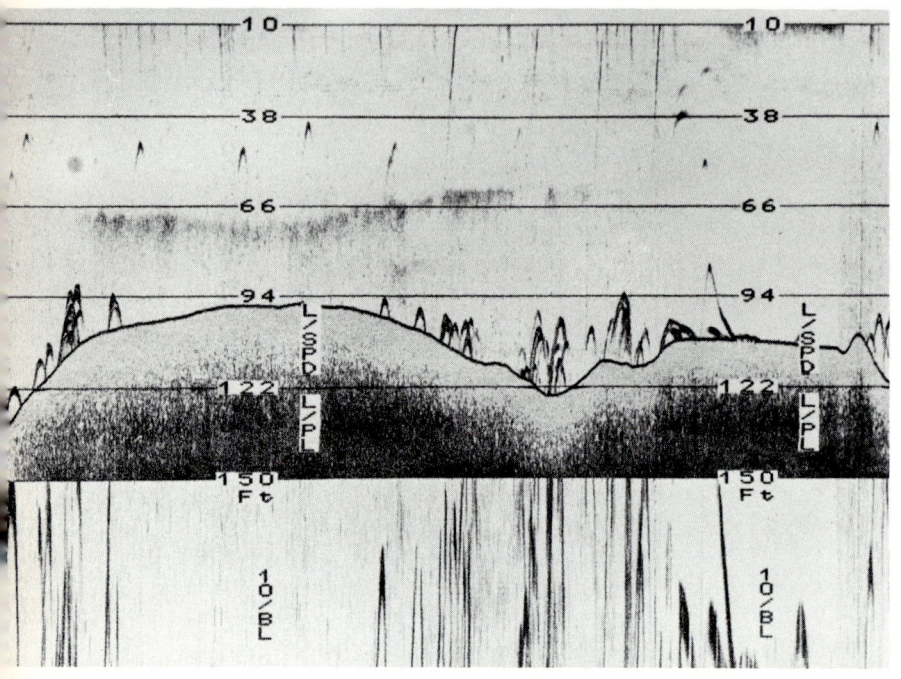

Fish are not always right in the thermocline. Notice these Lake Superior lake trout are oriented to bottom in 95 to 125 feet of water. The thermocline is in the 70-foot range (note stray fish above this range as well). Photo is of a King 1350 paper-driven graph.

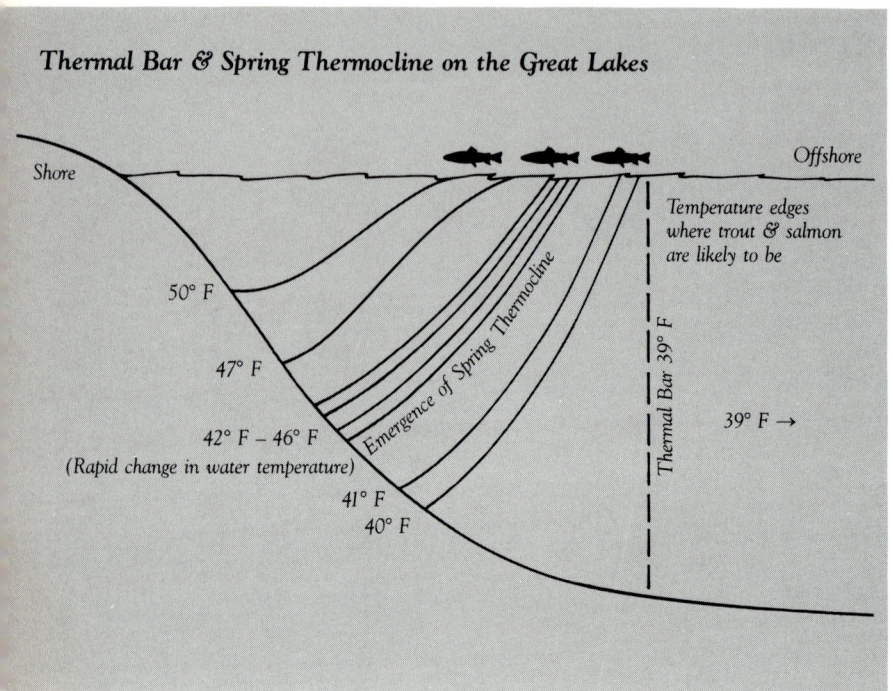

Spring trolling for king salmon in Lake Michigan is a hit-or-miss sport. On one day, Captain Kevin Hughes of Onekama, Michigan, put several chrome-sided kings in the fish box. The next day, just three hours after beginning our troll, the only thing in the cooler was pop.

It wasn't Kevin's fault. One of the best skippers on the lake, he had done all the right things. His six-downrigger setup of trolling lures would look like a giant M if viewed underwater. The two out-downriggers and the center-stern unit were deep-set from 30 to 35 feet with leads of 30 feet behind the boat. Captain Hughes had locked in the corner downriggers at 15 feet, setting releases at 80 to 120 feet. The last downrigger, also a stern-end unit, complemented these extremes.

We were running Lightning Lures and J-Plugs – proven baits for Lake Michigan spring kings – in all the fish-catching colors: white and orange, white and blue, green and yellow. We should have been weary from fighting fish. But we weren't. So we changed trolling speed and lure colors, even though we weren't marking anything.

Sometimes you have to hunt salmon in spring, and we had done that, too, following the darker plume of 47-degree F. water from the Portage Lake outflow as it seeped into a clean, cold (45-degree F.) Lake Michigan. When that failed, we broke out a planer board and an outrigger and headed for shoreline shallows. Still no strikes.

That's when Kevin noticed a change in the wind direction from northwest to northeast.

"This could blow warm air from land into the upper layer of the lake," he said. "Let's go back to the plume and check the temperature." When we began to troll down-lake from the southern pierhead, the surface-temperature gauge aboard the *Sandpiper*, Hughes' 28-foot Bertram, registered 49 degrees F., two degrees warmer than before.

We hadn't gone 100 yards when a rod went off, then began jabbing like a scorpion's tail. Fifty yards behind the boat, a 20-pound king salmon tried to tailwalk on Lake Michigan. A quarter-hour later that fish beat a tattoo on the boat bottom until Kevin subdued him and slid him into the cooler.

Temperature

Within a couple of hours, six more kings (from five to 20 pounds each) joined him.

Hard to believe that only two degrees of water temperature could turn around our troll from failure to success. But water temperature is always important, no matter what freshwater species you are seeking or where you are fishing; yet many anglers never even think to consider it. Thanks to a wide selection of competitively priced probes on today's market, temperature is a variable that fishermen can easily and cheaply monitor. No, they may not be able to control it, but at least they can be aware of temperature's significance.

Because fish are coldblooded, they take on the temperature of their environment. That doesn't mean they like it, though. Each freshwater species has an optimum temperature zone where it is most active and where important things like eating, migration and spawning occur. Hatchery experts know full well the importance of temperature to fish production. From hatchery conception until they end up in Joe Troller's cooler, gamefish such as trout and salmon prefer and prosper from specified temperatures. Studies show that Chinook eggs, for example, grow best at 52 degrees and Chinook fingerlings at 58 degrees. Once released, the baby kings seek temperatures from 54 to 62 degrees throughout the 2½ to 3½ years they live. Coho salmon like this same range. Lake trout prefer the cooler side at 48 to 52 degrees, and rainbow/steelhead favor the warmer side at 58 to 62 degrees. Brown trout like their water warmer yet – 65 to 75 degrees.

The angler who knows something about temperature, as it relates to the species he is targeting, will have a leg up on the fisherman who ignores it altogether.

It also helps to know something about the phenomenon of *water temperature change*. Dr. Michael P. Voiland, who administers the New York Sea Grant Extension Program on Lake Ontario, has done extensive studies on seasonal changes in water temperature there. His findings can be applied to the other four Great Lakes and, to some degree, large inland lakes. Here is what happens:

Freshwater becomes densest at 39 degrees F. During winter, as portions of the big lakes freeze at 32 degrees, this 39-degree water sinks to the bottom. Then, spring runoff and the sun's higher rays from the approaching summer solstice combine to warm the upper layer (the "epilimnion") of water, forcing the layer of cooler water (the "hypolimnion") down. When inshore water temperatures higher than 39 degrees meet offshore temperatures less than 39 degrees, a vertical wall of water called an "interface" or "thermal bar" results.

This thermal bar moves slowly offshore until sometime in late spring or summer when rollover is complete and the summer thermocline (a more-or-less horizontal band of water where the epilimnion and hypolimnion mix) forms. Before that happens, though, right behind the thermal bar is something called the "spring thermocline." It is an inclined narrow band of water from 42 to 46 degrees that is deepest closer to shore and yet comes to the surface farthest from shore. Thus, it offers both a surface and a deeper layer of water differing in temperature from its surroundings.

Baitfish, salmon, trout and other species are often drawn to the warmer temperatures produced by both the thermal bar and the spring thermocline. Great Lakes anglers are just now learning to look for these thermal bars and to fish along the edge or to "stitch the seam," that is, zig-zag back and forth across the interface. Besides monitoring surface temperatures with a probe, they watch for changes in the color of the lake and note baitfish schools on the graph, current swirls, flotsam and other debris that denotes a "color line," herring gull activity, and slicks.

"Slicks" – smooth water surrounded by ripples – often denote a thermal bar, which could be 100 yards to one-half mile across. Sometimes the difference is dramatic. Bill Muirhead, a Cannon field tester, says he found a Lake Michigan thermal bar one time that resembled a rip tide. "There was all kinds of junk in it – tires, lumber and debris," Muirhead said. "The temperature difference must have been severe – probably 20 degrees or so – because some of that stuff came shooting right out of the water. It was like something out of the *Twilight Zone*."

Some trollers with big, seaworthy boats are running out halfway across Lake Michi-

Fish Hawk Model 520 hand-held temperature gauge comes with 100 feet of line. Anglers either stop the boat to measure or hook the thermocouple to a downrigger weight before lowering.

Surface temperature probes, such as this Lowrance LDT-2000, fit right into the dashboard behind the steering wheel and give constant readouts while under power.

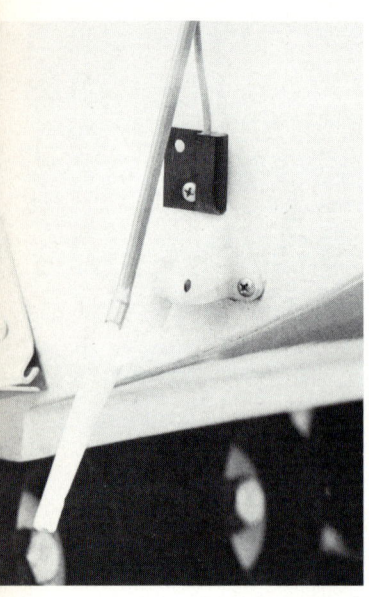

Thermocouple (black square-shaped object) fits onto rear of boat so that when craft is in the water, the thermocouple will be just under the surface.

gan as late as mid-July to look for the thermal bar. Bottom here may be 600 feet deep, right off their depth finders. Kevin Hughes said that on a hot summer day, as you approach the thermal bar, the air suddenly becomes decidedly cool, like walking into an air-conditioned room. Occasionally a fog bank will blanket the water. Steelhead, salmon and sometimes brown trout are often suspended just under the surface along the edge of the temperature break. Flatlines, shallow-set downriggers and side-rigged lures such as planer boards or outriggers are popular trolling tactics.

When rollover is complete and the summer thermocline forms, anglers can find it, too, with the help of a good temperature probe. Storms and variable winds can change the elusive thermocline, narrowing or widening its swath accordingly and sending it deeper or shallower.

One way to understand the thermocline is to think of it as a band of water with higher temperatures above and lower temperatures below. If you know the preferred temperature of the fish you are seeking, you may, indeed, find that species in or near the thermocline. As noted in the last chapter, each body of water is different. Snowmelt, stream discharge, prevailing winds, depth and structure all contribute to a lake's or river's temperature profile. Knowing the location of the thermocline in summer or the warmest water in spring helps anglers to fish the lake accordingly.

For example, in spring, besides seeking thermal fronts, Great Lakes trollers look for thermal plumes from power plant and factory thermal discharges, as well as color lines created from rivers and streams freighting warm water into the big lake. They take advantage of the sun-warmed shallows, too, along with targeting the chute between pierheads, wave troughs that parallel shore, and the lee sides of islands or points on days when cold winds blow from the north or west. They do this because they know that spawning smelt, alewives, gizzard shad and lake emerald shiners are among the many species of baitfish that seek spawning water in warm lake shallows or tributaries.

Stream discharge into an inland lake is nearly always a hotspot in spring and again in fall. As fall wears on, the sun's rays strike the water at a decreasing angle. Thus, the lake surface cools, forcing the warmer water deep. Once again, in winter when the lake is frozen, the warmest water will be 39 degrees, and it will be on the bottom.

But in summer, it is not always a good idea just to fish in the thermocline. Instead, scatter lines throughout, as well as above and below the thermocline, until you establish the strike pattern for the day. There are several reasons for this. One is that predators might be seeking food which has a preferred temperature range quite different from their own. Lake Michigan trollers are finding this phenomenon to be so true as the forage base shrinks and trout and salmon have to hunt harder for something to eat. These anglers are telling strange stories of catching salmon deep and lake trout near the surface some days, the exact opposite of what one would expect. Another reason for scattering lures is structure. Lake trout, for instance, may lie in the mud on lake bottoms several degrees colder than their normal preference of 48-52 degreees. Apparently, they are willing to forego the comfort of temperature for one of structure or food. Walleyes in Lake Erie, for example, usually suspend, often several degrees out of temperature, to take advantage of suspended gizzard shad and other good things to eat.

Preferred temperature is the place to *begin* looking for fish, but that does not mean they will always be found there. Each lake and each fishing situation is different involving temperature. Fall coho fishermen in southern Lake Michigan seek the warmest water available, just as they do in spring. Art Talsma, a Cannon field tester and savvy Lake Oahe fisherman, believes that Missouri River reservoir salmon are nearly always found at the shallowest depth where they can stay comfortable and still find plenty of food. He has further noted, along with many Great Lakes trollers, that salmon often move vertically, as well as horizontally, during the course of a day. Early morning, for example, might find them at 40 feet or even in the shallows off pierheads where they have been lunching all night on the smorgasbord buffet entering the lake. By midmorning, though, these salmon might be in depths of 70 or

Temperature

even 80 feet. Then, in the evening, they may return to shallows.

Remember that the thermocline is not exact, that its upper and lower boundaries are as elusive as quicksilver, and that instead of a definite size, it tends to undulate, sometimes as dramatically as a rollercoaster. Larry Colombo, a spokesman for Techsonics Industries, Inc. (makers of Humminbird electronics) says that fishermen can often "read" the thermocline on their charts, LCRs or flashers. Referrring to an illustration that he provided, Larry says that all three electronics were set on the 60-foot scale. The thermocline depicted in the illustration began at about 35 feet, with the heaviest indication at 40 feet. The heavy band on the chart paper shows this layer; you can see the fish for yourself.

The same conditions can be witnessed on the LCR display and flasher dial when you know what you are looking for. The LCR shows the thermocline as a series of dots (pixels) in a straight line across the face of the display. Once a fisherman recognizes the thermocline, he will not mistake it for any other signal. The same is true for the flasher dial; a constant flash, probably weaker than the normal return, will identify the thermocline at a fairly constant level on a given body of water.

Much is known about how fish relate to temperature. In 1974, the University of Massachusetts published an annotated bibliography of the effect of temperature on fish. The authors said they selected their 450 references from over 7,000 research projects. Even though much more has been learned in the past 12 years, much more remains to be discovered.

I suspect that the better fishermen will play a hand in those discoveries. They will also be the first to experiment with them.

Ways to Measure Temperature

Fishermen have four major ways to measure water temperature:

1. At any depth while hand-held. Inexpensive hand-held temperature gauges allow you to measure water temperature as deep as 200 feet. Some, like the Fish Hawk 510 (100 feet of cable) and the 520 (200 feet), even feature depth-readout in a digital display. Because the sensor probe itself is weighted, simply drop it over the boat side with your engine in neutral or attach it to a downrigger weight while under power. Cheaper yet are models sold by the HeathKit Company that you can put together yourself.

2. At the downrigger weight. Great Lakes trollers have recently discovered that, due to underwater currents, lure speed can be significantly different than boat speed. Several manufacturers are now producing temperature gauges and trolling-speed indicators that attach to the downrigger cable just above the weight or to the weight itself. These sophisticated electronics are able to measure the slightest change in temperature or lure speed. The Weller ProCombinator and the EMS Penguin are two such popular units.

An exciting product in this category is the Fish Hawk Thermo-Troll 800 Computer. Snapping a sensor to the downrigger cable allows accurate, wireless reading of temperature, speed and pH to depths of 200 feet. Trollers can compare this information with temperature, speed and pH at the surface. A compact receiver display mounts at the helm, transom or anywhere else the fisherman desires.

3. At the surface. Surface temperature is especially important in spring when trout and salmon seek the warmest water available. Pelican, Micronar, Si-Tex and Lowrance all offer surface temperature probes that efficiently mount within the dashboard. Other models mount on the dashboard itself, and some fishermen even like to secure the display units on the transom of their boats so they can monitor water temperature while setting lines. Special mounting brackets attach the sensor to the lower secton of the boat stern. Once in the water, the boat's draft puts the probe just under water.

4. On the graph or liquid-crystal recorder. Some manufacturers now offer liquid-crystal recorders and paper-driven graphs that measure surface temperature while detailing bottom structure and suspended fish. Ray Jefferson's Telescan 1000, Impulse Manufacturing's Micro Trac 6800, Lowrance's X-5, and Computrol's Bottom Line II are examples of liquid-crystal electronics featuring temperature probes. King's Model 1060 is an excellent chart recorder that measures surface temperature.

The trolling fisherman uses his knowledge of water temperature to eliminate one of the sport's biggest variables. Given the wide range of ways to measure temperature today, there really is no excuse not to do it.

Preferred Temperatures of Freshwater Fish

The following are preferred temperature ranges for major freshwater species caught on downriggers:

Bluegills 64-70
Brown Trout 65-75
Catfish 70-75
Crappie 65-75
Chinook salmon . . . 54-62
Coho salmon 54-62
Lake trout 48-52
Largemouth bass . . 75-80
Muskellunge 65-75
Northern pike 65-75
Rock bass 55-60
Smallmouth bass . . 68-70
Steelhead/Rainbows . 58-62
Striped bass 62-67
Walleyes 65-70
Yellow perch 66-70

Electronics

"Is the world of electronic gadgetry taking the sport out of sport fishing? The answer is 'no'."

Some trollers like to have a temperature and trolling-speed indicator near the work area so they can monitor these variables. A flasher or LCD works well here, too.

Available Electronics

Putting electronics on a boat equipped with downriggers makes as much sense as putting toothpaste on a brush. You can clean your teeth without the paste, of course, but the job is performed faster and more efficiently when you put something on those bristles. Likewise, you can catch fish on downriggers without the aid of electronics, but you will catch more fish with them.

You will have more fun, too, as well as learn plenty about fish habits and habitat and effective angling methods. Learning all they can is one big reason why many fishermen take up the sport in the first place. And the things you can learn, thanks to spaceage electronics, are nothing short of phenomenal.

Consider "sonar" (SOund NAvigation Ranging), developed many years ago by the navy for finding enemy submarines. The sonar unit or machine sends an electrical impulse to a transducer that the angler has mounted on or underneath his boat. The transducer converts these electrical impulses to sound waves, which travel downward in ever widening rings. The sound waves bounce off anything they meet – bottom, structures, fish, weeds – then return to the transducer where they are converted back to electrical impulses. Information, like depth, bottom composition and objects between the transducer and bottom, are displayed on the unit's screen. Thus, sonar is like having eyes underwater.

As is true with downriggers, electronics are changing the way we fish. Not surprisingly, then, the two modern developments go hand in hand – like, well, toothpaste and toothbrushes.

Early sonar units were bulky and expensive, but microchip technology and fierce competition among many manufacturers have given us sonar units today that are uncannily accurate, often measuring objects an inch apart at depths to several hundred feet. Sonar in its many forms – flashers, paper-driven chart recorders (often called "graphs"), liquid-crystal displays (LCDs), and video (both black-and-white and color) – can help the fisherman in many ways:

• Besides constantly knowing where bottom is, he can determine bottom type by the strength and shape of signal.

• He can identify fish-holding structures, such as weeds, logs, boulders, dropoffs, brush and trees.

• Depending on the sonar-unit type, he may be able to "see" the thermocline as well as monitor surface temperature, boat speed, even log his trip in terms of distance and time.

• He will be able to locate fish and, after some experience, may be able to identify them by species. If his unit is equipped with zoom capability, he will be able to focus on only a few feet of water at a time.

• He can track his downrigger weights and even his lures.

• He can be a safe fisherman, relying both on what the sonar display tells him are shallow-water obstructions and on listening for a warning alarm that he preset.

Besides sonar, VHF marine radios and Loran C (LOng RAnge Navigation) help a fisherman to be a safe boater and better angler. Sophisticated VHF radios with extended antennas project his "ears" to nearly a hundred miles and allow him to scan more than 80 channels, plus key on channel 16, the Coast Guard's emergency broadcast channel. Some scanning units actually lock on a receiving signal to pinpoint its location. Therefore, fishermen can tell where a successful caller is having his luck. In addition, if the call is coming from a harbor or land base, the angler can find his way home in the dead of night or in a pea-soup fog.

Loran C is such an exciting development as a navigational and fishing aid that we are featuring a special section on it in this chapter.

But sonar is the first consideration of most serious fishermen thinking about adding electronics to their boats. Choosing the right type and model number of sonar for you can be confusing and frustrating. To make things clearer and to help in your decision, consider these key thoughts:

1. Any sonar unit can help you become a better fisherman, and no one unit is "better" than another. Much depends on the type of fishing you plan to do and the waters you expect to visit. How successful you are also hinges on your willingness to learn and your ability to interpret what the sonar tells you.

Modern electronics have helped to change the way we fish.

2. Sonar does not frighten fish. Fish cannot hear the high-frequency signals that the unit sends out and that are bounced back to the transducer and, ultimately, to your display screen.

3. All sonar units are sensitive and should be handled carefully.

4. Cone angle varies from five degrees to 60 degrees and depends upon the transducer type. According to the Lowrance Company, in 15 feet of water a 20-degree transducer covers an area about five feet in diameter, while the eight-degree transducer covers only about a two-foot-wide circle. In terms of area covered, then, the 20-degree transducer covers 525 percent more than the eight-degree transducer. So the 20-degree transducer is better, right?

Not necessarily. Lowrance suggests using the 20-degree transducer when looking for fish or structure, or to easily find drop-offs or reefs, and to see more fish. In deep water, however, with the sound energy being concentrated in a smaller area, the eight-degree transducer can reach to greater depths. Because of the narrower cone angle, the eight-degree transducer can pinpoint sharp drop-offs better than the 20-degree signal.

Most downrigger trollers, however, generally like the wider cones to help them track weights. Using Lowrance's X-16 Computer Sonar with 45-degree transducer, it is possible for a fisherman to track six downrigger weights at once.

5. Linked to transducer cone angle is the frequency with which sonar units send and receive electrical impulses, which are measured in kilohertz (Khz). Low frequency sonar (50 Khz, for example) units generally feature wide cones, and high-frequency units (200 Khz, for example) have narrow cones. Some anglers purchase two sonar units with different frequencies — one for deep water and one for shallow. With some models, like the Lowrance X-16, you can get both high and low frequencies for a single investment.

6. Constantly fine-tuning your sonar unit will help it to consistently report back what it "sees" and is a big aid in interpreting the information. All models have sensitivity adjustments for filtering out interference and for delivering the strongest signal possible. The first and most important step in fine-

Available Electronics

tuning the unit is to establish a double echo at a consistent intensity. Doing that will help you to interpret any change in bottom composition. Most manufacturers include fine-tuning directions in the owners' manuals for the products they sell.

7. Testing your sonar on a familiar lake will help you to understand how it measures such variables as depth, soft and hard bottoms, weeds, structure, and even fish. Pick up a good topographic map of your favorite lake, then use the sonar to find any structure, depths and contours illustrated.

Electronics such as Color-C-Lektors, pH meters, temperature probes, trolling-speed indicators, marine radios, Loran C, sophisticated sonar and computerized downriggers are changing the way we fish. Future units will be more sophisticated than ever, and they will be even easier to use.

A fair question is this: Is the world of electronic gadgetry taking the sport out of sport fishing? The answer is "no." If anything, electronics add to the challenge and the fun, just like computers make math and writing more interesting and intriguing. All electronics do is help you to interpret a myriad of fishing variables, including the finding and identification of fish. Catching those fish is still up to you.

This paper printout from a sensitive graph shows clean marks made by fish. Smudges are clouds of baitfish. Diagonal lines were made by raising and lowering downrigger weights.

Sonar has a wide range of uses for fishermen. This small-boat river angler is using a portable LCD for monitoring depth and fish.

Few decisions to buy are easy, and the toughest decisions are those you have to make alone. This is especially true with buying sonar, when it is possible to bust a $100 to $1,000 bill and walk out of the store with a gadget that weighs a pound or so and fits in the palm of your hand. How do you know you want to spend the money in the first place? Then if you do shell out the cash, how do you know you purchased a product that will do the job for you?

Begin by knowing what type of sonar you might need, then learn all you can about the products available before you buy a unit. For example, would a $199 flasher serve your purposes as well as a $1,000 chart recorder? How good are the new liquid-crystal display (LCD) units? Would you be better off with video? It is not our intention to trumpet one type of sonar over another but simply to point out major differences in regard to using them to fish with downriggers. The truth is that any sonar unit will upgrade your fishing program. Still, we hope to offer some key considerations. Let's begin with a look at the four major types of fishing sonar:

Flashers

Flashers were the earliest sonar models available to fishermen some 30 years ago. Tremendous advances have been made in flasher resolution and sensitivity in recent years, and they remain popular enough that several manufacturers vie for an increased market share. Besides their relatively low price (when compared to more sophisticated sonar units), the advantage of flashers is their constant depth-monitoring capability and their portability. Many anglers use them to scan bottom while running wide-open. Flashers are easy to read; better ones feature variable depth options and audible alarm. Their disadvantage is that they do not give an ongoing or permanent record of structure or fish that are marked.

One of the newest developments in flashers is the appearance of in-dash units that resemble small digital depth-finders in size. Many fishermen like to monitor depth on the easy-to-read LED displays while they are running to and from fishing grounds as well as while trolling. Price can be as low as $150. It goes up when you add sophisticated

Sonar and Fish Finders

features like surface water temperature, time of day, and deep- and shallow-water audible alarm. The Lowrance 3400, for example, is a 600-watt depth finder with dual alarm. It sells for about $380.

Small-boat anglers like the portable or quick-mount flashers that attach to their dashboards, seats, gunnels or transoms. Prices for these flashers start at $100 or so for 30- to 60-foot models. The Micronar FL-6, for example, features 0-60 and 60-120 foot scales in one-foot increments. The company's FL-8 model has four ranges to 240 feet and marks bottom in red as well as intermediate echoes in orange or green, depending upon signal strength. If you need to go deeper, King Marine's 810 flasher operates from depths of 1-600 feet in six range steps, plus it features an audible alarm when the boat passes over fish and has adjustable alarms for keel watch and anchor drag. The 810 sells for about $300.

Portability in a flasher can be advantageous for anglers who rent boats or want to use their depth finder on more than one boat. The Fish Hawk 202A has a 60-foot scale and a powerful tranducer that reads through the hull. Humminbird's Birdtrap flasher is a completely portable unit weighing only eight pounds, five ounces. It runs off two six-volt lantern batteries. Lowrance also makes fine portable flashers.

Most flashers mark top and bottom with a constant band of color. Sharp drop-offs show a wide band at top and bottom of the structure with stab marks in between. Heavy weeds will most likely be several thin lines above bottom. Logs and boulders show up as prolonged heavy marks as long as you are over them. Fish are generally portrayed as flashes between top and bottom. The heavier the marks are, the greater the concentration of fish or the bigger a single fish is. Solid stab marks, however, can also indicate that you are directly over the fish. Faint or quick flashes could mean the edge of your sonar cone caught the object. Reading a flasher correctly takes some time to gain familiarity.

Graphs

The paper-driven graphs are also called "chart recorders." That's a good name because the units give a permanent record of what they see. Fishermen can go over the paper readouts immediately after a fishing trip or even months later if they wish to study structure and fish habits. But because the paper scrolls slowly across the screen, anglers can also track downrigger weights (sometimes even lures in the case of highly sensitive recorders with excellent resolution) while they troll. Such tracking capability allows them to adjust their trolling program on the spot.

For example, assume that you are marking fish – usually in the shape of inverted Vs when they are directly under the boat – at 35 feet in 90 feet of water. Your weights and lures are running at 50 to 60 feet. It is a simple matter to raise a lure or two to 30 feet where the fish can see them. And if you have long-enough leads, there will be time to adjust the trolling pattern before the lures enter the potential strike zone.

Like flashers, graphs have improved tremendously, thanks to microchip technology and consumer demand. When Lowrance brought out its X-16 Computer Graph Recorder in 1986, the company billed it as the "ultimate in sportfishing sonar." A thousand lines of resolution permit the X-16 to separate objects only an inch apart with over 30,000 possible range selections. The X-16 has dual frequency capability, too, allowing anglers to switch from 50 Khz to 192 Khz with the flip of a switch. Interfacing the X-16 to Lowrance's Loran C means anglers can print position coordinates directly onto the graph paper. Cost of the X-16 is about $1,000.

King Marine also has a graph that they call the Ultimate Recorder. The King Model 1350 (about $900 retail) mates with the 8001 Loran C and features audible depth alarm from three to 30 feet. The graph can be used in any of three depth-finding modes: one using the LCD, one with LCD and the chart, and a third with LCD and bottom lock on the chart.

There are cheaper graphs on the market, too, including several by King Marine for as low as $450. Si-Tex makes some fine chart recorders, too, including the HE-32 MK II model that has both an 18-degree and 36-degree cone. Seven depth scales begin at 0-12 feet and run to 1-1,200 feet. Digital window depth is displayed in feet, fathoms

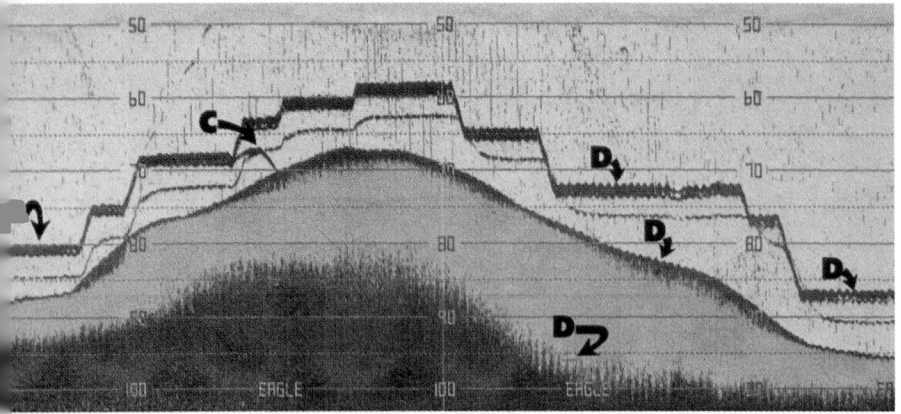

By relying on a transducer with wide cone (20 degrees in photo) a downrigger fisherman can watch his graph to (1) avoid obstacles and (2) put his lures on target. Graph letters refer to (A) downrigger ball stepping up from 83 to 58 ft., and down to 87 ft., (B) 4-inch lure following along, (C) fish looking, and (D) surface waves.

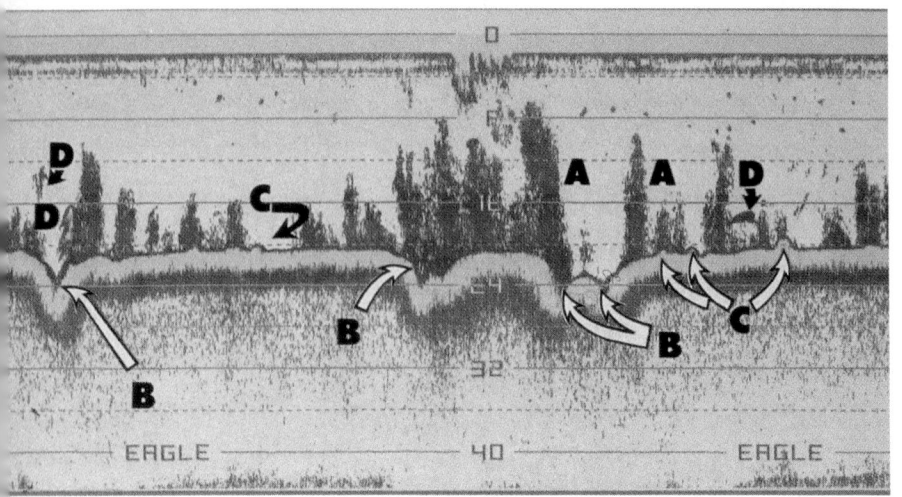

Graphs provide a permanent record of what sonar "sees." Without good electronics, it would be impossible for a downrigger fisherman to troll through this fish-rich though hazardous area. Letters here refer to (A) submerged trees, (B) creek channels, (C) rocks, and (D) fish.

or meters and can be used with or without recording mode to save paper.

Better graphs have a "gray line" (sometimes called a "white line") that blanks out everything below the bottom signal (temporarily eliminating the "echo") to produce a fine black or white line. This feature enhances bottom objects such as rocks, weeds and low-lying fish. With the gray line turned off and the echo restored, fishermen can determine (once they became familiar with their recorders) soft bottoms from hard.

It's important to realize that paper-driven graphs see and record on a horizontal plane under the boat, then print the details in a vertical mode. Further, because the cone angle varies according to depth, frequency and transducer, most of the objects the sonar "sees" will not be directly under the boat. Downrigger weights, for example, may actually be several feet behind the boat and several feet off the depth that the recorder says they are. The amount of time required to send a signal to an object, then retrieve the signal, determines how deep the object appears on paper. In other words, a fish or downrigger weight that seems to be 25 feet deep, could actually be only 20 feet or 15 feet deep.

Once again, familiarity with your sonar will help you to interpret what it tells you. Veteran fishermen, for example, can usually tell how deep a fish is and what it is doing (chasing a lure, fleeing from a downrigger weight, lying in the mud) just by the type of scratch marks it leaves on the paper.

There is at least one more advantage to graphs, and that is that they often can help a troller find and follow the thermocline. Plankton, baitfish and water density often appear to be a wide, fluctuating line quite different from the areas above and below.

Liquid-Crystal Displays

Liquid-crystal-display sonar debuted only a couple of years ago, but it is already sweeping through the nation's fishing fleet. Critics who scoffed at manufacturers' ad hype that billed the new electronic marvels as bridging the gap between flashers and graphs are not so quick to criticize these days. LCD

Sonar and Fish Finders

units are becoming so sophisticated that they can do everything but take the angler's blood pressure when he is fighting a world-record gamefish.

For example, consider these enhancements in the Lowrance X-5 and the Eagle Z-7000: (1) digital depth readings in one-tenth of a foot, (2) temperature gauge that reads in one-tenth of a degree, (3) a speedometer reading in miles-per-hour, kilometers or knots, (4) an odometer capable of recording 1,600 miles, (5) 3,000 watts of transmit power for deep-water penetration and finest shallow-water resolution, (6) a battery backup system that preserves indefinitely all functions programmed into the unit, (7) storage capacity for two screens of information. Zoom capacity, gray-line feature, and 1,922 dots per-square-inch enable these fine LCDs to separate targets of one inch or less from the bottom or each other.

On an LCD, the bottom and all objects between it and the surface show up as dots (pixels). The more pixels per-square-inch of display, the higher the resolution. This information scrolls across the screen at varying speeds to disappear and then start over. As a kid, do you remember those gray tablets with a wax base and thin sheet of see-through plastic that stuck to it? You would write or draw on the object with a leadless pencil, then lift the plastic sheet to erase your work. Liquid-crystal units remind me of those tablets.

Humminbird was the first major manufacturer to break through with low-priced models. The company's LCR 1000 can be purchased for as low as $150. At the other end of the scale, Humminbird's LCR 8000 offers split-screen capability, which means anglers can monitor a full depth-scale readout as well as zoom in on a particular level. The LCR 8000 will further memorize up to 16 half-screens for later recall, even when the power is turned off. A six-inch by four-inch viewing screen reads five depth-ranges from 0-15 feet to 0-240 feet.

Micronar offers a side-scanning unit, the Micro-Scan M-810, which searches an area 90 degrees wide on bottom and up to 45 degrees on each side of the boat as well as sweeping 30, 45 and 60 degrees to left, right and under the boat. Talk about eyes underwater! Touch-key operation allows you to program it accordingly. When you add vertical and horizontal cursor lines, the M-810 uses digital readout to pinpoint fish depth, distance and direction.

Vexilar's Model 481 LCD is available in either 50 or 200 Khz at about $700. For another $150, you can buy the Model 482, which features both frequencies. Computrol's Bottom Line II offers fish and submerged-hazard alarms, automatic or manual mode, cursor depth, surface temperature, and expand mode to zoom in on bottom details.

A nice feature of all LCDs is that they give you a sustained visual image – like the graphs – but without the hassle or expense of changing paper. As they grow even more sophisticated, they may well equal the sensitivity of the chart recorders.

Liquid-Crystal Displays

Video units like this Uniden MC 500 give a "televised" look at what's beneath the boat. The Fish Hawk Thermo-Troll 800 measures temperature and lure speed at the downrigger weight.

Video

Video units scroll along like the LCDs while reading what is underwater in two-color or full-color. Watching one is much like viewing television. Popular with saltwater commercial fishermen, they are catching on fast with freshwater sport fishermen as well as charter-boat captains.

Jon and Debi Belliveau, professional guides and Cannon field testers who charter out of Michigan City, Indiana, during the summer and out of Florida and the Bahamas in winter, are sold on video color sonar. Debi does the driving from the fly bridge of their 34-foot Silverton, the *Grande Dame*. At her disposal is a complete set of electronics, including and EMS temperature/trolling-speed indicator, Loran C, RDF radio communication, and a Humminbird Color Video Recorder 50. She feeds a steady flow of information to Jon, who shortens or lengthens leads, changes lures, and otherwise fine-tunes the trolling program according to what the electronics and Debi tell him.

Debi knows her CVR 50 so well that she can actually identify fish by the color and shape of marks that scroll across the screen. The way the Belliveaus explained it to me was that different species of fish have different sizes and shapes of air bladders. Sound waves from the sonar unit strike the fish, then are returned via the transducer to the screen. Strength of the signal determines color and shape of the image, which tells them what kind of fish is on target.

Frankly, I found this hard to believe, but when I fished with the Belliveaus one summer day, Debi proved it over and over. Long before the fish were netted (and in a couple of cases before they even struck lures), she correctly identified coho and Chinook salmon as well as Skamania steelhead. I could hardly believe what I was seeing.

Color videos offer most of the features already described with the other types of sonar. For example, Humminbird's CVR 50 and 200 models feature eight-color eight-inch screens, digital bottom readout, variable depth and zoom ranges, and zoom lock. An optional Tape Interface will let owners make color cassette recordings of their troll. Micronar's M-700 color video sonar has a four-inch diagonal screen that displays bottom contour, structure, fish, weeds and even the thermocline in five colors depending on echo strength. Five depth scales range from 1-10 feet to 1-600 feet. Zoom control, digital display of bottom depth, and water surface temperature are included. Impulse Manufacturing's Micro Trac 6100 is a four-shade black-and-white LCD that contains over 16,000 pixels on its 5½ inch screen. The company also makes full-color LCDs.

Color video units are not cheap; expect to pay about $1,000 for a good one.

Where do electronics begin and end, and to what extent should a fisherman invest in them? Neither question is an easy one to answer. There are still plenty of anglers who fish with proven tactics and ignore electronics altogether. There are many more, including most of the better fishermen, who rely on electronics, especially sonar, for their "luck." Consider Al Merfert, a Cannon field tester and savvy guide out of Port Washington, Wisconsin.

Merfert, who skippers a 42-foot Chris Craft, is a self-avowed "electronics nut." We suspect that he frequented pinball halls as a child and now spends his evenings in video arcades. Merfert's *C Eagle* has more electronics than a NASA launch control center. Included on the boat are two VHF radios, a ProCombinator, four Cannon Digi-Troll downriggers, auto-pilot, Wesmar SS265 side-scan sonar system, Wesmar SR3000 Omnicolor Digital Radar System, Gemtronics recording graph, Si-Tex Plotter and Si-Tex Loran C. The Wesmar side scanner (more correctly called an Omnicolor Digital Scanning Sonar System) is like something out of Star Wars itself.

The unit, which cost Merfert $7,100, acts like radar to scan up to one-half mile underwater in all directions. A gimbal-mount transducer probes under the boat for 18 inches and automatically scans in a 360-degree sweep. It can also be manually turned clockwise or counter-clockwise. Objects, such as fish, are pinpointed as to depth and range in feet. When Al notes a school of fish, he hunts them; and, because he has time to lower or raise his lures accordingly, Al is usually on the money by the time the *C Eagle* arrives. The Si-Tex Plotter, when mated with Si-Tex Loran C, allows Merfert to add "strike" zones (spots where fish hit)

Sonar and Fish Finders

to a screen and then steer right back to the hotspot. "It literally paints a picture for you," he said.

Are such electronics essential for catching fish? "I couldn't get along without them," Merfert admitted. "And, according to what my customers say, neither could they."

In the final analysis, to buy or not to buy sonar is probably not as hard as picking out the best unit for your needs. If you are really not sure, a good tip is to fish with anglers who use various types and learn from their experiences.

Selecting and Mounting a Transducer

Thoughtful consideration should be given to the type of transducer and to its placement. There are transducers designed to fit every application, and several standard mounts are available. They include the transom mount, trolling motor mount, through-the-hull, kickup, and portable mounts. According to Humminbird spokesman Larry Colombo, each type has its own advantages, though certain conditions must be met to achieve proper installation. Here are Colombo's suggestions:

Transom mount. The transducer is attached to the outside of the hull off the transom (stern end) of the boat with no gap between materials. This mount is recommended for flashers, LCDs and graphs.

Trolling motor mount. This transducer, which looks like a hockey puck, is attached to the foot of a trolling motor with the help of a stainless-steel hose clamp. The mount is especially useful with a bow-mounted sonar unit, such as Humminbird's Super Thirty II, because it allows the angler to maintain pinpoint control of the water depth beneath the trolling motor.

Through-the-hull. A puck-type transducer is attached to the inside of the hull with two-part epoxy. Shooting through the hull, the transducer allows excellent performance of a depth sounder or LCD, although some sensitivity loss will occur with graphs. It can only be used, however, with boats that feature a single thickness of fiberglass or aluminum. Attach the transducer in the center of the boat near the bilge, and be careful to eliminate any air pockets between the transducer and hull.

Kickup mount. This transducer is designed for boats with rough or irregular hulls, such as those on some aluminum boats. Proper installation means spotting the transducer face about a ¼-inch to ½-inch below the boat hull to avoid the stream of bubbles created from rivets, grooves and ridges. The transducer bracket is designed with a spring which allows the unit to kick up should an object be hit. The transducer returns to its original position once the object is passed over. The kickup mounts permit high-speed performance for flashers and LCD units.

Portable mount. This is a heavy-duty suction cup easily installed and removed from any fiberglass or aluminum boat. It is usually used with a portable depth sounder, such as the Humminbird BirdTrap, and is excellent for switching from boat to boat or when renting a boat. The portable mount works best at trolling speeds and is not designed for fast running.

In addition to Colombo's suggestions, we offer these considerations from King Marine Radio Corporation for mounting the transducer of the company's Color CRT Fishfinder. The suggestions may apply to mounting of all transducer types.

- The deeper the better.
- A place where there is no interference from bubbles or eddy currents.
- With inboard engines, ahead of the propeller.
- A spot with minimum vibration.
- A spot with minimum rolling and pitching.
- With either outboard or IO engines, not in line with the propeller.
- Never in the bow area.
- Always as level as possible.

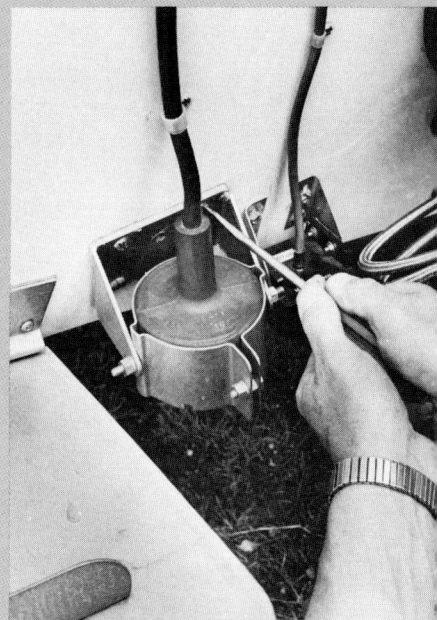

Transducers come in all shapes and sizes. Their purpose is to convert electrical impulses to sound waves and back again to electrical impulses to produce an image on a display screen.

Sonar and Fish Finders

Loran C

The windshield wipers were out of sync on the *Fishin' Machine*, Jim Beyer's 27-foot Sportcraft. The left-right, left-left-right tempo of the swishing blades was a small distraction to the six of us huddled in the boat cabin as Jim wheeled out of Monroe, Michigan's Riverfront Marina, and down the Raisin River. Frankly, we were more concerned with the weather. An inhaling earth on this foggy Saturday morning was sucking up the rain, which was falling in sheets from a sky the color of dull pewter. Although walleye fishing had been super in the Western Basin of Lake Erie, Jim, who is a charter-boat captain and Cannon field tester, wouldn't predict our luck today. There were four customers aboard. I was tagging along, hoping to find out how the highly respected Beyers catches walleyes on downriggers.

"We got 'em yesterday," he said, "so we'll go right back to the same spot where we left off and start there."

"How are you going to do that?" asked customer John Oldaker. "You said we'd be out too far from shore to see landmarks."

"With Loran C," Beyers said. "See, I enter certain coordinates on this computer, and it guides me to the exact location where I punched them in yesterday." We were just clearing the river entrance as Jim explained. Our captain shoved the throttle down, and the engine roared back.

"Unbelievable," Oldaker said, gripping a railing as the boat raced into the fog.

I, too, found it hard to believe. For 20 minutes Beyers watched the changing numbers on the little graph-like box, while landmarks shrunk, then disappeared altogether in the gloom. Satisfied, Jim throttled down to a whisper, turned the wheel over to me, and began trimming lines. "This is it," he said.

I'd like to report that we filled the cooler that day. In truth, we boxed only about 15 walleyes – far better, however, than most other trollers were reporting on the marine radio. Without Loran C, we might not have caught any fish, but what really impressed me about the little magic box on Beyers' boat was what happened just as we were finishing our troll. Suddenly, we chanced upon two power boats dead in the fog-shrouded lake.

"We don't know where we are," one driver said, tossing up his arms in frustration. "We want to get back to Toledo Beach. Can you point the way?"

"I can do better than that," Beyers said and disappeared into the cabin. A moment later he came back out and told the lost boaters exactly what course to run and how long it would take them.

Loran C. It is changing the way bigwater boaters and fishermen navigate. Developed by the U.S. military during the Second World War, Loran C (LOng RAnge Navigation) is a powerful radio transmission system that operates around the clock from 13 stations in the U.S. and overseas. Special receivers on boats that intercept the radio signals are able to plot courses that are extremely accurate.

Terry Walsh, another veteran charter-boat captain working western Lake Huron from his Au Gres, Michigan, home north to Harrisville, is a strong believer in Loran C as a fishing and boating aid. Walsh said that just seeing how well it worked on the boat of another professional guide one day convinced him to order a unit immediately upon returning home. "I would never be without it," he said.

Besides guiding, Terry is a freelance writer. In an article for *Great Lakes Fisherman*, he explained how Loran navigation works: "It is based on the measurement of the time delay (TD) between the reception of radio signals transmitted from a master station and at least two widely separated secondaries. The signals between the master and secondary stations are synchronized by the shipboard receiver and the position displayed on the receiver readout. This TD information is only useful when interpreted on a navigation chart overprinted with lines of position (LOP)."

Terry explained that the Loran C chart is nothing more than a map of a specific geographic area highlighting LOPs from transmitter stations within one or more chains. By locating the LOP on the chart that corresponds with the receiver's readout, the navigator knows his craft lies at some point along that line. A second measurement between the master station and another secondary will produce yet another time differ-

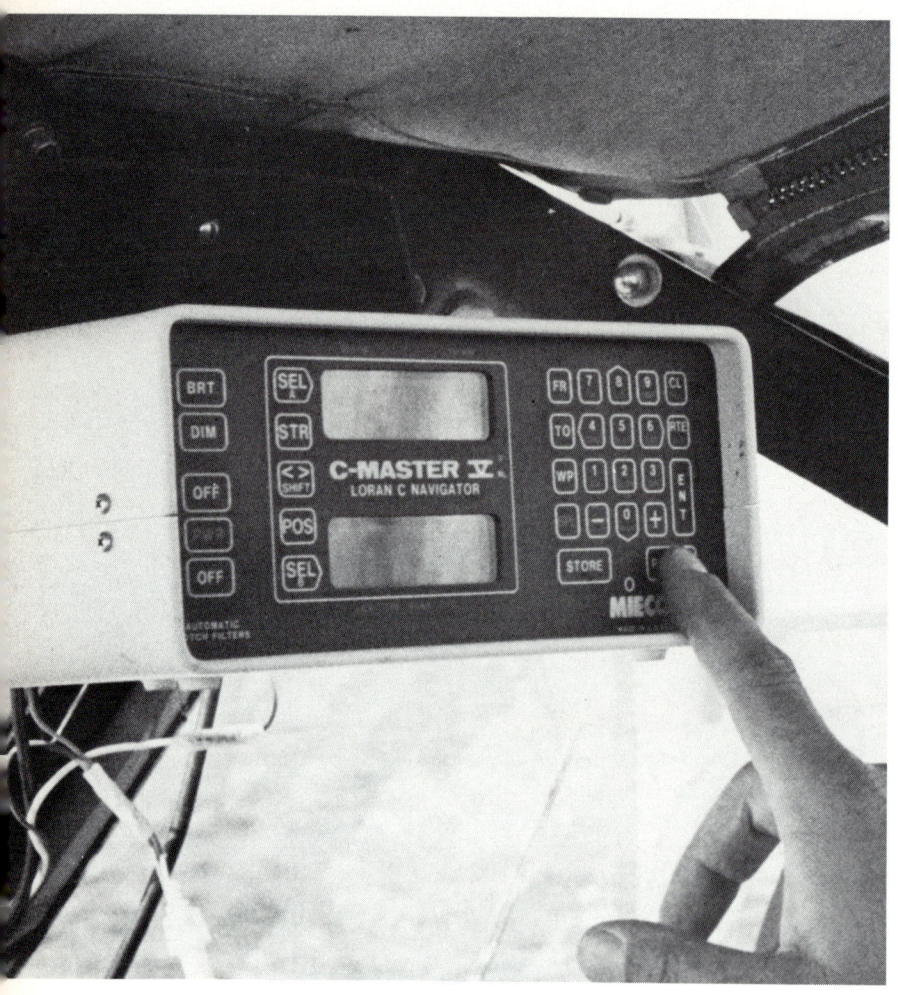

Mounting the Loran C unit away from the magnetic compass is one of several critical guidelines that must be followed for correct installation.

ence (TD) displayed on the Loran receiver. This will also correspond with an exact LOP on the Loran C chart. The intersection of the two LOPs on the chart indicates the exact position of one's vessel.

As the vessel moves, a continous display of changing TDs and their corresponding LOPs on the Loran C chart makes it possible for the boater to accurately plot his position. He can also determine his speed by measuring the distance the boat travels during a given time period.

How reliable and accurate is Loran C? Terry said that, based on his daily experiences as a charter captain, he gives it a 10 rating. The key, however, is proper installation. Once this requirement is met, the unit functions almost flawlessly, failing only when one of the transmitter stations is down. Even then if you own a quality unit, it's still possible to pick up another secondary and be back in operation.

"One of the things I learned right away is that proper antenna installation is a must," Terry said. "The antenna *must be* as high and as far away from *all metal objects* and *other antennas* as possible. Failure to do so severely reduces the signal strength of the receiver and thus its performance. My recommendation is to *temporarily* install the unit's antenna and then try the receiver. If the unit functions reliably (strong signals and no noise or other interference), the antenna can be permanently installed."

The veteran skipper said another area of concern is *proper grounding* of the antenna, which is every bit as important as antenna placement. On metal boats the grounding can be accomplished by connecting a metal strap to a mast or the hull. Wooden or fiberglass vessels require both the receiver and antenna coupler be connected to the ground plate and engine block by heavy-gauge copper wire.

Another important point is to mount the Loran C receiver in an area where it is out of direct sunlight and free from moisture and vibration. Also, keep it as far away from the magnetic compass as possible – up to three feet is recommended.

Walsh, who closely follows the development of Loran C by the major manufacturers, said that a great deal of innovation has gone

Loran C

into their construction. "The sets have become not only very compact but very affordable," he said. "There's a unit on the market that now meets virtually any boater's need and pocketbook limitations. Receivers (complete with antennas) sell for around $400 upwards to $2,000. Installation by a competent electronics specialist can add another $100 or so, but the extra cost is worth it."

Terry believes the more one pays for a Loran receiver, the more quality he is likely to get. On more expensive models the owner will enjoy the additional feature of latitude and longitude readouts in addition to TDs. Other enhancements include the following: (1) built-in ASF (Additional Secondary Factor) can correct differences in a given area between lat/lon and TDs, (2) a number of selectable waypoints (a preselected location where a change in course may be desired) are available instead of a relative few, (3) waypoint alarm to indicate the destination has been reached, (4) an anchor watch, (5) constant course correction, (6) speed and estimated time of arrival at the next waypoint as well as the present distance from it, (7) constant memory of all entered data from one season to the next, and (8) autopilot interface.

"The one great merit of Loran C, however, is its repeatability," Walsh said. "The unit will again and again guide the navigator to a preselected waypoint with a very high degree of accuracy. As a fisherman, the Loran receiver makes it possible for me to return to a school of fish over and over and keep track of them once I'm over the school. During heavy weather, poor visibility, or a nighttime return to port, I know the Loran will guide me back with uncanny accuracy. And should an emergency ever arise, rescue will be greatly facilitated by being able to give the exact position of the disabled vessel."

Is Loran C for you? "It is without question one of the best investments a serious boater or angler can make," Terry said.

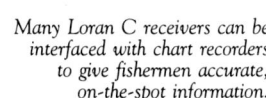

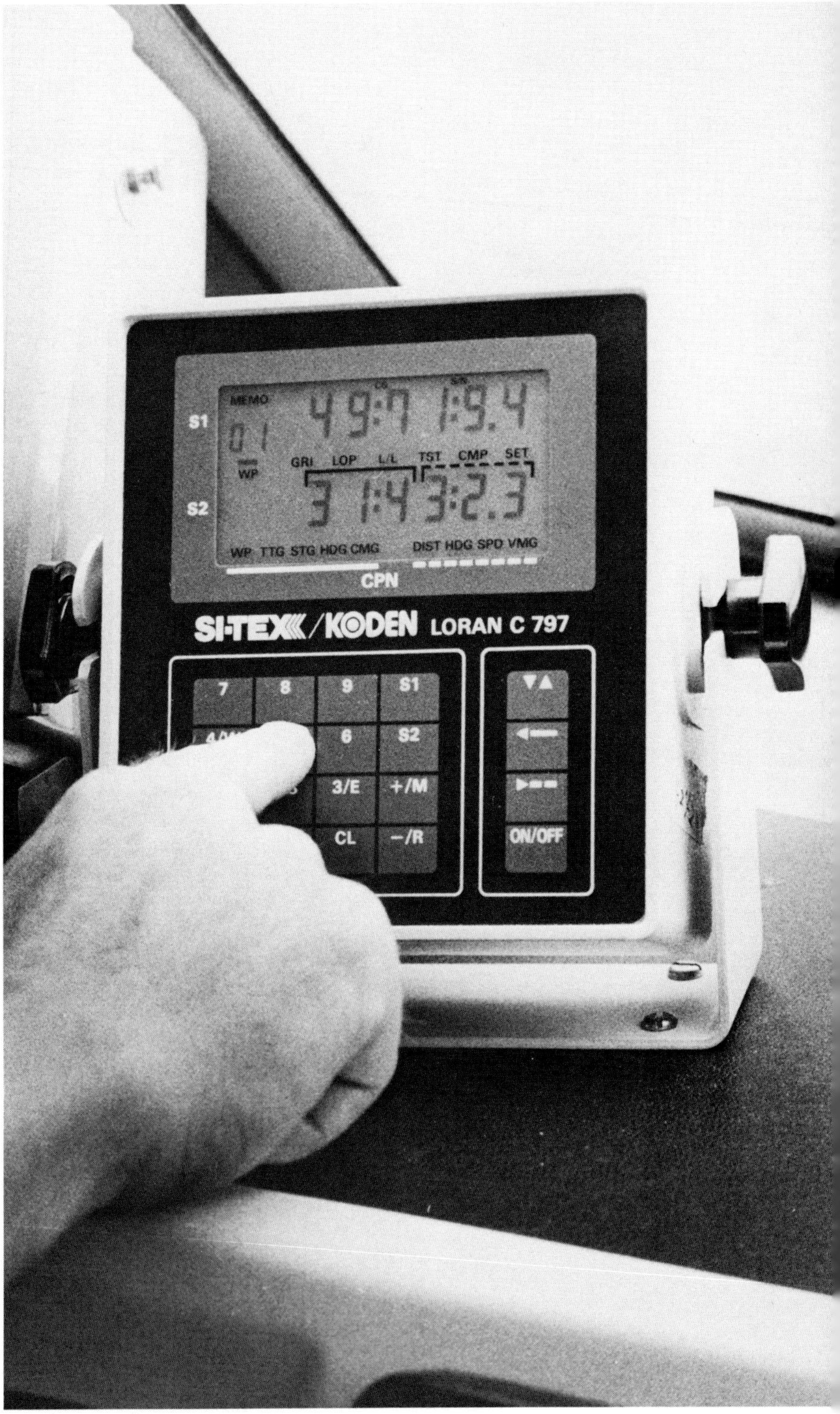

Many Loran C receivers can be interfaced with chart recorders to give fishermen accurate, on-the-spot information.

Trout

"Because downriggers take lures to any depth, then hold them there, they are one of the most effective (and newest) methods for catching trout."

Lake Trout are well distributed throughout Canada, the Great Lakes, northern New York State and New England, and Western high-country reservoirs. Downriggers are an exciting way to catch them.

Lake Trout

Like people, lakes are born, grow old and die. Lakes age over thousands of years due to enrichment of the waters with nutrients. These nutrients are leached from the soil and enter the lakes as erosion from runoff and rivers. Plant life, which begins in the shallows and spreads to deeper water, encourages the growth of animal organisms, such as plankton and insects, and gives off oxygen which helps support fish populations. As a lake matures, organic deposits begin to pile up on the bottom, making the lake warm and shallow. This process of organic decay uses increasing amounts of precious oxygen, which eventually suffocates animal life. The lake then becomes a marsh and dies.

Trout are the most delicate of freshwater fish. For a lake to hold trout, there must be a fine balance of the food supply, temperature and oxygen, and there must be suitable bottom composition and limited turbidity. In the cold waters of the Far North, many of the lakes are oligotrophic – old in a geologic sense but meagerly productive of food. One summer I fished Chantrey Inlet, a wide pool of the Back River 40 miles above where it sluices into the Arctic Ocean. I doubt if there is cleaner water anywhere in North America, perhaps in the world. But some of the lake trout we caught with downriggers had large heads and small bodies, a sign of malnutrition. So an abundance of trout in a lake indicates not only a clean environment but a maturing body of water in terms of food production.

Trout are special, indeed, and that is why many fishermen hold them in the highest esteem. All trout are of Arctic marine origin. The fish migrated south ahead of the descending glaciers and established their races in freshwater lakes and rivers of North America and Europe. Rainbows and cutthroats moved south through the Bering Strait to the Pacific Coast. Cutthroats found the rushing waters of mountain streams and the cold depths of high country lakes much to their liking, whereas the rainbows fed heavily in the ocean before mounting their spawning drives as silvery steelhead in West Coast Rivers from Alaska to California. The same ice movements pushed brown trout south between Norway and Greenland as far as Spain. It sent the brook trout as far south in North America as temperatures would allow him to live.

Because of the clean, clear waters which trout demand for survival, presentation of fishing bait or lures must be precise. Not only must the lure look real to a trout, it must be presented on target, and in no way can it be associated with the angler or his boat. Otherwise, the fish, especially the biggest trout, will ignore the bait or lure altogether. Wherever trout fishermen gather – in bars, at tackle shops, on lakes and rivers, and at Trout Unlimited chapter meetings – they endlessly discuss ways to catch more fish. Such is the grip that trout have on fishermen.

Because downriggers take lures to any depth, then hold them there, they are one of the most effective and newest methods for catching trout. Anglers are relying on downriggers to take huge cutthroats from Pyramid Lake in Nevada and giant Dolly Varden from Lake Pend Oreille in Idaho. Fishermen using downriggers report incidental catches of brook trout, splake (hybrid cross between brook trout and lake trout) and even golden trout, but it is the lake trout, brown trout and rainbow/steelhead that capture the interest of most trollers seeking trout. What follows is an in-depth look at these species and how downriggers can be used to catch them.

This Lake Superior lake trout tossed the lure after coming to net.

My first lake trout trophy was a 12½ pound sag-bellied fish caught out of South Haven on Lake Michigan many years ago. A powerful fish, she popped a port-side downrigger with a savage strike, then instantly squirted for bottom. The drag on my reel talked in a new language that I would come to love. A few minutes later, following instructions from our guide, I pumped a translucent fish into view. Twenty feet below in the cobalt waters of Lake Michigan, my laker twisted into ghostly shapes. The bowed rod threatened to break when I lifted her the final few feet, and the guide closed a net over her.

Along with the brook trout, lake trout are actually members of the char family, which have finer scales and different teeth structure than trout. Lake trout are well distributed in the Great Lakes and cold, deep waters of upper New York State's Finger Lakes, northern New England and throughout Canada as far north as Alaska. Deepwater reservoirs in Colorado, Idaho, Washington, Oregon and California are also home to transplanted lake trout, except in the West they are called "mackinaw trout" or just simply "macks."

Wherever they are found, lake trout are structure-oriented fish that school. These habits concentrate them over reefs, boulder fields, drop-offs, ledges and other breaks. Sculpin, freshwater shrimp, crayfish and various minnow species (gizzard shad, alewives, lake emerald and golden shiners, sticklebacks, smelt and so on) often swarm to such structure. They come for protection from predators, to propagate their own species, and to feed on zooplankton and other microorganisms.

Lake trout know these things.

Sometimes the fork-tailed predators lie in structure mud, making it difficult to pick them out with graphs and bottom probes. This is especially true when structure is accompanied by 48- to 52-degree F. water. Lakers will leave this preferred temperature zone, but not often. When they do, it will usually be to spawn in fall or to feed. In spring, for instance, they usually seek the warmest water available and, therefore, may be found off creek mouths or sun-warmed shoreline shallows. Gullets full, they sink

Lake Trout

back to structure and living-room temperature. When three key living conditions – temperature, structure and food – are in one place, lakers may stay put for weeks, lounging like well-fed hogs.

In the Great Lakes, at least, that is why many fishermen call lakers the "bread-and-butter fish." Lake trout are, for the most part, dependable, and they are not all that difficult to catch once you find them. Tactics vary around the country but nearly always involve some kind of attractor, such as a flasher or string of shiny blades, ahead of a lure. In the dimly lit world of 150 to 300 feet, the flash of stainless-steel or silver-plated metal shows. Schooling lakers associate this twinkling flash with baitfish and so, when one fish strikes, its strugglings trigger a predator-pack response from others. Most veteran laker-takers say it is a rare experience, indeed, to catch only one lake trout when fish are known to be over a specific structure. When I fished Chantrey Inlet, for example, as one lake trout came to net, we often saw up to a half-dozen others shadowing the struggling fish.

The key to catching forktails is making sure that your attractor and lure are working in harness. Variable boat speed, from one to four miles per hour, is one way to achieve that. Another is to put lures the correct distance behind attractors so that maximum action is imparted to the lure. Generally, 20 to 24 inches behind in-line strings of blades is about right. For the oval-shaped flashers, put your lure one and one-half times the length of the attractor behind it. In other words, if you are using a 10-inch flasher, the lure should go about 15 inches behind it. Release lengths (the distance of the attractor from your downrigger weight release) are generally close – two to five feet because lakers are often attracted by the weight itself and because at great depths, tangles will be less common.

Good lures behind bladed strings include small plugs such as Clatter Tads, Fire Plugs, Wobble-Glos, L'il Guys, Spin-N-Glos, Rapalas and Rebels and small spoons such as Eppinger Thindevles or Flutter Chucks, Southport Slammers and Andy Reekers. These same lures, as well as streamers and large trolling flies (Michigan Squids, Sparkle Flies, Flash-Tail Flies and Twinkle-Squids, for example), work well behind flashers. Several manufacturers produce attractors. Earl's Pearls, George Richey Whirl-A-Gigs, Les Davis Cowbells and Odd-Balls, and Luhr Jensen Ford Fenders, Main Train, and Beer Can lake trolls are popular bladed strings. Flashers in demand include Mehler Hot Spot Flashers, Babcock attractors, Jensen Dodgers, Abe and Al Flashers, and Les Davis Herring Dodgers.

You can kill favorable lure action by overpowering it with a big string of flash. Conversely, too little blade turnover may deaden the lure. Always test your offerings over the boat side until you determine the speed which imparts best action to your lure. Blades should turn over slowly; flashers should rock back and forth – to give a jerking motion to the trolling fly – without turning over. Slowing down or speeding up will dampen action or increase it accordingly. Other means to slow the action include downsizing to smaller attractors to taping swivels with electrical tape.

Fine-tuning an attractor trolling system for lake trout involves knowing how much flash to rig, what speed to troll, and exactly what lead lengths to set from release to attractor and from attractor to lure. Experimentation is the key. How much and what kind of flash is best varies according to locale. Generally, in clear-lake or shallow-water conditions, back off on flash, and increase it when the water is stained, dirty or deep. Silver or 50/50 (half-silver, half-brass) blades seem to work best on bright days while copper or brass is effective under cloudy skies. Chrome is the color of choice in flashers. Stick with it or white on bright days, then consider switching to hot colors (yellow, red, kelly-green, chartreuse) singly or in combination for dark-day conditions, especially if chrome isn't paying dividends. These same colors are effective in lures, too. In fact, you don't always need attractors to catch lake trout. Plain lures or sewn minnows will do the job, too. When a hungry laker sees your lure or bait, he'll have no qualms about belting it if it looks like food.

Still, attractors account for 90 percent of the lakers coolered, and so there is nothing new about trolling with them. For years,

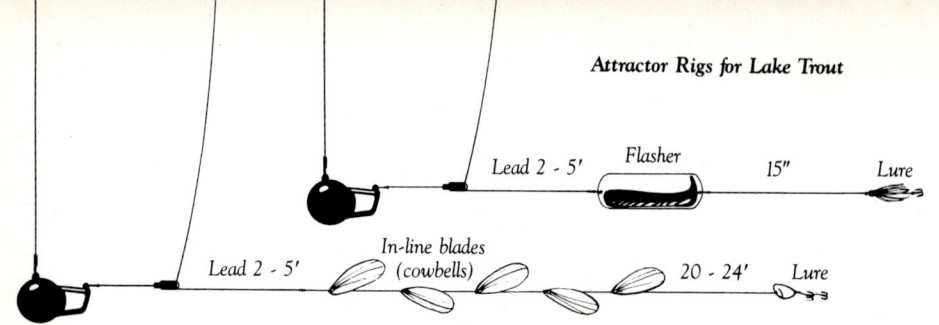

Lake trout can grow to huge size. This 20-pounder was caught at Chantrey Inlet Lodge on the Back River in the Northwest Territories. The Inuit guide is Tommy Anguttitauruq of Gjoa Haven.

savvy fishermen have been relying on wire or lead-core line wound to heavy-duty reels and run through the guides of short, stiff rods to pound attractors and lures into lake-bottom mud. It's tough work, though made much easier when one turns to downriggers. They do the job because lure wandering is minimal, thanks to short release lengths. Once you put your downrigger weights on target – usually on or near bottom structure – you're in business. And you won't have to fight heavy lead weights or lead-core line when a laker strikes either. We interviewed several Cannon field testers around the country to see how they catch lake trout on downriggers. Here is what they had to say:

Sport fisherman Ron Kolodziej of Amsterdam, New York, bumps the bottom of Lake George while trolling at only one or two mph. The technique calls for lowering downrigger weights to bottom, then bringing them up a half-turn of the pulley wheel, or just so they skip bottom every few feet. Sometimes Kolodziej will fine-tune one of his four electric Mag 10A downriggers, raising and lowering it inches at a time. This results in stirring up the bottom, which results in lakers thinking someone is ringing the dinner bell. "If suspended fish are showing on the graph, I'll occasionally stack another lure at mid-depth," Ron said, "and then adjust my speed accordingly."

Dennis Bidigare, a charter-boat captain from St. Clair Shores, Michigan, has three Digi-Trolls mounted across the stern of his 25-foot Luhrs and a pair of Mag 10A electrics for out-downs. When fishing specifically for lake trout, Bidigare relies exclusively on his Digi-Trolls. The center-stern unit gets a 20-pound weight with corner downriggers receiving 15-pound and 12-pound weights accordingly. Such rigging allows Dennis to bounce bottom with all three downrigger weights at three different angles without fear of tangling. The dual-memory of his computerized Digi-Trolls also permits for fast rigging, including stacking for salmon or other suspended fish. For example, if the stern-end unit bounces bottom at 100 feet on the counter in 90 feet of water (the difference is due, of course, to cable bow), the captain sets M-1 at 60 feet and M-2 at 100 feet. As the weight is descending, he can tend to

Lake Trout

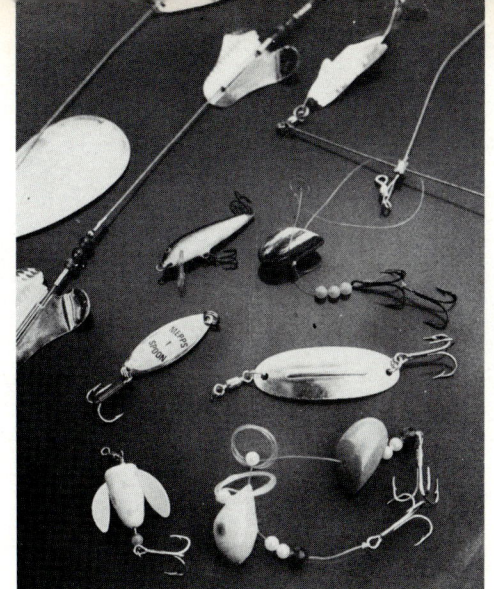

Flasher-type attractors (left photo) include this Mehler Hotspot Flasher (left) and three Luhr Jensen Dodgers, including the famous Les Davis Herring Dodger with Silver Plate. A variety of small spoons, plugs and trolling flies can be run behind dodgers for lake trout. Moving left to right, top to bottom, those in the photo include (over Dodger #1) Luhr Jensen Alpena Diamond, Acme Flutter Cleo, Eppinger Flutter Chuck, Mehler Apex; (over Dodger #2) Pro Spoon, Andy Reekers, Worden's Herring Plus II; (over Dodger #3) Flash King, Eppinger Thindevle, Mainliner; (over Dodger #4) Williams Wabler, Worden's King Fish, and Burke Banana Bait.

Flashy laker-takers (right photo) include these lures, clockwise from Mepps No. 1 Spoon: Floating Rapala, Wobble-Glo, Williams Wobbler, Burke Soft Touch plugs (2), and Worden's Spin-N-Glo. Attractors in photo are in-line blades. They include (from upper left) Cowbells, Richey's Whirl-A-Gig, and Luhr Jensen School of Shiners.

rigging another unit. When the first Digi-Troll stops at 60 feet, Dennis adds a rubber-band stacker, then punches M-2 to complete the descent.

Robert Ribarsky of Port Huron, Michigan, also relies on Digi-Trolls for lake trout fishing, except that he has mounted them as out-downriggers, rather than across the transom. A pair of Mag 10 As goes off boat corners. Like most other fishermen using multiple downriggers, Ribarsky runs his attractor offerings (sometimes called "junk lines") off the stern end, except that he then cycles his Digi-Trolls to work higher water for suspended fish. He, too, believes in stacking, but with a twist. Eight to 10 feet above downrigger weights and the bottom-running lure, Bob will sometimes add a fixed-depth stacker of the same lure (just in case fish are off bottom a little or want to chase a lure). Then he adds a slider rig, usually a spoon of a different color, thus giving him three lures off the same downrigger.

Ken Coleman, a sport angler out of Willsboro, New York, catches Lake Champlain lakers on small floating Rapalas and other small plugs that imitate the smelt and perch that lakers feed upon there. Key depth in summer is the 85- to 100-foot range near bottom. Coleman picks up occasional whitefish with his method, too.

Many Lake Superior and Canadian trollers like to sweeten their lures with cut bait, ususally a chunk of sucker or cisco. Further, because lakers lie on bottom at depths to 300 or more feet, innovative anglers are learning that they sometimes have to provide all the flash possible to get fish to see and hit lures. By stringing together two sets of blades – such as Les Davis Odd-Balls – they can create a five-foot run of flash with nine blades of up to four inches each. Another trick is to mate a Cowbell string with a flasher. Besides all the twinkling chrome, the aroma of cut bait helps lakers to home in on the offering.

Some lake trout fishermen are trying really unusual things with downriggers, too, especially the exciting Digi-Trolls. Lake Huron charter-boat captain Bill Thede, for example, is experimenting with jigging, setting his Digi-Trolls to just touch bottom on the five-foot, five-second cycle while drifting or slow trolling. And, as we reported in the section on Digi-Trolls, Steve Payne of Post Falls, Idaho, is using his computerized downrigger to jig for huge mackinaw trout through the ice on Priest Lake, a deep, mountain lake in northern Idaho.

The trick is so new, and so different, that we repeat it briefly here. Payne, a freelance writer and sport fisherman, relies on a generator with power reducer to throttle down to the 12 volts necessary to operate his Digi-Troll, which he mounts to a snowmobile or board across his ice hole. Lake trout to 35 pounds (most are five to eight pounds with occasional fish in the 20-25 pound class) lie on bottom in 80 to 90 feet of water. By using the pulse cycle on his Digi-Troll, Steve jigs Deadly Dicks, one-ounce pieces of lead with a treble hook, in chrome color. A piece or two of flash prism tape seem to help trigger strikes as does an occasional flasher ahead of lures. Most macks hit on the drop.

However you catch them, lake trout are deep-water, exciting fish. Downriggers make the sport especially fun.

Casey Richey caught this 24-pound monster brown trout on a Long A Bomber run off a planer board while spring trolling in Lake Michigan's Platte Bay.

April 13, 1985. Casey Richey of Honor, Michigan, has been trolling the Platte Bay shallows of Lake Michigan since dawn. A veteran fisherman at only 19, Casey has been trying to catch a monster brown trout since his eighth-grade year of school. Spring is a good time to do it because hungry browns enter shoreline shallows of the Great Lakes then in quest of smelt. Casey and other knowledgeable fishermen go after them with small boats, relying on side-rigging tactics, flatline trolling, and shallow-set downriggers. Casey's 14-foot aluminum boat is equipped with a Cannon Mag 10 downrigger on one side and a Cannon Uni-Troll downrigger on the other. He also relies on Cannon Plane-R-Boards to put his lures practically on shore where the biggest browns lurk. And although he has yet to break the 20-pound mark with a trophy fish, he has caught many smaller browns. Just the previous spring, for example, he and a buddy boated 25, keeping a two-man limit of 10 fish from three to eight pounds each.

"I want a big fish, though," Casey has repeatedly said, especially after hearing the news that another small-boat fisherman 20 miles south of Platte Bay broke the state and national record with a 34-lb., 6 oz. brown.

There are no other boats out this April morning as Casey and his friend troll along a deserted strand of beach. A few herring gulls hovering over the naked hardwoods on shore watch their slow progress with idle interest. Then at 9:30, a rod springs loose from the planer board release. You wonder, sometimes, how a person knows when it is a big fish. ESP or just a hunch? In young Richey's case, you can't rule out experience either. But as soon as Casey grabbed the bucking rod, he knew a buster brown trout was on the other end.

"Long A Bomber!" he hollers. "Wonder Bread color. Big fish, big fish!"

The trout wallows once on the surface like a fat carp, then races for Wisconsin as Casey's reel talks back. The fish saws back and forth, then rushes the boat, allowing the excited fisherman to spool back some slack before stripping it away again. Ten minutes pass and the fish shows no signs of tiring. Then 15 minutes. Meanwhile, Casey keeps up the pressure, his rod bent over almost

Brown Trout

double, monofilament to the breaking point. The brown is tiring; its runs are brief and it has stopped shaking its head. After 20 minutes of battle, Casey inches his football-fat trophy to the boat. Slipping a long-handled net behind the spent fish, Casey's buddy scoops him aboard.

Twenty-four pounds of brown trout sags deeply in the net. For Casey Richey, five years of determined fishing has finally paid off.

To many anglers, the brown is the prize of prizes among trout. Moody, shy, unpredictable as a junkyard dog and sometimes as ornery, browns can also be tough to catch. Introduced from Europe to North America over a hundred years ago, brown trout now live in all but a handful of states. Their primary range, however – approximating that of the brook trout – is across the northern United States. They live in rivers with brookies and rainbows, often to the detriment of those species since browns are exceptionally predatory, even cannibalistic at times. Hatchery-planted browns are fairly adept at reproducing themselves. In Western reservoirs, such as Flaming Gorge, and in the Great Lakes and in some lower Midwest, New England, and upper New York State lakes, they grow to massive size. Consider these current state records: Wisconsin – 32 lb. 8 oz.; Michigan – 34 lb. 6 oz.; New York, 24 lb. 8 oz.; Illinois, 28 lb. 8 oz.; Utah, 33 lb. 10 oz.; Wyoming, 25 lb. 13 oz.; Missouri, 29 lb.; Idaho, 28 lb. 8 oz.; California, 26 lb. 5 oz.; Arkansas, 33 lb. 8 oz.

Many half-truths and outright myths have attached themselves to brown trout and brown trout fishing. Although it is true that browns gorge themselves to the bursting point, they do not eat themselves to death as some people believe. True, they are shy fish, and that is why most trollers rely on light line and long leads to catch them; but they will, on occasion, grab lures right in the prop boil, too.

One of the best times to catch browns is in the spring when the hungry fish target river mouths, factory and power plant runoff, and sun-warmed shoreline shallows. Warm water attracts baitfish, which, in turn, draw brown trout. Anglers that exclusively target spring browns usually rely on planer

In spring and fall, and sometimes in summer, browns can be taken near the surface by using longline trolling techniques. In summer, brown trout will also target deep-water structure.

Spring fishing in the shallows for Lake Michigan brown trout. This angler uses a shallow-set downrigger to catch this small three-pounder. Note trolling-speed indicator, graph and temperature probe on transom. These are keys to catching browns at any time.

boards for up to 75 percent of their action. The planer swings lures away from the immediate boat wake, engine noise and boat shadow. Fish that fan away from an approaching vessel often will bust lures flashing through the shallows to either side, especially when they do not associate the artificials with the disturbance.

Those techniques that Ed Mendus, a Cannon field tester and sport troller from Ballston Spa, New York, uses to take Lake Ontario brown trout each spring. "Very long lines and minnow-imitating lures are what we use in the Point Breeze and Oak Orchard Creek areas," Mendus said.

That is also why longlining with flatlines and shallow-set downriggers is a good spring method, too. Downriggers are especially helpful for spreading multiple lures to avoid tangles. Release lengths may be 50 to 150 feet behind downrigger weights, and from 100 to 300 feet on flatlines. Because planer boards are usually far enough away from the boat, release lengths can be shorter. Most brown trout trollers spot lures from 10 to 40 feet behind planers. Outriggers, incidentally, are another good tactic for spreading lures and allowing more setups.

Some brown trout trolling experts, like Ron Gusse, a Cannon field tester and charter-boat captain from Oshkosh, Wisconsin, rely exclusively on downriggers in the shallows. Gusse targets warm water off nuclear plants at Kewaunee, Point Beach and Sheboygan and shoreline shallows at Baileys Harbor. By dropping downrigger weights only a foot or two under the surface, Ron keeps Little Cleos and Mr. Champ spoons in red, orange and green in the upper 20 feet of water. When browns are deeper than that, he breaks out 0 sized Dodgers and attaches his own homemade trolling flies in yellow-green, black or blue. Leads for both clean-run spoons and attractor/fly offerings are reasonably short at 25 feet or so.

Different lures take browns from different locations. In shallows of the Great Lakes, effective spring lures include minnow-imitating plugs (Rapala, Long A Bombers, Finnigan's Minnows); small crankbaits (Fat Raps, Storm Hot 'N Tots and Texas Shads, Bill Norman ZX-10s and Wiggle Warts); and small, thin spoons (Krocodiles, Sugar

Brown Trout

Spoons, Cobras, Thindevles).

In summer, browns often haunt deepwater structure such as rocky ledges, strewn boulders and jagged reefs. They prefer a hard bottom that is uneven and are especially fond of rocky dropoffs. Many fishermen in summer report excellent success by adopting lake trout trolling tactics with attractors (especially in-line blades like Cowbells) and small lures or sewn minnows. Putting bait on target to deep-water browns is the key to catching them because fish don't actively chase food to the degree that they do when on top. Downriggers not only spear the offerings on target, they keep them there, even allowing discriminating trollers with dependable sonar to work lures in and out of structure.

However, it is not uncommon to see brown trout, which prefer 65- to 75-degree temperatures, on or near the surface, too. In fact, one method that some fishermen use on hot, muggy summer days when the lake surface is calm is to watch for porpoising activity of cavorting or feeding browns. Often, the big fish will look like carp thrashing topwater.

You can catch these summertime browns while slow-trolling surface lines with X-5 or U-20 Flatfish, Kwikfish, Tadpollies, Hot 'N Tots, Rapalas, Sugar Spoons, Rattlespoons, Andy Reekers, McMahon Spoons, Finn Spoons, Little Cleos, Krocodiles and Locos. Choice colors, at least in the Great Lakes, are pearl, silver, silver-and-orange, yellow, gold, and chartreuse. Many successful anglers add flash to these and other lures with punch-out prism tape. Once again, flatlining and dropping downrigger weights a couple feet under the surface are the top-rated tactics.

In fall, when brown trout return to the shallows – only this time to spawn – anglers go back to spring side-rigging methods to get lures in close to shore. Flatlining is also effective. Browns sometimes spawn as late as Thanksgiving, and so there is usually some excellent fishing late in the fall and even through the ice in winter.

Brown trout fishermen go the extra mile when it comes to getting top action from their lures. Fine-tuned tactics include tying loop knots to split rings instead of swivels and using monofilament as light as six- or four-pound test. A few use rod-length leaders of the light line, then back it with a couple hundred yards of 10- to 20-pound test. Because long leads make for stretch in fishing line, and therefore missed strikes, most anglers rely on adjustable line releases, such as Cannon's *Quick Release* or *Offshore Release* or rubber bands like Cannon's *Elasti-Clip* release. Rubber bands in particular help trollers to keep a sharp eye on rod tips for lures running out of synch as well as for strikes.

Trolling speed, of course, is tied to lure choice. The object is to get the maximum amount of action from your lures, usually at the slowest speed possible. Slow speeds also help fishermen to make wide S turns, which tend to speed up outside lures and hold inside ones motionless for a moment or two. Lures that hesitate, then suddenly dart ahead often promote strikes. So does slowing down and speeding up and raising and lowering downrigger weights. Cannon's *Digi-Troll* downriggers and *Excitor* flatline agitator automatically sweep lures and are ideal for brown trout trolling.

How do you catch a trophy brown trout, one of 20 pounds and up? To begin, adopt the determined attitude of one gutsy Casey Richey. Also, consider the advice of Ray Johnson of Salt Lake City, Utah. Johnson, who was called "a living legend beyond anyone's question" by the National Fresh Water Fishing Hall of Fame, has taken more trophy trout than anyone in North America and perhaps the world. Because huge browns are Johnson's specialty, he devoted a chapter to them in his book, *Big Trout!* Here is what a fisherman has to do, according to the expert:

1. Learn to fish in the dark and always be on the water just as day begins to break.
2. Learn to fish in cold weather and to survive while doing it.
3. Concentrate on spawning (or soon-to-spawn) browns in the fall.
4. Troll slowly, *very slowly.*
5. Target small areas where you believe lunkers live (a good graph and topographic map are helpful).

Yes, brown trout can get a mysterious hammerlock on some fishermen. One fish can do it.

Brown trout takers include these lures (left to right): Finnigan's Minnow by The Producers, J-9 Normark Rapala, Storm Texas Shad and Hot 'N Tot, Normark Fat Rap, Bill Norman Little N, Luhr Jensen Krocodile spoon, and LumaLure.

The author caught this sleek-sided Skamania steelhead in southern Lake Michigan. Bright-colored lures like this silver J-Plug with orange ladderback are the best choices.

One look at a rainbow trout is evidence enough that these fish are built for battle. Besides a vermilion racing stripe down each side, rainbows are sleek, well-muscled fish, strong enough to run rivers for long distances, powerful enough to be acrobats above water when hooked. Originating on the West Coast from Alaska to California, rainbows are called "steelhead" when they descend rivers to the ocean, grow up, and then come back to spawn. In the sea, they exchange the pink-sided "rainbow" look for the sleek, steel-blue look of the steelhead.

These popular fish have been introduced throughout the northern and western U.S. and elsewhere in the world. Rainbow trout provide tremendous sport for river anglers using flyfishing and spincasting methods. In reservoirs and lakes, they serve up year-round sport, and open-water fishermen use a variety of tactics, including trolling with downriggers, to catch them. Rainbows that remain inland often reach huge size, 20 pounds or more, and develop beautiful spawning colors complete with those handsome slashes.

Steve Payne, a Cannon field tester and outdoor writer from Post Falls, Idaho, trolls for huge, Gerrard-strain rainbows in 1,300-foot deep Coeur D'Alene Lake. The rainbows, introduced from Kootenay Lake in British Columbia, have, on occasion, reached 30 pounds. Payne said they are always suspended although depths vary from season to season, day to day. Early spring tactics call for flatlining with No. 11 Rapalas in black and silver, Rebel Fastracs in green and silver, and Cisco Kids in brown and gold. As summer comes on, Steve uses his Digi-Troll downriggers to lift and drop these lures, as well as Mehler Hot Spot Flashers ahead of Mac's Squid Hootchie Trolling Lures, at various depths. Since only one rod is allowed each fisherman, stacking the attractor rigs with small spoons is a popular technique. Clear water from surrounding high-country streams dictate release lengths of 40 or 50 feet.

Landlocked rainbows tend to be chunky fish. On the other hand, steelhead return from the ocean or Great Lakes to run natal rivers as slim, torpedo-shaped fish. Most steelhead strains enter streams to spawn

Rainbow/Steelhead

in late winter or very early spring, discharging their eggs and milt when water temperatures reach 45-degrees F., then dropping back to the big water. Sometimes, steelhead ascend rivers in the fall, mostly to gobble salmon eggs that break free from redds, although a few steelies also spawn in the fall. It is not uncommon for steelhead to winter-over in Great Lakes rivers. Certain summer-run strains – fish from the Skamania, Umpqua, Rogue and Siletz rivers, for example – enter natal flows in August or September, drop eggs in February and March, and then return to the ocean or great lake to do it all again a few months later. Unlike Pacific salmon, steelhead don't die after spawning.

Whether you catch them in the open lake, harbor, drowned river mouth or river itself, rainbow/steelhead are tremendously exciting fish to catch. Some anglers say the summer-run Skamanias, which have had southern Lake Michigan fishermen wired in recent years, are the next best thing to hot dogs at a baseball double-header. There are several reasons for this reputation: they grow faster than eighth-grade kids. Skamanias are predictable in knowing enough to come home and stay home. They're also scrappers that knock out lures, invent new pretzel bends in midair, and have a phobia for trolling boats and poised landing nets.

The first Skamania steelhead I ever saw was already eight feet above Lake Michigan when he caught my attention. After he spit a Sutton Spoon at our boat, I realized the downrigger rod had gone off. Later, when I tried to wear down a spirited nine pounder, I had the feeling someone had already cornered this fish, then poked at it with a punt pole. In Alaska, they shoot fish that threaten anglers, but this was no 200-pound halibut nor did we have a .357 magnum aboard.

You'll have to forgive me, but Skamanias can carry a fellow away. Thanks to successful egg-taking efforts at Indiana Department of Natural Resources' hatcheries, Skamanias are already available to Michigan fishermen and soon will be available to Missouri River reservoir fishermen and to anglers in Wisconsin, Ontario and New York. Skamanias are exciting gamesters that freight-train lures and fight like they were bred on city streets.

Then again, I've never caught a steelhead, summer-run strain or not, that didn't earn my respect. In the Great Lakes, they become available at ice-out, along with salmon and brown trout, to shallow-water fishermen. In fact, most spring steelhead are caught off river mouths incidentally to other species. Other salmonids are in the warming shallows of these river mouths to chase spawning baitfish; steelhead are there mostly to spawn.

Steelhead prefer 58-62 degree F. water, and so they will remain in lake shallows until well into spring. For the most part, they are a topwater-oriented species, occupying the upper 10 to 40 feet of water, even over depths to several hundred feet deep. For years, charter-boat captains with seaworthy vessels have known that they could catch steelhead miles from shore in the upper lake levels. Along with cohos and an occasional brown trout or Chinook, the steelhead cruise near the surface in loose schools to pick off emerging insects and floating insects such as honey bees. Why the steelhead are there was a mystery until discovery of the thermal bar, which we explained in the chapter on temperature. Apparently, steelhead like to lie inside such temperature breaks and gobble available food. Trolling with flatlines, downriggers set from 10 to 50 feet deep, and even outriggers are favored tactics. Lead lengths and trolling speeds vary from day to day.

While some fishermen are out in the middle of Lake Michigan, others, like professional guide and Cannon field tester Jon Belliveau of Michigan City, Indiana, are targeting Skamanias poised in the shallows where they are mounting spawning drives. By mid-July most years, Jon and his wife, first mate Debi Belliveau, catch the silvery bullets in the upper 25 feet of water over depths of 60 feet. Hot lures off downriggers are white-and-orange Stainless Steelers, silver-and-red Marek-L-Lures, and silver J-Plugs with orange or red skeletal patterns. Good outrigger offerings include silver or white Wiggle Warts and Hot 'N Tots.

Although heavy mid-day boat traffic will spook these steelhead, it is also true that the period from 10:00 a.m. until 4:00 p.m. is often the best time to try for them. Debi, who steers their boat, the *Grande Dame*, from the fly bridge, targets untrolled water away from the trolling fleet. When I fished with the Belliveaus one scorching day in July, we quickly hung a 10-pound steelhead that flashed purple and silver as it curled in the net. After four fish in the box, we decided to experiment. Jon set up a 12-pound noodle rod with four-pound test line, adding a tiny swivel and a small white Northport Nailer. Next, he sent the offering far out on the port-side out-downrigger and slid the delicate rod into a holder. The sensitive rod tip thrummed in tune to the diesel-engine beat on the *Grande Dame*. Our next three strikes came off the fragile setup and, although we took turns fighting these racehorse steelhead for up to a quarter-hour each, we never got one closer that 50 feet to the boat. Each fish shook off. I have yet to catch a tail-walking steelhead on light line.

Dick Swan of Clare, Michigan, does it every summer on both Chinook salmon and Skamania steelhead. In a letter to me on the subject, this is what the rod builder and highly respected guide had to say:

"After jigging for early-run Chinook in Manistee Lake (a drowned river mouth on Lake Michigan), for 12 years, it was easy to make the transition of light-lining from a 12-foot cartopper to trolling the same light stuff aboard my 25-foot *LiteLiner*. Downrigging with two-, four- and six-pound test line on long noodle rods has proved to be the most exciting, most sporting technique on the Great Lakes. Downrigging with ultra-lights requires very few adjustments in the techniques already established.

"No. 16 rubber bands have long been accepted by trollers as their release. This same rubber band is a *must* release for light-line fishing. We spool the small-diameter lines on quality level-wind reels and tie directly to our lures. No shock leaders are necessary. We give our hooks the consideration that others do — keeping them sharp and fishing those of top quality. Such consideration allows the rubber band to be the sole source for setting a hook. We don't set hooks with a limber noodle rod.

"Small-boat trollers often stop whenever a rod releases. We also stop. It is far more sporting to fight a fish from a standing platform, than fighting it with a moving boat. The only way we differ from other trollers is that we don't fish with attractors or trip planers like Dipsy Divers. It is more enjoyable fighting fish without the added weight of such artificial objects anyway.

"We land Skamanias and Chinooks within 20 minutes and our netting success is 75 percent. landing these large fish has never been a problem. Our best fish to date is a 22½ pound Skamania on six-pound test and a 23-pound Chinook on two-pound test. We have also boated a 30-pound king on four-pound test line. To my mind, fighting and landing these trophy fish on ultra-light tackle is the ultimate in downrigger fishing."

In fall, steelhead are again available off river mouths, shoreline shallows, in harbors, and in rivers themselves. A popular tactic then is to slow-troll along the channel of drowned river mouths or wide sections of steelhead streams where the current is not too swift. Flatfish in big M-2 or L-9 sizes, jointed Kwikfish, magnum Tadpollies, and Ping-A-Ts are popular plugs that can be slow trolled on flatlines or shallow-set downriggers. Fluorescent colors with or without silver seem to work best. Water temperature often dictates how fast one should troll. In warm water, a faster speed may work best; then, some fishermen opt for J-Plugs. When the river is under 45 degrees, however, they break out the slower-working plugs. Cowbells with small lures or sewn minnows will also work at all temperatures.

Where currents are swift and unpredictable, boat fishermen have learned specialized techniques with hot-colored crankbaits such as Wiggle Warts, Hot 'N Tots, Bug Plugs, River Runts, Fat Raps and Mann's Razorbacks. "Drop-back fishing" is the practice of anchoring with heavy chain links, winch-driven spuds, or Cannon's *Chain-of-Weights* river anchors to hold a canoe, aluminum boat or jet-powered river craft ahead of steelhead holes. Fishermen then run crankbaits through the steelhead lies, and "drop back" — that is, release a few feet of line at a time. This causes the lure to dig down in front of a resting or spawning steelhead's nose. Few of these aggressive fish can resist belting it, and that is why strikes are unusually savage.

Downriggers open up new possibilities for such on-the-money fishing and for keep-

This big river steelhead hit a Hot 'N Tot that was backed down, with the help of a downrigger, through her lair.

Rainbow/Steelhead

ing non-digging lures at depths of the fisherman's choosing. Flatfish, for example, work exceptionally well on slower streams, especially below power-generating dams that fluctuate water levels at will.

A second method, called "drift-boat fishing" or "hot shotting," involves the use of double-ended, rocker-bottom craft patterned after the famous McKenzie River Drift Boats developed on West Coast rivers. These boats, about 16 feet long, resemble the seagoing New England dories used by Grand Banks cod fishermen. The center section rides in the water, and the prow and stern are turned up to crest out of the water. The oarsman sits in the middle and, using light oars (that usually turn over because they lack gunnel pins), holds the boat in a current by lightly backstroking. Once a drift boat is properly balanced and the oarsman has the hang of things, it is easy to propel and steer. A drift boat can turn on a dime, hold steady in a raging current, and be easily maneuvered in white water.

They are growing in popularity among Midwestern and Eastern steelhead fishermen. Anchoring a drift boat above or beside salmon beds, you can catch steelhead by bouncing spawn bags along the gravel bottom. However, most drift-boat fishermen prefer to run wiggling crankbaits in those hot colors that seem to enrage steelhead. Because the oarsman can operate his boat with all the skills of a Pac-Man wizard, lures stay on target. Fishermen can literally herd steelhead to the lower ends of holes where most strikes occur.

Dave Keene, a river guide and Cannon field tester from Flint, Michigan, has a couple of Easi-Troll downriggers which he sometimes mounts to the front of his drift boat, left and right of the bow. The downriggers help Dave to pinpoint his lures in the Manistee, Muskegon and other Michigan steelhead streams. He relies on 14-pound test, quality mono with good stretch but will lighten up to 10-pound test in clearer streams in mid-winter when fish are more sluggish. Level-wind or bait-casting reels work fine when paired to two-piece rods of seven to 8½ feet in length. For winter fishing, Keene prefers fiberglass ferrules and ceramic guides which he says ice-up less often than wire loops.

Drop Back or Drift-boat Fishing for Steelhead

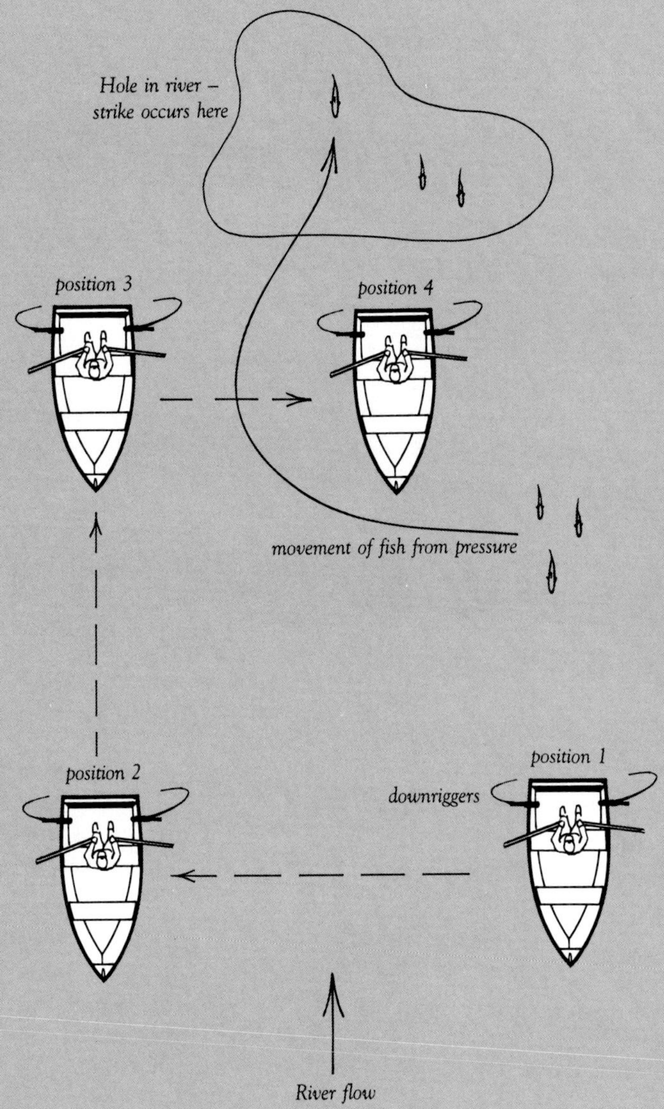

Salmon

"When used with other trolling tactics, such as flatlining and side-rigging, downriggers allow salmon fishermen to spread lines, run more lures, and fish at all depths."

Big, brawling kings return to natal-release sites as 3½ and 4½ year old adults. Heavy-duty tackle and sharp hooks are required to catch them.

Salmon. To me, the name suggests many things: mysterious wanderings in the oceans and Great Lakes, thousand-mile journeys up tundra or mountain streams, lightning-quick strikes on flies and lures, powerful runs on light line with the reel drag screaming and the rod tip jabbing like an accusatory finger, walk-on-water acrobatics, 10 or 20 or 30 pounds of kicking-mad fish in the net, grinning anglers receiving congratulatory thumps on the back.

The electrifying salmon does all these things and more. And now that these ocean-dwelling fish have been brought inland, more and more fishermen are able to experience the thrill of catching them. Five Pacific species include the Chinook (king), coho (silver), humpback (pink), sockeye (red or Kokanee) and chum. Kings, cohos and pinks live in portions of the Great Lakes where they were introduced in modern times. Chinook salmon have also been released in Lake Sakakawea and Oahe, huge Dakota reservoirs on the Missouri River. Kokanees are native to Washington, Idaho, Oregon and British Columbia lakes and have been successfully introduced in California. The Atlantic salmon is called the "landlocked salmon" in certain New England states, New York's Adirondack lakes, and eastern Canadian provinces. A one-time native to Lake Ontario, Atlantics are being restored there. Lake Michigan and Lake Superior are home to small numbers of Atlantic salmon, too.

"Salmon fever" was the way some observers described the 1967 return of the first Great Lakes spawning cohos to Michigan's Platte River. Because the Michigan Department of Natural Resources continues to release nearly a million coho "smolts" (18-month-old fish reared in hatcheries) each year to the Platte, salmon fever continues to rage. Eight Great Lake states and Ontario now plant out millions of salmon in the five inland seas. Once for a magazine article, I tallied the releases of all salmonids (trout and salmon) in the Great Lakes for a single year. There were over 20 million. And salmon, in particular, are successfully reproducing in some streams, too.

Twenty years is not a very long time to learn all the nuances of salmon behavior in freshwater as well as successful catching

Chinook Salmon

techniques. There is much yet to discover, especially in new waters like the Missouri River reservoirs. Still, much is known, at least about Great Lakes migration patterns, temperature preferences, and feeding habits of salmon. Supported with sensitive electronics, specialized tackle, and increasing knowhow, many fishermen are turning on to salmon. Downriggers have become synonymous with their angling success. When used with other trolling tactics, such as flatlining and side-rigging, downriggers allow salmon fishermen to spread lines, run more lures, and fish at all depths.

Catching a salmon with any technique is quite a thrill indeed. Read on and we'll show you how.

Chinooks

Planted out as six-month-old spring fingerlings, Chinooks provide trolling sport for the next 2½ to 3½ years (males usually spawn and die as three-year-olds, females in their fourth year). A second-year king will weigh from two to five pounds, in the third year from five to 15 pounds, and in the fourth year from 15 to 30 pounds. Fish beyond 30 pounds have either eaten exceptionally well or are older fish that, for some reason, spawn later than the norm.

Like the other salmon species, kings prefer 54- to 62-degree F. temperature but will leave this comfort zone for various reasons. In spring, for example, they simply seek the warmest water available, knowing that baitfish will ususally be found there. In summer, they will go out of temperature to find food, too, and when the spawning urge overtakes the appetites of the older fish, temperature grows less important. Kings spawn earlier in the season than do cohos. In the Great Lakes, the kings begin staging off natal-release sites in late July, entering streams sometime in August or September when water levels and temperature are right. They may run these rivers as late as October and, on occasion, will hole up in downstream pools until rains raise the water level enough to trigger an upstream surge. Spawning has been documented as late as March with deteriorating fish nearly black in color. Some ripe fish hang back in the open lake, too,

then return the following July to reproduce as brawling five-year-olds. Like all salmon, kings die after their first spawning.

Jim Beyers of Mt. Clemens, Michigan, is a good salmon fisherman. A charter-boat skipper and Cannon field tester, Beyers has been taking the *Fishin' Machine*, his 27-foot Sportcraft, to Oscoda, Michigan, on Lake Huron each July for the past 15 years. He times his arrival with that of schooling king salmon, staging offshore in preparation for running the AuSable River. Beyers' records show that kings generally approach shore in three stages lasting from one to two weeks each.

The first stage begins when lake trout trollers begin taking salmon on stacked offerings or highlines. This normally occurs from mid-July to early August with suspended fish over 90 to 110 feet of water. Spoons such as Kingfishers, Southport Slammers, Flutter Chucks and Lucky Lures in silver with combinations of blue, green, orange and chartreuse are preferred hardware, especially when trolled at 2.5 to 4.0 mph. Most catches occur from 50 feet deep to bottom.

Within a week or two, the salmon move to the next stage – troughs that are 80 to 90 feet deep. Then, Beyers and other savvy anglers break out flashers and flies. Popular are 0-sized chrome Luhr Jensen Dodgers with Michigan Squids in black or blue or Sparkle Flies in green or blue. Stacking the attractor rigs with small spoons is also productive.

The dodger/fly game ends soon after it starts, and kings will now move to the final stage – 40 to 50 feet of water – of the summer/fall fishery. Beyers shifts his lure program to plugs, such as No. 4 and No. 5 J-Plugs in green, chrome, pearl, khaki and black; blue Bang-O-Lures; Topkats in various colors; and clear-lemon Ping-A-Ts. Lure choice often depends upon the trolling speed that kings want that day. A fast clip calls for the speed-forgiving J-Plug; crawling speed means Ping-A-Ts or even Flatfish.

As trolling depths lessen, Beyers lengthens leads to 20 or 30 feet behind downrigger weights and up to 150 feet for highlines. Outriggers and planer boards figure in the shallow-water program, too, although heavy boat traffic may preclude running the latter.

Al Lindner caught this small Chinook salmon while trolling off Montague/Whitehall, Michigan, in Lake Michigan.

Before kings begin to stage near release sites, finding them can be difficult, especially in late May, throughout June, and in early July. Salmon that flee the warming shallows can generally be found in or near the thermocline; but that, too, can be gypsy-like, ever elusive and changing. Thunderstorms with resulting lightning, high winds and waves may scatter salmon, requiring several days of trolling effort to find them. That's when the better fishermen use every trick in the book.

In the chapter on rigging, we discussed trolling patterns that Cannon field tester, Bill Muirhead, a charter-boat captain from Milford, Michigan, employs. Besides the special rigging patterns explained there, Muirhead oscillates his corner-set Digi-Troll downriggers to lift and drop lures at five-foot intervals every 15 seconds. Also, to make sure his lures are all running at a certain distance behind the boat (in order to imitate a schooling effect), he blood-knots 30-foot-long leaders of clear 20-lb. test Stren line to 20-lb. test Golden Stren line on his reels. The two colors help him to quickly set lines and to mark the movements of hooked fish.

The ability to oscillate lures is a tremendous advantage when hunting king salmon in summer. Not only can trollers cover both ends of the thermocline, but the lifting and dropping action helps create fluttering of the lures. Kings often pounce on such lures when they hesitate or change speeds. Bill Thede, a Cannon field tester out of Harbor Beach, Michigan, has five Digi-Trolls on his 25-foot Cherokee charter boat, the *Country Bumpkin*. Last summer by specifically targeting king salmon on Lake Huron, Thede put nearly 400 fish in the cooler.

Besides oscillating, Thede runs stationary lures in and above the 54-degree range, relying on a Weller ProCombinator to measure both lure speed and temperature at the downrigger weight. He said that deep-water currents and the fickle nature of the thermocline require the use of such electronics in order to find fish, then stay on them. Thede stacks each downrigger with Cannon Offshore Stackers. Best lures in summer are Southport Slammers, Locos and lighted ET Spoons, with J-Plugs and Producer Tiger Plugs getting the call as fish begin to school up.

Another highly respected fisherman, Larry Pressnall, tests for Cannon on Lake Michigan out of Kewaunee, Wisconsin. Pressnall has a "hunting" philosophy that works exceptionally well for him and the customers aboard his 31-foot Slickcraft, *Southern Comfort*. He trolls certain corridors, subtle depth lines of structure that go unnoticed by other anglers. "Most fishermen look at Lake Michigan as having little structure," Pressnall said. "But by concentrating one season on running north of the harbor and the next year on trolling south, I learned the structure. I began by choosing a depth line that seemed to hold fish. By working that certain depth line north, then turning around and trolling south, I found that I could catch fish in certain places perpendicular to shore. Next, by running in and out from shore, I began to see the little rises and falls on bottom. To me, those little spots of structure are king-holding corridors. The best ones are when two corridors meet."

Like Muirhead and Thede, Pressnall runs the gamut of lures after finding fish at rapid trolling speeds while pulling J-Plugs. He said the biggest problem that most king salmon fishermen make is that once they find fish, they keep on trolling with the same lure. Trolling back and forth over marked fish while slowing down by degrees and cannonballing compatible-running lures, Pressnall finds out what the kings want for supper that day. Spoons are the biggest early- and mid-summer producers, and Pressnall is not at all shy about trying out plenty of colors and styles. Andy Reekers and Hooksters provide throbbing action. When those fail, Pressnall breaks out Northport Nailers and Flutter Chucks, which impart a darting action. If the salmon want lazy lures, down go Dodgers and flies.

Pressnall's summertime king trolling program involves four downriggers, a couple of side-rigged Dipsy Divers on steel line, a suspended steel line, and a highline off the stern. The rigging pattern gives him coverage on both horizontal and vertical planes. Like most other salmon hunters, Pressnall stacks his downriggers, but he does it differently than most. He uses a small Crane swivel that will pass through rod guides. Adding a 12- to 14-foot strip of monofilament to the swivel

Good Chinook lures include J-Plugs and their many imitations (top row) along with various spoons in many colors. Spoons (left to right) include Manistee Wobbler, several colors of Northport Nailers, two Eppinger Flutter Chucks, Loco, and KC Spoon.

gives him the lead to his bottom lure. A five- to seven-foot leader containing a second lure goes on the swivel. Pressnall then attaches his downrigger line release halfway between the swivel and the bottom lure. Both lures, consequently, will sport five- to seven-foot leads and will be separated by the same distance.

Another tip from Pressnall is the use of single-barb hooks on lures instead of treble hooks. He claims that single hooks, especially when touched up with a sharpening stone, drive deeper into the jaw of a king salmon and therefore hold better.

Pressnall's reliance on diving planers — such as Dipsy Divers — along with downriggers, is being echoed on Lake Huron. According to veteran charter-boat captain Bob Bingle, the Dipsys have replaced Dodgers as salmon attractors. "In addition to trolling with my Cannon downriggers, I always run at least two Dipsys and sometimes as many as four on a side," Bingle said. "In fact, I have replaced my outriggers with them." How does one put out four of the little diving planers without tangle? "You have to set the first one the farthest back and the deepest," Bingle explained. "Then as you come forward up the boat, shorten the depth. When the Dipsy trips from a strike, it will run up and back, out of line from the other divers. I have no tangles whatsoever."

Bingle said that big lures like Silver Streaks are ideal because they won't spin behind the Dipsys, plus fish tend to hook themselves deeply when barbs are pin-prick sharp because the diving planer acts as a bolo of sorts. Hot colors in the Dipsys, which apparently act as attractors to salmon, are orange on dark days and chrome on bright days. Green works well all around. Good Silver Streak colors are chartreuse and lime, green, and Wonder Bread.

Cannon field testers are among the most innovative of fishermen. We asked Al Merfert of Muskego, Wisconsin, how he catches so many king salmon. Besides relying on advanced electronics, which we explain in the chapter on Electronics, Merfert credits his rigging program. Basically, he applies V-shaped rigging, with starboard and port lines higher and featuring longer leads than stern-end offerings, which tend to be deep and close to downrigger weights. A pair of Digi-

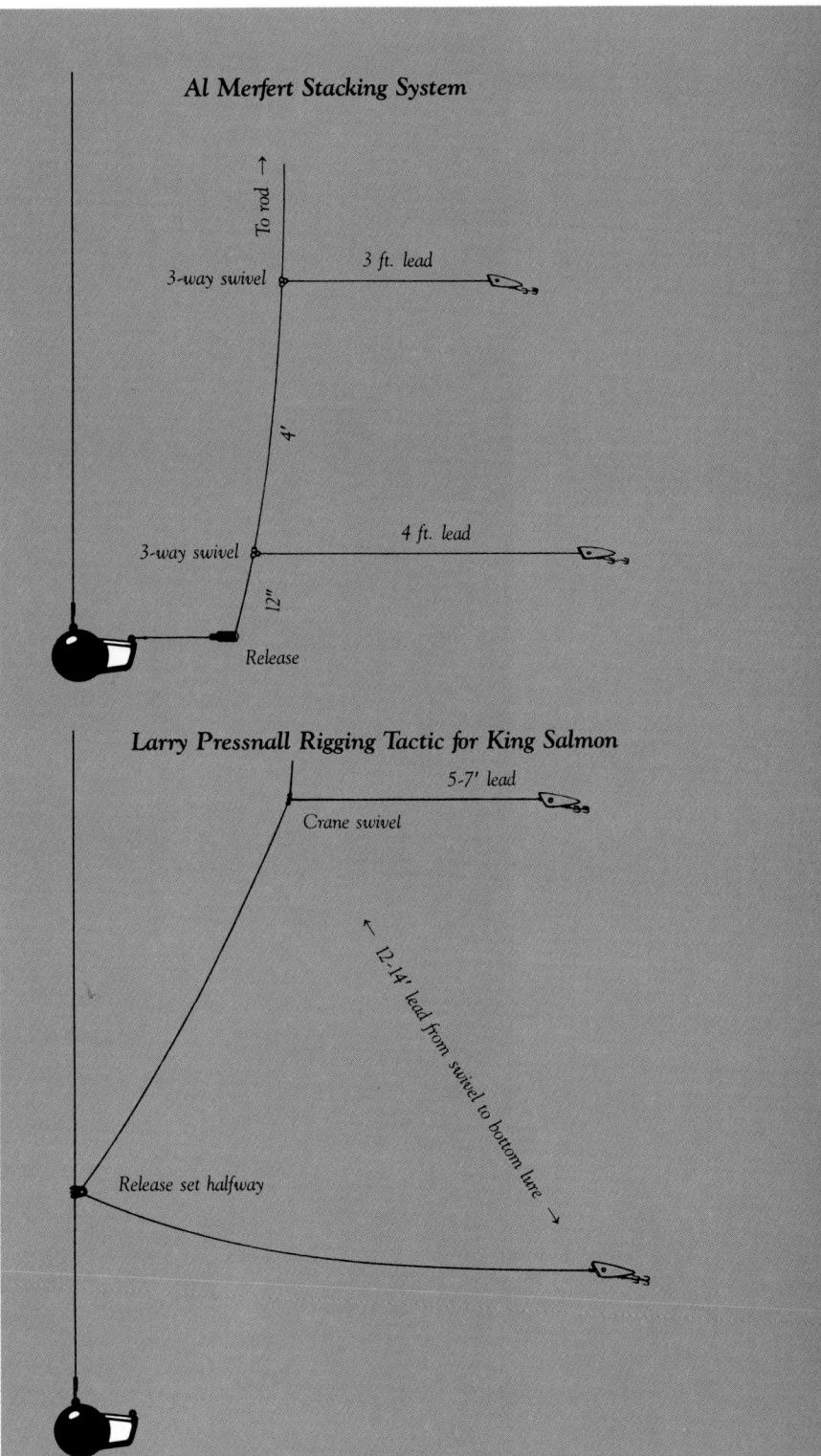

Troll out-downs have 66-inch booms whereas corner-set Digi-Trolls feature 44-inch booms and are locked on swivel bases at 45-degree angles. A single Mag 10 electric has a two-foot boom and is spotted in the center.

Merfert stacks his out-downs with sliders and inside lines with a unique double-stacking system that employs a three-way swivel. Twelve inches above his release on the downrigger weight, Merfert adds a three-way swivel. The bottom loop goes to the release, the top loop goes to his rod, and the side loop contains a four-foot lead and a lure. About four feet above this three-way swivel, Merfert adds a second three-way swivel. The bottom loop attaches to the line coming off the top loop of the bottom three-way. The top loop goes to the rod, and the side loop holds a second lure on a three-foot lead. Merfert said that large split rings work as well or better than the three-way swivels.

Salmon takers in spring are jointed Rebels in blue and silver, or green and silver with orange bellies. Lucky Louies in silver and various other colors are good summer salmon baits, especially when stacked with Lucky Lures in silver with green, orange or blue. "I depend on downriggers to do the job," Merfert reports, "but I also put out a couple of outriggers and run a flatline or two. Rebels or Northport Nailers are the mainstay on those rigs."

On his charter boat, Carl Gibson of Wood Dale, Illinois, runs six Cannon electric downriggers, four across the stern and a pair of out-downs. Also a Cannon field tester, Gibson begins adding sliders in spring when salmon are in 30 feet of water and seas are calm. He claims that 50 percent of his catch on some days come off the added lures. Gibson has also discovered that king salmon in the late summer or early fall will sometimes lie right in lake-bottom mud. To stir them into striking, the innovative skipper has experimented with bending a two-foot piece of stainless-steel wire into a hairpin shape, then attaching it with duct tape to a cannonball into which he has drilled a small hole. Using his electric downriggers, Gibson lowers the cannonball to within a foot of the smooth southern Lake Michigan bottom, then "tickles" salmon there.

"I know it sounds crazy," Gibson said, "and I'm even reluctant to report it, but I caught several king salmon with this method last summer."

These and other tactics will likely work in other freshwater places where Chinooks are being released. One of the best spots to go for a trophy king is Lake Ontario where salmon have yet to impact a lush forage base. Kings are also available to eastern basin Lake Erie trollers, southern Lake Superior fishermen and, of course, to anglers in Lakes Huron and Michigan. The newest Chinook hotspot, however, is Lake Sakakawea in North Dakota and Lake Oahe in South Dakota. Fishermen in the two reservoirs are just learning catching tactics for kings. South Dakota's Lake Francis Case, which received its first king salmon releases three years ago, could be the next Missouri River hotspot.

Art Talsma, a charter-boat captain and Cannon field tester from Pierre, South Dakota, grew up fishing the Great Lakes from his former Michigan home. Consequently, Talsma is in the forefront of Missouri River reservoir salmon-catching tactics. "It's different out here," Talsma said. "First, whereas in Lake Michigan we could troll everywhere; in Oahe, we must avoid 50 percent of the places due to sunken trees and quick contour changes. Second, we are still learning how to track salmon migrations seasonally. Oahe fish tend to run north and south from their release location at Whitlocks Bay to the dam about 60 miles down the lake. Because we have no large streams, we target flats areas. Still, most of the fishing activity occurs near the dam because it is the deepest, coldest spot in the lake and because the flow of water there attracts baitfish and salmon."

Shallow-water effective lures are mostly flutter-type spoons such as Southport Slammers and Westport Wobblers. Small J-Plugs, Rebels, Bombers and Shad Raps, along with rattle-producing crankbaits, such as Willy's Worms, are hot tickets for fish from 70 to 100 feet deep. Attractors and flies or squids are popular for deep-water salmon, too. Leads shrink as depths increase and because Lake Oahe water tends to be dark, Talsma said that glow lures sometimes produce.

"By the end of August, our salmon simply disappear," said Talsma, who is then likely

Gerry Gibbs, fishing editor of Outdoor Life, *caught this dandy Lake Michigan Chinook in late summer.*

Chinook Salmon

Carl Gibson's Method of Getting Salmon on Bottom to Strike

"Tickler" made from stainless steel wire

Lake bottom

to trail his boat back to Lake Michigan for salmon action. "In mid-September, however, they are back in Whitlocks Bay to spawn. Peak fishing occurs by the middle of October."

It is a foregone conclusion of most fishermen that once salmon enter rivers, they can't be caught with sport-fishing methods. In some places where it is legal, and in other places where it is not, a snag fishery has developed. Snagging advocates say they might as well take the salmon, destined to die anyway, since the fish won't strike lures.

Bob Kingsley disagrees. A veteran sport fisherman and Cannon field tester from Muskegon, Michigan, Kingsley has recently begun to guide for Chinook salmon in the Muskegon River. He said that 90 percent of the time, he can get limit catches and that his success has caused some former snagging enthusiasts to turn thumbs down on that practice.

"The lower end of the Muskegon River is narrow with deep pools featuring plenty of drowned timber, cuts and runs behind logs," Kingsley said. "Fish stack up in these pockets, and the only way to catch them is to run lures straight off the back of the boat. Bank or wading fishermen lose a ton of tackle."

Kingsley adopts the drop-back technique explained in the chapter on steelhead fishing. He relies on pearl-colored M-2 Flatfish which dig down to the level where the brutish kings are lying. The problem that occurred, however, when Kingsley tossed a pair of Flatfish out, one to each side of his 14-foot Mirrocraft, was that the currents pulled the two lures to the river center and quickly tangled the lines. That's when Kingsley began lowering the Flatfish with his Cannon Econo-Rigger and Easi-Troll, one of each downrigger he has mounted to the boat. Thanks to the downriggers, he can now put his lures on the money and keep them there. Kingsley uses heavy-duty size 32 rubber bands for releases off the downrigger cables. "When a salmon pops one of those rubber bands," Kingsley said, "you can bet he's hooked."

By switching to the downriggers, Kingsley opened up space to each side of the boat for adding a spawn bag setup. He pierces a size 4 Eagle Claw style 42 hook to a big chunk of fresh spawn or knotted bag of salmon eggs. Eighteen inches above the bait goes a single No. 4 split shot. Kingsley quarters across the river with his cast, then allows the spawn to skip along bottom. Lifting his anchor a few seconds at a time or releasing a few feet of line periodically helps him to drop his two lures and two baits through the salmon hole by degrees. As with steelhead, strikes are particularly vicious.

"I can't tell you why these salmon strike," Kingsley admitted, "but they definitely do hit both the Flatfish and the spawn. We never foul-hook (snag) a fish. I know they're not hungry because their stomachs are atrophied, and I doubt if aggression is the cause because the salmon don't spawn in the lower river. I have a theory, at least to maybe explain why they take spawn. The theory is survival of the species."

Kingsley explained that salmon usually cover their nests with gravel to keep eggs from washing away and to prevent predators, mostly steelhead, from destroying them. But loose eggs dribbling with the current help predators to home in on the nest. By eating the spawn they see rolling along, salmon may, knowingly or unknowingly, be helping the species to survive.

It's an interesting theory, one which proves at least one key point about Chinook salmon: They are fascinating fish. Further, much remains to be learned about the species and how to catch them.

Low-light conditions are ideal for catching king salmon. Prime times are early morning and late afternoon.

Jon Belliveau nets a Lake Michigan coho salmon for a young client aboard the Grande Dame.

Sometimes when the fish aren't biting, trolling can be about as much fun as watching new paint dry on bathroom walls. Your fishing trip turns into a long boat ride, and you find yourself nodding off to the lull of waves, the hum of wind in downrigger wires.

Then, there's the coho salmon. Get into a school of hungry cohos, and you can experience more fun – and confusion – than a power outage at a three-ring circus. Fishing rods go off two and three at a time while silver salmon pirouette above the lake. Anglers holler "Fish on!" while passing rods under and over each other to avoid tangles, looking like they are crocheting something with huge needles. When everything goes right, the result may be up to a half-dozen silver bullets trying to kick the cooler apart. When it goes wrong and the cohos succeed in making a shambles of everyone's tackle, the boat can look like a set from a Three Stooges movie.

Coho fishing is like that, an all-or-nothing affair. Some of the hottest action occurs in spring in southern shallows of the Great Lakes. Because these areas warm first, cohos begin drifting back in late fall and winter to such spots as southern Lake Michigan; Lake St. Clair and the St. Clair River; Marquette and Duluth harbors on Lake Superior; from Erie, Pennsylvania, to Buffalo, New York, on Lake Erie; and Lake Ontario west of Toronto and from the Niagara River outflow east to Oswego, New York. Most of the cohos are one- to three-pound fish, planted out the previous spring as 18-month-old smolts. They are hungry in spring, so hungry that most will triple weights by fall when they spawn and die as three-year-old adults.

In baitfish-rich Lake Ontario, cohos grow bigger than eight pounds, than 10 pounds, than even 12 pounds. Twelve- to 15-pound fish are not uncommon; those that win the fishing derbies are nearly always hang-belly salmon of 20 or more pounds.

In spring, cohos are not all that hard to find. Simply look for the warmest water available. Nuclear and coal-fired powerplants are top prospects as are factory warmwater discharges, rivers and streams, slicks (pastures of warm water surrounded by cold,

Coho Salmon

choppy water), and shoreline shallows. Cohos don't seem to mind the glitter and racket from trolling hardware (namely lures and attractors) and engine propellers. In fact, they may even be drawn to it, perhaps mistaking the activity for a baitfish slaughter. Trollers report cohos snapping lures in the prop chop right behind the boat, plus they often bust lures fluttering to the surface after the angler deliberately has broken his line release to change baits. Some fishermen even paint their cannonballs in eye-catching fluorescent colors, claiming that the feisty little salmon are drawn to them.

Rigging tactics from spring through fall are basically topwater-oriented. Cohos often cruise just under the surface and in the top level of the thermocline, once it forms in summer. Ron Yagelski, a charter-boat captain and Cannon field tester from Michigan City, Indiana, catches Lake Michigan cohos beginning about the second week in April. Yagelski runs five Mag 10 downriggers off the back of his 30-foot Trojan while seeking the upper 15 feet of water over depths to 40 feet. Light spoons go on the downriggers, which are often doubled with sliders, while small Rapalas and Tadpollies go on several flatlines and a pair of 22-foot outriggers. The outriggers are pointed straight out so that lures enter the water sooner and dig down faster. Various combinations of chartruese, red, black and orange are the colors of choice. Yagelski starts trolling at 2.0 knots, as measured by an EMS Pelican, and moves up or down from that mark, depending on what the salmon want.

By the first week in May, king salmon usually move in and the cohos move out – with Yagelski and other coho fishermen staying with them. Until early June, the trollers catch them in the upper 15 to 30 feet of water over depths to 240 feet – 15 or more miles from home port. The same tactics work, but Yagelski now adds 00 orange Dodgers ahead of black-and-silver or black-purple-and-silver Bead Flies. When cohos return in late September, anglers break out bigger lures – Silver Hordes, J-Plugs, jointed Rapalas and Northport Nailers – for the bigger fish. Fishermen that tough out late-fall weather can catch the following spring's vanguard when two-year-old salmon, released six months

These are effective dodger/fly combinations for king and coho salmon. Richey Custom Flies pictured are (top to bottom) yellow and black Michigan Squids, blue and green Sparkle Flies, and the Dazzler.

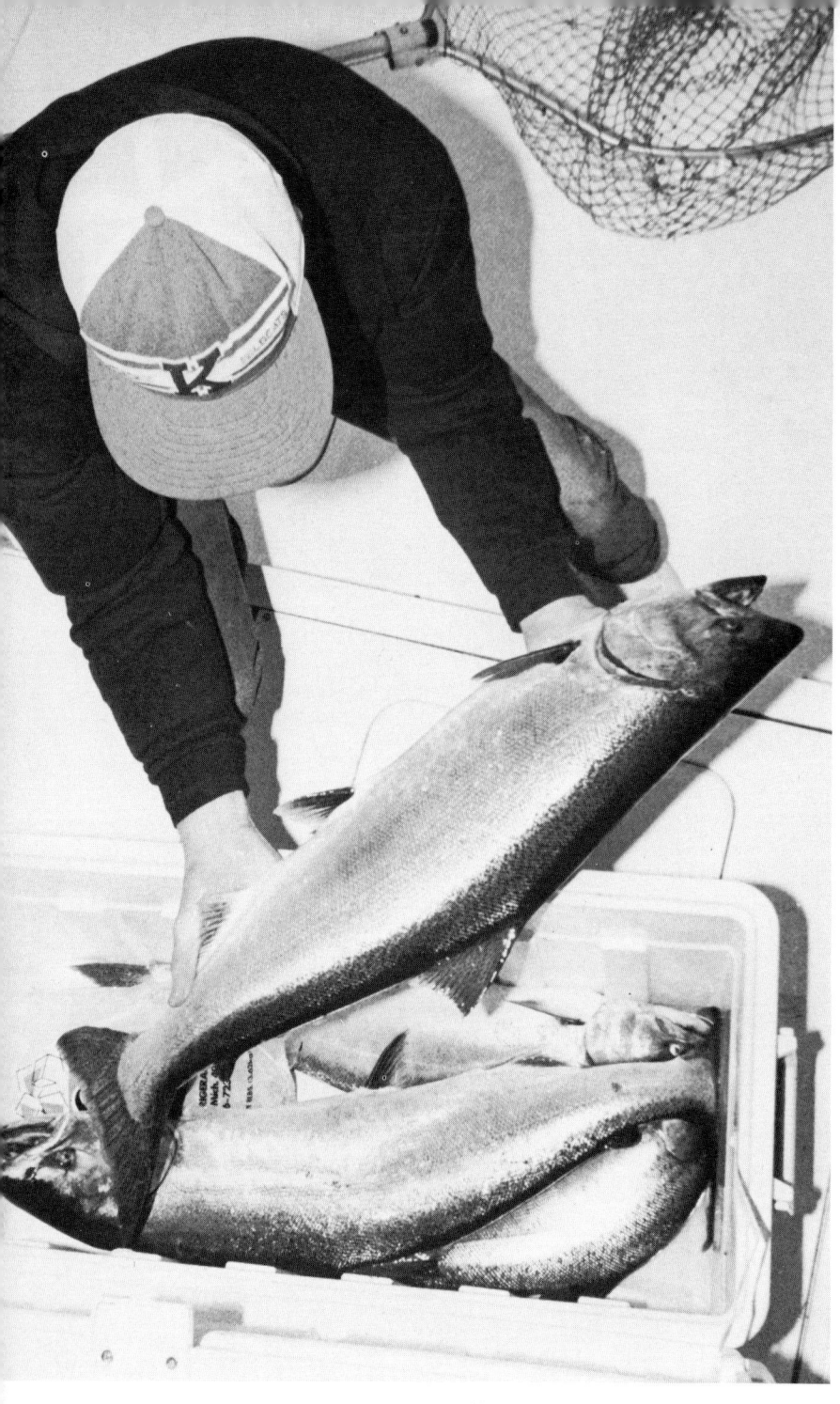

A mixed bag of spring Chinooks and cohos. The angler's success was due to finding warm water, then trolling the right lures in the right colors for that day.

earlier, show up in the shallows, about Thanksgiving, to winter-over.

Although cohos provided the first chapter in the Great Lakes Cinderella story – with their initial release by the Michigan DNR in 1966 – the silver salmon have taken a back seat, of sorts, to their brawling cousins, the Chinooks. Not only are Chinooks bigger, but they are released by hatchery personnel as six-month-old fingerlings, thus requiring only a third of the supervision and care that cohos demand. Also, kings provide more bang for the public buck because they are available for up to 3½ years. Cohos, on the other hand, yield about half as much catching opportunity. Further, cohos are great wanderers, even though they can be successfully imprinted to return to natal streams.

On the other hand, cohos have some pluses going for them, too. Besides their fighting ability and excellent table quality (the flesh is a bright-orange color), cohos are available to small-boat fishermen. So you don't have to own a 30-foot charter boat to catch them. In fact, anglers working out of smaller boats have the edge in spring because they are able to get close to shore with planer boards and can work in tight traffic much better. The biggest advantage, though, is their flexibility. Small-boat fishermen can trailer their craft to any port that is hot. That's especially important because, in the case of cohos, catching action can change as fast as the score in the Super Bowl's closing moments.

Consider Jim Friedel, a sport fisherman and Cannon field tester from Fond du Lac, Wisconsin. Friedel regularly port hops in spring with his 18-foot Lund Tyee 5.5. Armed with a Plane-R-Boom and two Plane-R-Boards in the bow, two Digi-Trolls on the corners, and another Cannon downrigger at the stern center, Friedel is fully rigged for spring fishing. About one-fourth of his early-season catch are cohos with the balance split among kings, browns, steelhead and lakers. He takes full advantage, too, of Wisconsin law which allows each fisherman a total of three rods. Typical rigging with a partner aboard calls for two downriggers, two wireline setups, and a pair of Dipsy Diver rods to act as outriggers.

Friedel likes two lines in the prop wash with three- to four-foot leads off downrigger weights. Flutter Spoons and Little Cleos in silver and/or green are first picks in early spring. Wire lines are usually used for pulling Dodgers with flies or spoons. A hot combination is a silver 0-sized Dodger with a green Apex spoon (locally called a "shoe horn"). Friedel attaches a two-foot leader to a three-way swivel with a rubber snubber in-between to take up shock. Dipsy rods are run out to each side of the boat at about a 10-degree angle above the water. A 20-ounce ball takes lures to a suspended depth of Friedel's choosing. There, bouncing waves impart tantalizing movement to them.

If Friedel has a third angler aboard, he may add a flatline, another downrigger and a planer board. Small Rebels and Rapalas are good lures off boards or flatlines.

Many summertime and even fall-spawning coho trollers like to run "license plates" (another term for flashers or Dodgers) with flies or squids. Again, hot color combinations prevail. Here are some good ones to try: chrome flasher with green or blue lure; green-and-yellow flasher with green, yellow or white lure; chartreuse flasher with yellow or green lure; red flasher with black or green lure; white flasher with black lure; orange flasher with black or blue lure. Put your offerings in, above and below the 50- to 55-degree thermocline, then stack one or more setups with flake-thin spoons. It is not uncommon to get a double-header when you troll through schooling cohos.

Cohos are here today, gone tomorrow, and back the next day, sometimes making them a frustrating target. But when you can find at least one, it won't be swimming alone.

Because cohos are schooling fish, most anglers run multiple offerings. Doubles and triples are common when trollers can stay with the salmon pack.

 Atlantic Salmon

Author Tom Huggler holds 12-pound Atlantic salmon he caught in Lake Michigan on a jointed Rapala.

Atlantic salmon are often called "landlocks" when found in lakes and reservoirs of eastern Canada, upper New York State, and northern New England. Average size is three or four pounds although Atlantics can grow much larger. In Vermont, the record is 12 pounds (Lake Champlain); in New York, it is 19 lb. 3 oz. (Lake George); in Minnesota, 12 lb. 8 oz. (Lake Superior); and in Massachusetts, 9 lb. 11 oz. (Quabbin Reservoir). The Michigan record, a Lake Michigan fish caught in 1981, weighed a whopping 32 lb. 10 oz.

Great Lakes trollers catch Atlantics incidentally to other species. In New England, however, anglers fish specifically for these exciting gamesters. One of the best fishermen is professional guide Pete Grasso, a Cannon field tester from Laconia, New Hampshire. Grasso goes after landlocks from spring through fall in sprawling Lake Winnipesaukee, where his best fish to date is a six-pounder.

"Spring fish are up high," Grasso said, "in the top 25 feet. From ice-out until early May, we troll a lot of spoons in silver and copper. Flutter Chucks, Flash Kings, Sutton Spoons and Mooselook Wobblers are good ones when slow-trolled because they resemble smelt, the principal forage species in the lake."

Grasso said typical rigging with a pair of Digi-Trolls is to triple-stack each one at 10 feet apart with staggered depths. For example, on one side of the boat, the veteran guide will drop his weight and bottom lure at 25 feet, then stack respectively at 15 and five feet. The other side will feature lures at 30, 20 and 10 feet.

Grasso also runs flatlines and planer boards because the water is clear, and topwater salmon are easily spooked. Rapalas are good lures for these techniques. By early May when the salmon switch from smelt to emerging insects, Grasso begins to rely on streamer flies – Meredith Specials, Gray Ghosts, Red Ghosts and Spirit of 76 patterns. As spring merges into summer, fish go deeper, and so Grasso hugs the 50- to 55-degree F. thermocline, which he finds with the help of a Lowrance X-15 graph. Lake trout are often in the thermocline or below, too, and so stacking of lines may produce both species.

Pink Salmon

As water temperature cools in September and Atlantics once more seek the upper lake levels, Grasso jacks up his trolling speed and begins to cycle his Digi-Trolls. The combination produces continued success until the season ends on September 30.

Ed Mendus, a sport troller and Cannon field tester from Ballston Spa, New York, goes after Atlantics in Lake George in the foothills of the Adirondacks with an 18-foot Boston Whaler. Downrigger and planer-board rigging tactics are similar to those of Pete Grasso's except that Mendus relies on ¼ oz. to ⅜ oz. pencil-thin saltwater jigs with white skirts. Mendus ties the jigs directly to four- or six-pound test line, adjusting tension accordingly on his Cannon Quick Releases and trolling at a fast six mph clip.

Mendus also makes his own flies in a Gray Ghost pattern. The streamers are 3½ to four inches long and are designed so that the wings fan out when trolled. Another trick the veteran employs is to use 10-pound Salmon Tracker downrigger weights. These are long, thin weights with adjustable tail fins which, when trolled fast, veer to the boat side and impart appealing action to Mendus' lures.

Lake Champlain guide Ken Coleman of Willsboro, New York, catches three- to five-pound landlocks in spring by targeting river mouths and points in 20 feet of water. Typical rigging aboard the Cannon field tester's 18-foot boat is two downriggers pulling Rapalas at 10 to 15 feet deep, a pair of flatlines featuring smelt-imitating streamers on sinking flylines, and dual planer boards with Mooselook Wobblers in silver, brass or fluorescent red.

"You've got to have lures with good action to catch Atlantics," Coleman said.

Pink or humpback salmon first appeared in the Great Lakes about 30 years ago when Canadian fisheries biologists accidentally dumped some hatchery leftover fish (destined for Hudson Bay) into Lake Superior. Within a few years, stream anglers began catching the little odd-year spawners (mature, two-year-old pinks average only a couple pounds each), but they didn't know what they were. Slowly the pink salmon (not pink at all, but rather silver throughout the year until they take on spawning colors of olive-brown) spread throughout the Great Lakes. In 1985, they reached huge numbers in Lake Huron. Fishermen expect them to return in 1987 and every odd year thereafter.

Anglers also learned that the scrappy pinks will hit small plugs and spoons, especially those highlined or in the upper reaches of the thermocline. Previously, even the fisheries biologists assumed that the littlest Pacific salmon subsisted on zooplankton and other small organisms.

Pinks can be sporting fun on light line of two- or four-pound test. They will smack small lures such as Andy Reekers and Eppinger Thindevles that are gingerly set into thin rubber-band or adjustable releases like Cannon Quick Releases or Cannon Offshore Releases. Although some fishermen view the little humpies as a nuisance — especially when a school sets off half their lines in one flurry — others see them as a windfall. Two things are certain: (1) they are in the Great Lakes to stay, (2) they can be caught on downriggers and other sport-trolling methods.

This tiny, yet adult, pink salmon hit a Flutter Spoon in Lake Huron.

Walleye Bass

"Most importantly, it's fun to fish for walleyes with downriggers . . . Downrigger fishing is the fastest-growing tactic for striped bass angling in the country."

Catching walleyes on downriggers is not as crazy as it may sound. When walleyes suspend, downriggers do the job.

Walleyes and downriggers. Not a very promising combination, is it? Makes me think of something weird, like eating a rye-bread sandwich of Dijon mustard and blackstrap molasses. Everyone who fishes walleyes knows he is up against a bottom-hugging species. After all, that's why drifting, trolling and jigging tactics with live bait and lures skipped over bottom work so well. And that's why the first time I was asked to tag along on a downrigger trolling trip for walleyes, I wondered if our host was from outer space.

He wasn't. He also knew what he was doing here in the western basin of Lake Erie. While trolling 12 lines with downriggers and planer boards, we caught and released 78 walleyes from one-to-four-pounds each during a four-hour charter. I learned some things on that trip. First, walleyes *do* suspend at certain times, mostly when they are hungry and food is in places other than on bottom. Second, downriggers and their related rigging tactics – planer boards, flatlines and diving planers – allow for multiple-line walleye fishing without tangles. Third, you can quickly get lures to any depth, including bottom, with downriggers.

Fourth, and most importantly, it's *fun* to fish for walleyes with downriggers. Walleyes are a schooling species. Catch one and you'll probably catch two, three, maybe four – and sometimes all at once.

"Walleye," "walleyed pike," "eye," "marble eye," "pikeperch," "yellow" or "pickerel" – call him what you will – the walleye is quickening anglers' pulses nationwide. Though long considered a midwest gamester, walleyes are now found in all 48 contiguous states, and their range extends as far north as Great Slave Lake, Hudson Bay and Labrador. Most everyone has heard about the east/west walleye booms in Lake Erie's western basin and the Missouri River reservoirs. But walleyes are coming on strong in several other places, too, including the central and eastern basins of Lake Erie.

Roosevelt Reservoir and the Columbia River in Washington are now serving up beerbelly walleyes to 16 pounds. In addition to super action in Lake St. Clair and in the Detroit and St. Clair Rivers, Michigan anglers are talking about twin hotspots in

Walleye

Lake Huron's Saginaw Bay and in Lake Michigan's Muskegon River and Muskegon Lake, as well as in the St. Joseph River. At the top of Lake Michigan, Little Bay de Noc recently yielded its finest walleye fishing in 20 years, and Wisconsin's Green Bay is ready to explode with walleye-catching action.

Even so, the nation's most untapped, most undiscovered walleye fishing may well be in Western reservoirs, large and small. Melvern, Milford, Kirwin, Glen Elder and Kanapolis lakes in Kansas, for example, bear watching. So do smaller impoundments in Nebraska, Montana and the Dakotas, the names of which will be on walleye anglers' lips by the end of the decade. Just now, Texas, Oklahoma and New Mexico fishermen are getting a taste of what "walleye fever" is all about.

Lake Stockton in Missouri and Greer's Ferry in Arkansas are getting hot for walleyes. So are many of the big bass lakes in the South, like Dale Hollow in Kentucky and Tennessee. Bass anglers in this region are sitting atop a gold mine of walleye action – not many fish, perhaps, but hefty hogs that stretch a spring scale beyond its limit. A long growing season in warm, forage-rich lakes is the reason. And, consider northern Florida: Two years after lakes there were stocked, they began serving up four-pound marble eyes.

Along with yellow perch and sauger, walleyes belong to the perch family. The only resemblance to a pike – even though they are often called "walleyed pike" – is their predatory nature. Walleyes are yellow- to brownish-green in color with overlaid darker mottling and a white-tipped tail on the lower fin. The average-sized walleye will scale a tad under two pounds and will tape less than 18 inches, but these fish do grow to impressive sizes. Most anglers consider an eight-pounder to be a lunker, but 10-, 11-, even 12-pound bruisers are not uncommon. The world record, a 25-pound walleye, was caught in 1960 from Old Hickory Lake in Tennessee.

Not noted as a scrapper the likes of trout, salmon or bass, walleyes nevertheless can test tackle and equipment. The males in particular sock bait hard and fight well soon after spring spawning when they go on a feeding spree. Females soon follow. Mid-summer is another time that produces hot action from

These fishermen teamed up to land a fine six-pound walleye.

Jon Nissen, a charter-boat captain and Cannon field tester, swings aboard a small Lake Erie walleye.

aggressive fish, although initial hits then are still somewhat on the soft side. Fall is a good time to nail a lunker for the wall, but walleyes become less active then and don't fight as well as in summer. What the walleye lacks in slugging ability he more than makes up on the table. Some veteran fishermen, pointing out that supermarket fillets sell for $6 per pound, claim "nothing eats finer" than a plate of golden-fried walleyes.

Walleyes breed in early spring (shortly after ice-out in northern states) anytime from early March to mid-May. The species prefers gravel or rocky shoals of lakes and reservoirs and will run suitable river (those containing gravel stretches) a short distance to drop eggs. A single female may hold several thousand eggs.

Walleyes prefer relatively clean lakes that feature areas of hard bottom. Because of a layer of retina pigment, their eyes are extremely light-sensitive, and in clear lakes they often feed at night or during days of heavy cloud-cover. In murky lakes, they may feed off-and-on during daylight hours. Few angling experiences equal the thrill of a prize 'eye thieving your bait as it swipes monofilament off the reel spool, or the glow of golden eyes like twin-beamed flashlights when a walleye comes to net in the sun.

One of the walleye's biggest trump cards is his year-round catchability. You will find fish schooled off river mouths, hard-bottomed reefs, points, drop-offs, river channels and contour breaks. Normally bottom-holders, spring fish often stay in shallows to mug baitfish. Anglers then catch 'eyes by slow-trolling shallow-running crankbaits, minnow-imitating plugs, or jigs sweetened with a small minnow. Spawning rivers, shallow-water reefs, shoreline rip rap, and dam trailraces are likely spring fishing spots.

By summer, warming water temperatures and the sun's rays force walleyes deep. In the Dakotas' Lake Oahe, for example, they may be found from 80 to 140 feet where they seek rainbow smelt. Downrigger trolling with plugs and spoons is a good method to wake them up. Fall-catching tactics again call for slow-trolling in shallows with small cranks or drift-fishing with jigs tipped with minnows or crawlers.

Cannon field testers around the country have some dependable techniques involving downriggers for catching walleyes, too. One of the best fishermen is guide Jim Beyers who charter-fishes out of Monroe, Michigan's Bolles Harbor on Lake Erie, each June and July. To give his customers the maximum fight with the average-sized 1½ to 2½ pound walleyes here, Beyers uses Zebco Quantum open-face reels mated to Shakespeare Ugly Stik ultra-light rods that are only five feet long and that feature light-action tips. On the other hand, planer-board and flatlined lures get medium-action six-foot rods.

Beyers runs five Cannon Digi-Troll downriggers across the back of his 10-foot beam charter boat. Typical rigging involves heavy use of spoons – Flutter Chucks, Northport Nailers and Lakeview Nailers mostly – in purple, blue, black-and-silver, green, chartreuse or watermelon colors. One day in early June when I fished with Beyers in 25 feet of water, he staggered the above lures from left to right at these depths: nine, 16, 20, 12 and one foot. Release lengths varied from 10 to 20 feet.

Planer boards are a key part of Beyers' rigging program. If he has enough customers aboard (Michigan law permits two rods per angler), Beyers triple stacks each board. Until Cannon came out with its Offshore Planer Release, Beyers used plastic clothespins for releases. The boards are run out about 60 feet to each side of the boat, and each lure is attached to a line release. Lures are then allowed to slip via a ring down the planer board tether where line pressure from the boat's forward progress will hold them. Beyers thus controls how far from the boat each lure will run by simply increasing or decreasing the amount of fishing line he lets out. The lure closest to the board (and farthest from the boat) gets the longest release length. Release lengths shorten respectively as lines are stopped closer to the boat. The innovative captain also adds a flatline or two to cover the wake immediately behind his boat. Then, when a planer board trips from a striking fish, Beyers replaces it with a flatline.

The most popular lure for planer-board trolling is the rattle-producing Storm Wiggle Wart in five different colorings: blue, chartreuse with orange back, chrome with char-

Walleye

treuse back, deep purple, and chartreuse with green.

Far at the other end of Lake Erie, walleye-catching tactics with downriggers are quite different. Years ago, Jerry Heffernan, a Cannon field tester and charter-boat captain from North Tonawanda, New York, began trolling at night for eastern basin walleyes in both Canadian and American waters. Although he also relies on planer boards, Heffernan said he cycles his two Digi-Trolls (he also has three Mag 10A electrics on his boat) on the maximum 60-second pause. "I run my lures (principally Flutter Chucks) back 100 feet," Heffernan explained, "and the oscillation causes them to increase activity on the upward motion. Walleyes typically strike when the lure is dropped back on the downward motion." Heffernan opts for crankbaits on his planer boards. Good ones are magnum Wiggle Warts and Hot 'N Tots in silver, blue, purple, green or various combinations of these colors. In deep water, he may add four ounces of lead to get the cranks down to 20 or more feet.

As mentioned earlier, reservoir fishing for walleyes is sweeping the nation. Sport fisherman Ken Coleman of Willsboro, New York, has been testing a pair of Cannon Mini-Mag downriggers for fall walleyes on the Sacandaga Reservoir. He has been catching walleyes, too, relying on a depth finder and his downriggers to spot Rapalas just over drowned stone fences and flooded buildings where the walleyes suspend in concentration.

Another Cannon contact, Steve Payne of Post Falls, Idaho, reports catching walleyes to 14 pounds on downriggers from the Columbia River in Washington State. "Probably less than four percent of the fishermen there rely on downriggers," Payne reported. "Instead, most fishermen jig with Twister Tails in the deep, wide, slow-moving river. However, we have had excellent success in summer while downrigger trolling at 50 to 70 feet near bottom, which is reasonably smooth, with some humps and hollows. By watching the sonar and keeping downrigger weights a few feet from bottom, we allow our lures to move along close to bottom." Good walleye-takers for Payne include gold-and-orange Hot 'N Tots, Lindy Shadlings, Finsel Spoons, Eppinger Five of Diamonds spoons, and Luma-Lures.

This St. Joseph River fisherman prepares to unhook an Indiana walleye.

A growing number of Missouri Reservoir trollers are relying on downriggers to summer fish for deep-water walleyes. Some, like Cannon field tester Art Talsma of Pierre, South Dakota, like to fish the flats at night. Flats are flooded agricultural lands that average 20 feet in depth and two or three miles in length. Feeding walleyes cruise the flats at night. Talsma reports catches of fish to six pounds on Rapalas, Rebels and Hot 'N Tots run 200 feet behind downrigger weights. The walleyes normally suspend just off bottom, and the object is to keep lures there, too. Depending on the digging ability of the lure, Talsma adjusts downrigger trolling depth accordingly.

Fishermen like Beyers, Heffernan, Coleman, Payne and Talsma are proving that walleyes can indeed be caught on downriggers. More than that, these experienced anglers *prefer* to fish for walleyes – that's right! – with *downriggers*.

Largemouth and Smallmouth Bass

If it were allowed, sooner or later it would happen: Someone would win a bassing tournament while trolling with downriggers. Don't laugh. Downriggers could be the slickest thing yet for finding an elusive school of bigmouth or smallmouth bass. Both species suspend at certain times – largemouths in or over weeds, smallmouths along rocky ledges or drop-offs. Both bass travel in search of food, oxygen-rich water, and preferred pH and temperature. Smallmouths like water under 70-degrees F., largemouths above 70 degrees.

There are times when bass can be harder to find than a missing sock from your favorite pair. Bass vanish for lots of reasons. Cold fronts can bury them in the thickest cover around. So can periods of muggy weather with bright skies. Warming water temperatures, changes in food availability, and fishing and boating pressure are other reasons that bass head for parts unknown. Anglers that do locate them are often surprised to find largemouths at 30 or more feet. Although smallmouths and spotted bass are more deep-water oriented than bigmouths, nevertheless, the two species may descend to an unheard-of 100 feet.

Reams have been written about tough-to-find, tough-to-catch bass, but I have yet to read a magazine article about trolling for them with downriggers. Whether these Houdini bass are deep or shallow, buried in weeds or suspended over humps, downriggers can help get them on your stringer or in your cooler. In the case of largemouths, anglers can pinpoint-troll the weed line around a lake, keeping their lures within a foot or two of the vegetation. If bass are home and hungry, they'll drill lures as they come wiggling by. In mid-summer, bigmouths often suspend along the upper reaches of the thermocline; you can find them with sonar and fast-trolled crankbaits. In Western lakes both largemouths and smallmouths hang around points, drop-offs, spires of drowned rock as well as timber, brush and gravel bars. Smallmouths head for shipping channels and river channels in the Great Lakes as the shallows heat up and their spawning chores are over. Downriggers help there, too, as well as over reefs, boulder fields and contour breaks.

Largemouths are native in 33 states and have been successfully introduced to the other 15 contiguous states. Hatchery experts have spread the smallmouth's distribution from its original Great Lakes watershed range to all but a handful of states. No wonder bass are probably our most sought-after gamefish in freshwater.

Several Cannon field testers are reporting success while trolling for bass with downriggers. Bill Vanderford of Lawrenceville, Georgia, is an excellent largemouth bass fisherman, who also happens to be a professional guide and outdoor writer. Vanderford wrote a book about Lane Lanier, the world-famous reservoir outside Atlanta, Georgia. Lake Lanier has served up largemouths to 17½ pounds, striped bass to 43 pounds, and spotted bass (which look like small largemouths) to eight pounds. The lake also contains rainbow trout, crappies, walleyes and silver bass. Vanderford is as intimate with the sprawling 40,000-acre reservoir, which averages 60 feet in depth and is fed by mountain streams, as most people are with their neighborhood. He recommends that first-timers try trolling because it is the fastest way to learn the lake. When Vanderford is after largemouths, that could mean trolling with downriggers, especially during the transition periods before and after spawning.

Vanderford, who has caught stripers to 35 pounds and largemouths over nine pounds from Lake Lanier, mounted a Digi-Troll and a Uni-Troll on 12-inch pedestals to the back end of his Ranger bass boat. He uses his hand-cranked Uni-Troll to fish the upper lake levels for suspended bass. Lure choices are Rapalas or Cordell Red Fins in plugs and Sidewinders or Sutton Spoons in hardware. His electric Digi-Troll takes similar lures deep, often just over underwater treetops where bass like to hide. A Cannon Helmsman allows Vanderford to fish from the back of his boat while steering it. He has also caught spotted bass to two pounds each while downrigger trolling with a grub or bucktail Hair Jig.

"I rely on a Lowrance X-16 graph," Vanderford said, "to zoom in on 20 or 30 feet of water below the downrigger weight, which I can always see on the graph. If I spot the fish or see that I'm going to get into a tangle, a flip of the Digi-Troll switch and I'm out of danger."

Although we have reports of other fishermen incidentally catching largemouths on downriggers, Vanderford is the only angler we know who specifically targets the species with the technique. On the other hand, there is a growing number of good fishermen turning to downriggers to help them catch smallmouth bass. I had a chance to experience the excitement firsthand when I trolled with Jim Rutkowski and his son Robert ("Charlie Brown") out of Erie, Pennsylvania, on a muggy Sunday in mid-June.

Rutkowski, who owns a small manufacturing firm and field tests for Cannon as a sport fisherman, powered his 22-foot Chris Craft, *Island Princess*, out of the state-operated Walnut Creek Habor. During an hour's run east we flew past Presque Isle Harbor, then shut down to trolling speed within hollering distance of Rutkowski's friend Doug Van Tassell of Erie. A charter-boat captain, Van Tassell had a full house aboard his vessel. His customers had already coolered a nice Chinook salmon, a couple of smallmouth bass, and had lost a 10-pound walleye at the net.

"You guys really get a mixed bag out here, don't you?" I said to the Rutkowskis.

"You'll see," Charlie Brown said.

While his dad ran the boat and watched the graph, Charlie Brown set the four downriggers. We were trolling over a shale bottom, 34 to 40 feet deep, about a mile offshore. According to my hosts, smallmouths should be in a prespawn state, waiting for 70-degree temperatures so they could move into rocky reefs near shore and drop their eggs. The water temperature now was 59 degrees F. "We got a lot of fish here," Jim said. "Check out these marks." The graph paper looked like someone had splattered black paint on it. Fish were scattered from top to bottom.

"Are those smallmouths?" I wondered, my eyes widening.

"You better believe it," Rutkowski said, "although some are probably other species, too."

Rutkowski tests tackle for his friend, Jim Bagley, of the Bagley Bait Company. Consequently, everything we cannonballed that day was a Bagley lure, mostly crankbaits. Charlie Brown put out a pair of Mighty Minnows, one in black and silver and the other with a dark-green top/light-green bottom. He also ran a Kill'r B 2 in Chartreuse with orange top and a five-inch Bang-O-Lure in double-green color. Rigging was in the inverted V-shape pattern with outside lines set at 29 and 27 feet deep respectively. The young veteran sent down his stern-end lures to 22 and 15 feet. They featured shorter leads of 15 feet while the outside lines were allowed release lengths of about 60 feet.

"Here's the theory," his dad explained. "Outside lines attract the bass into our setup. Then they hit the inside lures. Besides, if we hook a Chinook salmon, he is less likely to tear everything up because he'll go up and away." Reinforcing his theory, to his outriggers Rutkowski added a pair of black-and-chrome Kill'r B 2s with sound chambers, then sent them back 150 to 200 feet behind the boat.

We didn't have to wait long for action. A few minutes later, the No. 3 rod went off and I found myself tangling with a hefty smallmouth. If you know smallmouths, you know how well they scrap, even against a moving boat. Several times this one got a good look at the world above water before I could wear him out and lead him to the net. Over the next three hours, we boated a 14-inch yellow perch, a five-pound walleye, several 1½ to two-pound smallmouths, a slab-sided rock bass, and a couple of sheepshead – all on downriggers. Then, just as we were ready to clear lines, a rod went off. Charlie Brown shoved it into my willing hands.

"Last fish for this spot," he said. "You take it."

"It" turned into another bookend bass. Hours later when we put them on the state scales at Walnut Creek Harbor, the smallmouths weighed 4 lb. 12 oz. and 4 lb. 10 oz. We figured them at five pounds each, live weight. Along with the rock bass, which tipped the scales at one pound even, I entered the bigger smallmouth in the Pennsylvania Fish Commission Angler Award Program.

I credit downriggers and the Rutkowskis' knowledge of bass habits and the local habitat for our success. Later, we motored out to 72 feet of water off Erie to see

Jim Rutkowski shows graph paper liberally marked with prespawning smallmouths.

Largemouth and Smallmouth Bass

if we could catch a salmon and steelhead for a "grand slam" of Lake Erie gamefish. Had I not had a five-hour drive ahead of me and asked to cut short our fishing trip, we might have done it, too.

Prespawning smallmouths are fun to catch wherever you find them. Because fish are hungry then – trying to gain all the strength they can before the rigors of spawning – they willingly strike lures. "They are ferocious fish," Jerry Heffernan, a professional guide and Cannon field tester from North Tonawanda, New York, told me when I fished with him and his brother, Billy, in eastern Lake Erie. "We troll as fast as our lures can take – from 2.7 to 3.5 mph is about right. If we start catching sheepshead, we are trolling too slow."

Heffernan fishes structure (humps, drop-offs and channels) on both the American and Canadian sides for spring walleyes and smallmouth bass. He typically runs a couple of planer boards to boat sides and two oscillating Cannon Digi-Trolls down the stern to either side of center. He cycles the Digi-Trolls at five-second intervals, claiming that rapid oscillation promotes strikes from bass. "It (oscillation) is the same thing as pumping your rod," Heffernan explained. "Most strikes come on the dropback."

Effective lures off both planers and downriggers include pencil baits (Rebel Minnow Floaters, straight or jointed Rapalas, Bill Norman Baltic Minnows, Long A Bombers) and small crankbaits in chartreuse with red or green.

Downriggers work well for smallmouths in the St. Lawrence River, too. Denis Leger, a native of Cornwall, Ontario, uses Cannon downriggers on his 20-foot Sea Ox to fish for a variety of species, including smallmouths. If Leger, a sport fisherman and professional photographer by trade, has enough people aboard (Ontario fishing regulations allow only one rod – although four hooks – per angler), he will rig all four of his downriggers – two Digi-Trolls and a pair of Mag 10As. All feature long, 66-inch booms which help to spread lures and avoid tangles. This is especially important on rough-weather days when boat control is difficult in the current.

"Boat control is the whole key to fishing this area of the St. Lawrence River," Leger explained. "When targeting smallmouths, we look for structure such as sunken islands, which we then zigzag over from shallow water to deep water. Downriggers do the work of keeping our lures close to bottom while I can concentrate on boat control." Also, Leger sometimes staggers the depths of his lures, occasionally stacking one or two units. Lead lengths are typically 50 feet, and the lures of choice include Shad Raps, Fat Raps, Wiggle Warts and Hot 'N Tots.

"I firmly believe, though," Leger said, that boat control and trolling speed are far more important than the type or color of lure. We get our best action at 2.0 and 2.5 mph, as measured by a Fish Hawk trolling speed indicator."

Downriggers will also work for smallmouths on other lakes and rivers around the country. For example, Ed Mendus, a full-time outdoor writer and Cannon field tester, trolls for suspended smallmouths on Lake George in New York State. Small, jointed floating Rapalas in silver color work best off downrigger weights or sliders at various depths to 90 feet, and over water that may be 160 feet deep.

Another sport fisherman and Cannon contact, Ron Kolodziej also fishes Lake George with Cannon downriggers. "One time we were trying to catch lake trout suspended at 80 to 90 feet deep," Kolodziej said, "but every time we sent our attractors and squids down, smallmouths would hit the lures. The bass were suspended at only eight to 10 feet deep. It was the one time in my life I was frustrated from catching four-pound smallmouths." To solve the "problem," Kolodziej moved into 120 feet of water, dropped his downrigger weights to bottom, then raised them as he trolled back to the lake trout.

Lake George holds not only a lot of smallmouths but some big smallmouths, too. Mendus, who has caught them to 7½ pounds, believes the next world record could come from this lake.

Don't be surprised if it is caught on a downrigger.

Good bass plugs to troll with downriggers include (left to right) Hi-Catch by Genuine Crankbait, K-11 Kwikfish, Burke Hunchback, Helin Flatfish and a Normark Shad Rap.

Striped Bass

Straddled by Arizona before touching Nevada and California, the Colorado River corkscrews its blue way south from the Grand Canyon for hundreds of miles through deserts and mountains. In spite of the dams, the cities, and the increasing flow of recreational traffic, the Colorado passes through areas that seem unaffected by time. It is the perfect river for the perfect fish, powerful striped bass, released here a few years ago and upriver in Utah's Lake Powell and Nevada's Lake Meade. Indeed, the world record for landlocked stripers, a 59 lb. 12 oz. monster was caught in the Colorado River in 1977.

I thought about all that at dawn one June morning. A high-powered bass boat that had raced by us found itself quickly swallowed by monolithic canyon walls. We were fishing the topwater bite for striped bass just upriver from Lake Havasu on the Arizona/California border. Steve Griffin, a fellow outdoor writer from Michigan, and I cast surface plugs to a fast-water break – a rocky outcropping sluiced by the five mph current. I had seen the water boil once or twice behind our lures – "follows" our guide Wayne Holmes called them – but had yet to experience the hook-throwing antics and raw power of a Colorado River striped bass.

In fact, I had never caught a striped bass anywhere. I was retrieving a Cordell Pencil Popper when suddenly the slim lure stopped in mid-current, then exploded from the water. A two- or three-pound "linesider," as stripers are often called, made a silvery U in mid-air, then crashed back to the swift current. About five minutes later I led the little battler alongside Holmes' bass boat, then scooped him aboard. It was the only striper I would take on our brief trip to the desert reservoir, where both largemouth and striped bass are the calling cards. I caught my striper just in time, too, because soon afterward a roasting sun peeked over a mountaintop. As Holmes had predicted, the bass went deep and we never got another strike. The temperature in this thirsty country was already crowding 100-degrees F.; before the day was over, it would climb to 115 degrees.

"Might as well call it a day," Holmes said, starting his outboard engine, which caught with a roar. Then he turned his cap around, bill backwards, so that it wouldn't blow away during the high-speed return to Lake Havasu. Our guide reminded me of Satch in those old Bowery Boys movies with Leo Gorcey. He was as enthusiastic and fun as that comedy team, too. Twenty-five years of fishing on the Colorado River had not lessened Holmes' appetite for a good time one bit.

"What do the fishermen do on the big lake when stripers go deep?" I hollered in our guide's ear as granite outcroppings whizzed by.

"They go deep, too," he shouted back. "They jig off the bottom with anchovies, water dogs (salamanders) and shiners."

"Why don't they troll with downriggers?"

"They do!"

And, sure enough, as we broke from canyon walls into the open lake, where heat waves shimmered mirage-like, there in the distance was a fishing boat, its back end bristling with bent-over rods pinned to downrigger weights. Later at the dock, Holmes explained that river-channel inclines and drowned trash such as cottonwood trees and mesquite thickets often hold stripers, which suspend nearby. "They get 'em on big Rapalas while trailing a marabou jig as a stinger," Holmes said. "Some downrigger fishermen use anchovies, too, specially rigged to plastic sleeves."

One of the greatest things that ever happened to freshwater fishermen was the introduction of the ocean-living striped bass to inland waters. More than half the states in waters as diverse as those found in New York and Nevada, Alabama and Arizona, are home to scale-busting stripers of 20, 30, 40 and more pounds. The best places around the country are reservoirs formed from damming big rivers. Stripers run these rivers to spawn, even though their efforts at reproduction are rarely successful. The problem with fishing inland stripers is the tackle-eating structure that lies underwater – flooded timber, brush, gullies, ravines, hills and even canyon and mountain walls. Most serious striper fishermen arm themselves with a quality sonar unit to read bottom and snags. They also rely heavily on inexpensive lures, such as jigs, or fish with live bait pinned to hooks.

Striped bass, like this four-pounder (left), are now found in over half the states in this country. Landlocked stripers grow to huge size, and fish of 20 to 40 pounds are not all that uncommon.

Downrigger fishing is the fastest-growing tactic for striped bass angling in the country. Stripers like the wide-open spaces of the big reservoirs where they have been introduced, but they especially like to suspend near the kind of structure I described above. They also move around like wolf packs to find food such as suspended threadfin and gizzard shad, shiners, smelt and other minnows. Trolling with downriggers helps striper fishermen to cover more potential water much faster than with other fishing methods. Stacking lures on the same downrigger helps them to cover the range of depth, too. When relying on a good graph, downrigger fishermen can mark fish as well as keep an eye on their weights and lures in the snag-infested waters.

Cannon's *Banana* weights were specially designed with the downrigger striper fisherman in mind. Banana weights slide over debris that will snag conventional round weights. The slim shape also keeps the Banana weights tracking on course.

Ken Milam is a Cannon field tester and professional guide fishing Lake Buchanan from his Tow, Texas, home. Lake Buchanan, which houses linesiders to 30 pounds, is one of several impoundments on the Colorado River in Texas. Sunken trees and other trash are everywhere, and it is not uncommon, even with the use of sensitive electronics and electric downriggers, to lose up to 25 jigs per day. Milam fishes with jigs most of the time, except in spring when fish are in shallow water and there is less chance of getting snagged.

Because shallow-water stripers are usually spooky, Milam may increase lengths from 15 or 20 feet to 60 to 70 feet, occasionally going as far behind the boat as 100 feet. It all depends on what the stripers seem to want. Dependable lures are 15A Shallow Water or 16A Heavy Duty Bombers in silver flash/orange belly and chrome/black back. Storm Little Macs in baby striper or blue mackeral colors are also rated. When fish go deeper in summer, often suspending at 25 to 35 feet over 48 to 60 feet of water, Milam breaks out Tad's horsehead jigs or Blakemore Road Runner jigs. A spinner on the bottom of these jigs helps to attract hungry stripers. Adding worm "flirts" such as Bill Norman

Striped Bass

Snatrix in white, yellow or chartreuse may also provoke reluctant bass to strike.

"I experiment a lot with these fish," Milam admitted. "For example, I try green yellow or other colored cannonballs because sometimes stripers are attracted to them. I'd love to give Dodgers and flies a workout, but there are just too many trees to risk losing the expensive tackle."

Jigs, then, are inexpensive and reliable. To maintain a schooling effect of supposed forage minnows, Milam runs four rods off two out-downriggers and a pair of rods off two stern-end units. His 26-foot Starcraft Islander is equipped with four Cannon Digi-Trolls. On the out-downs, Milam puts 1 oz. jigs on bottom setups, then stacks ½ oz. jigs six feet higher. "On turns, the jigs don't fall the same," Milam explained, "and so stripers are constantly getting new action to think about. Variety is important because I get 40 to 50 percent of my strikes on turns."

He relies on the oscillating feature of his Digi-Trolls when fish appear stationary and won't chase lures. Another trick the skipper uses, with the help of his electric 'riggers and a Lowrance X-16 graph, is to run lures close to underwater humps, then steer around them. "It's gotten to the point where I can just about predict strikes from marked fish," Milam said. "For instance, on an inside turn, one or two rods might go off. Then when I turn the other way, which straightens out my lures on the other side of the boat, they often get hit, too."

Milam uses 20-pound test T Line made by the Mason Tackle Company. Because stripers have sharp gill plates and teeth, Milam adds a steel leader of 44-pound test to his jigs.

Dick Dawson, a sport fisherman from Spring Hill, Kansas, fishes stripers in his native state as well as in Beaver Lake, a reservoir on Arkansas' White River. The Arkansas state record, a 48 lb. 6 oz. behemoth, came from Beaver Lake, and even though Dawson believes bigger fish swim there, he said a "good average" is 18 to 35 pounds. Also an advocate of downrigger trolling, Dawson customized his 15-foot Glastron boat to accommodate four Cannon Mini-Mag electric downriggers.

Because Beaver Lake stripers also suspend around trees in 20 to 40 feet of water,

Good downrigger-trolled plugs for striped bass include (left to right): Bullcat by Genuine Crankbait, Bill Norman Little N (top) and Rapala (bottom), Floating jointed Rapala, Bill Norman Jointed Minnow, Lindy Shadling, Bagley's B Flatt II (top) and Storm ThinFin Silver Shad (bottom), and Bagley's Kill'r B2.

careful fishing tactics are similar to those of Ken Milam's. Dawson reaches for big Blakemore Road Runner striper jigs in white color, then often adds a six-inch white Twister Tail. "It's just a theory," Dawson admits, "but I believe that stripers in the ocean are used to hitting squids. At any rate, they sure go after those white skirts."

To ensure a good hook set, Dawson adds a pair of Eagle Claw 5/0 trailer hooks. The first one goes through the eye of the jig, and the second trailer hook passes through the eye of the first trailer hook. Using 92-pound test Dacron line, Dawson then ties a half-hitch to the shank of the jig hook and passes it through the eye of the first trailer hook. Next, he adds another half-hitch, only this time to the shank of the first trailer hook. Finally, he secures the line through the eye of the second trailer hook.

"I run figure-eight patterns," Dawson said, "on a very slow troll. To start with, I hold my speed at 1,000 rpms. If I pick up fish on the inside turns (when lures slow down), I know I've been trolling too fast; so I might cut back to 800 rpms. On the other hand, if strikes come on the outside lines, I might speed up to 1,200 or 1,500 rpms."

Reports about big stripers caught on downriggers are becoming commonplace. Just the other day, for example, I received a news release about how a lucky troller named Bud George broke the Kansas state record with a 42-pound striped bass from Wilson Reservoir near Russell. When you think about it, though, he wasn't so lucky. After all, he was trolling with a downrigger.

Pike Muskie

"Several Cannon field testers are reporting good success while downrigger fishing for northern pike . . . Trolling is an excellent way to catch a big muskie, and downriggers are an excellent way to troll."

This nice female taped 42 inches. Big pike like this often suspend over deep water during hot periods in summer.

Members of the pike family are noted for their voracious appetites and generally solitary nature. Similar in appearance, the five species that live in North America all feature soft fins that are rayed, a head shaped like a duck's bill, and a mouth full of sharp, dangerous teeth. Pike family members like weedy areas near structure and can often be caught near the edge of weed lines, two types of vegetation, river-channel inclines and drop-offs. At other times, they will suspend in deep water. The five species include northern pike and muskellunge – both of which can attain huge size – and three types of pickerel: chain, redfin and grass. Chain pickerel average two or three pounds and sometimes grow to six or eight pounds. They live in the eastern half of the country from Canada to Florida. Redfin pickerel and grass pickerel are much smaller. The former lives in East Coast drainages, the latter in lakes and streams of the Mississippi River drainage.

Downriggers can be used to catch all five members of the pike family, but because some innovative anglers have devised specialized tactics for northerns and muskies, we will concentrate on only those two.

Northern Pike

Northern pike are also known as "jackfish" or "jacks." They live in rivers and lakes in northern latitudes around the world. Their home in North America extends from Alaska to Arizona, and they have been successfully introduced as far south and east as Georgia. Canadian biologists estimate that half of Ontario's 400,000 lakes contain pike, some to 40 pounds. Any northern over 20 pounds is considered a trophy by most fishermen, but much larger fish have been caught. The American record is a 46 lb. 2 oz. wallhanger caught in 1940 from New York's Sacanadaga Reservoir, which, incidentally, continues to serve up huge pike. The world record is a 55-pound Czechoslovakian monster.

The smaller pike are not very difficult to catch. Fish of two to 10 pounds readily hit bright spoons, spinners and plugs. Once in a Boy Scout camp in the Ontario bush, a friend of mine won a "weirdest-lure" contest when he caught an eight-pound northern on

Northern Pike

a red toothbrush with a treble hook. Larger pike are much more difficult to catch except for the period immediately after spawning. Most northerns over 10 pounds are females, which go on a feeding binge after the rigors of spawning, usually soon after ice out. For the rest of the year, however, big pike often become loners. To catch one requires stealth, patience and luck.

Several Cannon field testers are reporting good success while downrigger fishing for northern pike. In fact, Ron Kolodziej of Amsterdam, New York, said that until three years ago, he was the only angler successfully downrigging for northerns on Saratoga Lake. Now at least half the boats fishing the lake are equipped with downriggers. When I talked with Kolodziej on the telephone in July, he said he was hoping to score on big Sacandaga Reservoir northerns. "I believe they head for cooler, deeper waters of the northeast arm," Kolodziej said. "I plan to spend a lot of time investigating this theory over the summer."

Kolodziej's tactics involve trolling green or chrome Mepps Spoons set 10 to 12 feet behind downrigger weights and pulled at two to 2½ mph. He has four Cannon electric Mag 10A downriggers on his boat. A typical summer day finds Kolodziej running two to four lines in 25 feet of water while he threads the lake's weed line. Shore-side lures are sent down about 15 feet while those on the other side of the boat are locked at about 22 feet or just off bottom.

Another New York downrigger fisherman, Ken Coleman of Willsboro, catches suspended northerns up to a dozen pounds from Saratoga Lake on No. 11 jointed Rapalas in silver color. "In June and July, fish seem to suspend in 25 to 30 feet of water over depths to 40 feet," Coleman said. "I find them with the help of a Lowrance X-15 graph, then pass over them with long leads on a slow troll."

"I've caught pike to 26 pounds in the St. Lawrence River with my method," Kolodziej said, "and although there are pike that big and bigger in Sacandaga, I have yet to hook one." Kolodziej said that hot days in August seem to produce well. "Last summer on four consecutive Saturdays, it was brutally hot, yet we caught no less than five northerns on each trip."

By setting cannonballs a foot or two under the surface, muskie trolling-ace Denis Leger of Cornwall, Ontario, has caught St. Lawrence River pike to 10 pounds on gray giant Lindy Shads. Leger likes to troll with downriggers because he can stack his lines (Canadian regulations permit up to four hooks but each angler is limited to one rod) and because the downrigger cables pick up weeds and other trash in the water and shortstop the debris from fouling his lures.

That is the same reason that inland-lake guide Tom Richardson of Mt. Morris, Michigan, keeps a couple of Cannon Econo-Riggers in his 16-foot Sylvan Backtroller. A reputable muskie guide on southern Michigan lakes, Richardson sometimes switches to downriggers for both northerns and muskies at mid-day when fish go deep. Downriggers allow the guide to use bucktail spinners and floating lures that are normally cast. Plus, because the big predators are rarely afraid of a boat, Richards can troll his lures on short release lengths and therefore maintain better boat control.

In high mountain lakes in Idaho, Cannon contact Steve Payne has caught northern pike in weedy shallows on downriggers. "The bigger fish, though (pike to 20 pounds), will usually be 30 to 50 feet deep," Payne said. "Weighted lures with big lips will dig down, all right, but fishermen tend to lose them when they hang up. Downriggers solve that problem." Payne prefers Storm Hot 'N Tots and Shallo Macs on short, 10-foot leads off downrigger weights held within 10 feet of bottom. The lures (green or fluorescent red are rated colors) wiggle down the last few feet to bottom-lying pike.

On a recent spring bear hunt to Ontario, I shoved a Cannon Econo-Rigger with C-clamp base into my backpack, then stowed the pack under my airplane seat. The portable downrigger came in handy for fishing drops and humps when the spawned-out northerns left the flats for deep water. We caught pike to 15 pounds on spinners, spoons and plugs. There are plenty of Canadian lakes from Quebec to the Yukon Territories with lunker northerns that have yet to see a fishing boat – especially a fishing boat with downriggers aboard.

Post-spawn females go on a feeding binge.

Downrigger fishermen on the St. Lawrence River report excellent fall success for huge muskies like this fish.

The word "muskellunge" (*Esox masquinongy*) supposedly means "ugly fish" in the Indian tongue. I'll go along with that. Muskies certainly are vicious-looking fish with cold, flat eyes and a mouth full of wicked teeth. Muskies live in eastern North America from southern Quebec to western Vermont to Tennessee, north to eastern Illinois into Wisconsin, Minnesota and western Ontario. They also reside in Lake Erie, the Allegheny River and in northwestern Pennsylvania.

Muskies grow to immense size. The world record is a 69-lb. 15 oz. fish caught in the St. Lawrence River in 1957. The Chippewa Flowage in Wisconsin yielded a 69 lb., 11 oz. muskie, and Middle Eau Claire Lake served up a 69½ pounder.

There are three kinds of muskies. The Great Lakes variety features a color pattern of dark spots over a light background. Such fish live in bays and connecting waterways, including the St. Lawrence River, of the Great Lakes. Northern muskies, on the other hand, have lighter-colored bars less pronounced. They live in rivers and inland lakes. A sterile, hybrid muskie – hatchery bred by crossing eggs and milt of northern pike and northern muskellunge – is called the "tiger muskie." Tigers have neither the spots nor bars of the two purebred strains but rather resemble northern pike in appearance. Like pike, tigers grow fast and are easier to catch than the other types.

Catching a muskie is not easy. One reason is that, for the most part, they are great loners. Second, they are not always the voracious predators that many people think. According to one study, a muskie requires only four pounds of food to gain one pound in weight. A fish that is, say, five feet long and weighs 60 pounds, might be 20 years or older. In other words, he doesn't eat much.

Still, muskies go on feeding binges at certain times – for example, right after spawning in spring and again in fall. Muskie addicts then sometimes fish around the clock to catch a 30- or 40-pound trophy.

Muskies like to hide out along the edges created by two types of weeds, drowned timber, river or channel inclines, and contour breaks. They are nearly always found in shallow water – three feet to 12 feet deep –

Muskies

although on bright mid-summer days, they may go deeper. Sometimes in the fall, they are taken to depths of 40 feet. Favored angling tactics include casting bucktail spinners and spoons, bobber- or bottom-fishing with a large sucker or chub, and trolling. Where it is legal, trolling is an excellent way to catch a big muskie, and downriggers are an excellent way to troll.

Cannon field tester Allen Benas of Clayton, New York, is one of the most respected muskie guides in the business. Benas has 30 years of fishing experience in the 1000 Islands region of the St. Lawrence River, one of the country's best-known giant muskie holes. For the last 10 years, Benas has been guiding for pay. An innovative angler, Benas helped redesign the Radtke Pikie Minnow to include three sections, which at times can drive muskies wild, especially in perch, brown, and orange-and-black colors. Experimentation naturally led Benas to downriggers, and now he has a pair of Digi-Trolls on each of his two guide boats.

"Along with fellow guide, Russ Finehout, we were the first guides on the St. Lawrence to use downriggers for muskies," Benas said. "We caught the first two fish on downriggers on our very first day out, 10 minutes apart. The date was September 24, 1980, and we tagged and released both fish. Since 1983, downriggers have grown in popularity on the river, especially with the average weekend angler. Although we use downriggers exclusively now, many of the guides try them while still relying on standard trolling methods. Perhaps it's a confidence factor."

Benas said October is a prime month for muskies because the fish are coming back from Lake Ontario. November is good, too, except Benas doesn't like to guide then because he can't depend on the weather. Apparently wind, temperature and brightness of day make little difference as Benas has registered strikes under all conditions at all times of day in the fall. He said the key is good action to lures when trolled over places where he knows muskies should be. These include the edges of drop-offs within a couple miles of a marsh.

Traditional methods of fishing river muskies call for the use of two rods rigged with heavy Monel Metal line. Lures are trolled around 150 feet behind the boat, using the weight of the line to get them down to about 20 feet deep. A third line, usually monofilament, off the stern center is run back some 300 feet to get a lure to dig down about 12 to 15 feet. Benas said the long leads restrict mobility of the boat and that can result in tangles.

"When we initiated the use of downriggers, we continued the two long lines with Monel, using the downrigger to replace the one high line," Benas said. "Putting out two lures on the downriggers, about 12 to 15 feet down and 35 feet behind the weight, we were able to operate the boat much better. After gaining confidence that the downriggers produced as well, or better than the long lines, we did away with those altogether. Now, we use two downriggers with two rods on each unit. Deep lines are spotted 35 feet behind the weights at a depth of 15 to 20 feet. The stacked lines go 25 to 30 feet behind the boat at a depth of eight to 12 feet."

Benas said the exclusive use of downriggers allows him to fish areas that were previously off-limits. "We can turn on a silver dollar without hanging up," Benas said. "As far as I'm concerned, the use of downriggers seems to be limited only by one's imagination."

At the other end of Lake Ontario, Cannon field tester, Jerry Heffernan, fishes for muskies along 30- to 40-foot drops on the Canadian side of the Niagara River with the aid of downriggers because they help keep moss and weeds off his lures and because, simply put, they are productive. Pikie Minnows and Buck Perry Spoonplug 800 series lures are rated baits in natural pike and perch colors along with silver, gold or copper. To help get lures deep, Heffernan relies on 28-pound-test lead-core line, which he uses both with and without downriggers.

Little things count, Heffernan said. For example, bending lip corners up or down on his Pikie Minnows adds pizzazz to the lure, making it buzz left and right. Also, when using lead-core line with downriggers, Heffernan wraps a piece of inner tube around the line inside the release to both protect the line and to make for a cleaner break when a fish strikes.

The above-mentioned colors plus frog

Outdoor film-maker Jerry Chiapetta shows off a big muskie from the St. Lawrence River.

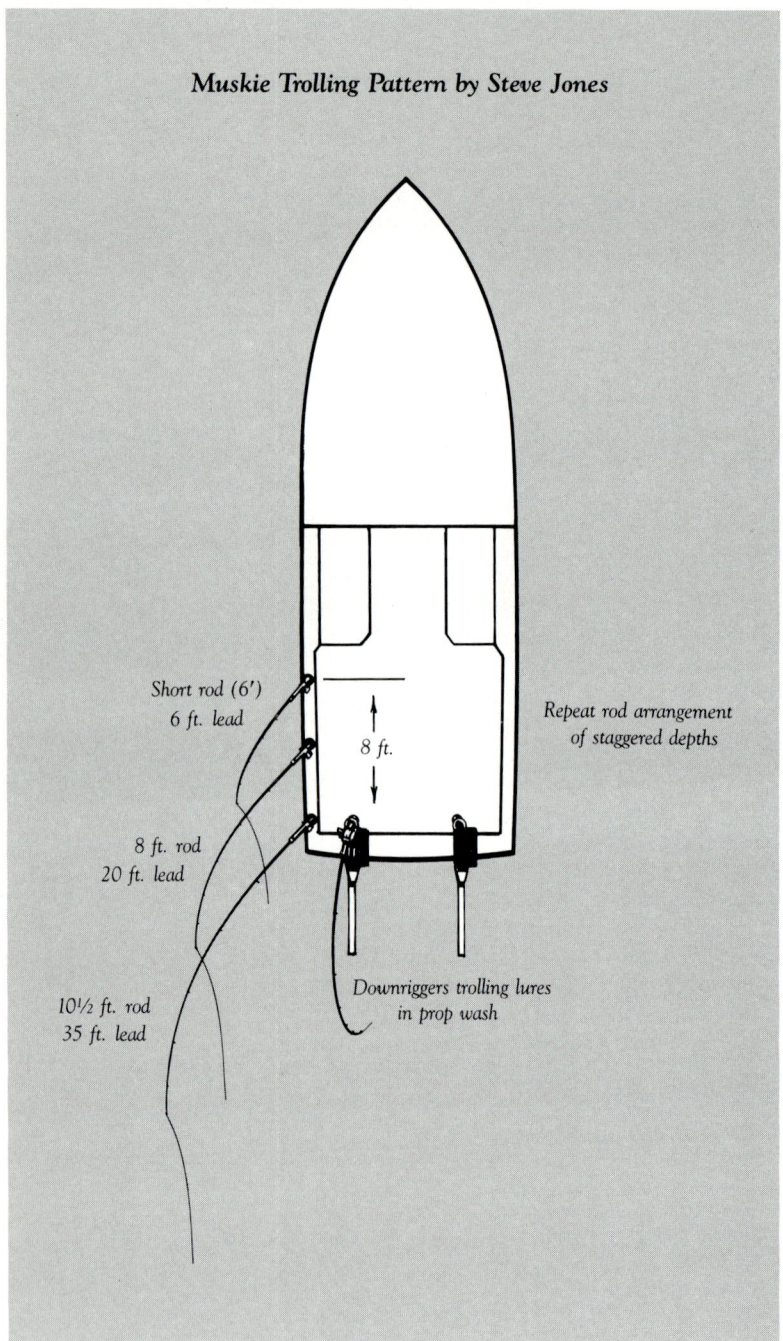

patterns in yellow, green, olive and black helped Steve Jones, a charter-boat captain and Cannon contact from Mt. Clemens, Michigan, boat 137 muskies from Lake St. Clair last year. Jones' best fish for the season was a 30 lb. 4 oz. giant, and he caught four others over 25 pounds. Jones has five Digi-Trolls and Mag 10A electric downriggers on each of two boats, which he uses for Lake Huron salmon trolling as well as muskie fishing. Actually, when Jones is after muskies, he relies on only two downriggers to run lures right in the prop wash at burn speeds of five and six mph.

"Muskies in St. Clair relate to the surface when they feed," Jones explained. "They are not thinking bottom (the deepest spot in Lake St. Clair is only 24 feet), and so the contrast of bait to sky is very important. That's also why muskies come to the prop wash. To form an effective trolling pattern, I like to build higher lines around a deep center-run lure or two.

Here is how Jones rigs: On one side of the boat six feet from the transom, he angles a rod tip down and puts a lure on a five-foot leader of 50- or 60-pound test monofilament. A one-pound lead ball slurps the lure, which is allowed to go back no farther than the transom, under the surface. Halfway between that rod and the transom, Jones rigs an eight-foot rod with 10 ounces of lead and a lure to run 20 feet behind the boat. At the transom itself goes a third rod, a custom-made 10½ footer, with the lure (with or without weight depending on the digging action of the lure) run back 35 feet. Next, Jones duplicates this three-rod setup on the other side of the boat, although he takes care to stagger release lengths. Then, he runs one or two lures off transom-mounted downriggers in the prop wash.

On the downriggers, Jones likes lures that don't pull so hard because line twist can cause a problem. Cisco Kids and Believer plugs work well, both on the downriggers and the other setups. Additional lures that get the call are bucktail spinners, Pikie Minnows and Swim Whizzes.

Jones' muskie-rigging program is a dynamite technique to catch a dynamite fish!

Downriggers for Other Freshwater Species

There is a dual thrill to being an outdoor writer. One is that you get to learn new methods of fishing and new places to fish. The second is that you get to tell others of your discoveries. Although some fishermen are reluctant to expose their hotspots or pet tactics, that is rarely the case with downrigger anglers. I suspect the reason is because the sport is so new and there is so much to learn. At any rate, I wish there were space to tell about all of the things I learned while interviewing Cannon field testers around the country. Unfortunately, I have nearly run out of time and space.

Perhaps the biggest thing I discovered, though, was that downriggers can be used to catch any freshwater gamefish (and most of the "rough" species). Pete Grasso of New Hampshire, for example, told me about trolling through a school of yellow perch on Lake Winnipesaukee one time, "when all the rods went off together. Talk about fun!"

And Bill Thede wrote these lines in a letter to me: "Believe it or not, two years ago on a morning charter (Thede skippers out of Harbor Beach, Michigan, on Lake Huron), we hooked a king salmon on the main line and a channel catfish on the slider. On the afternoon charter, we had a repeat. Then, just at dusk, a king hit a main line pulling a black Northport Nailer with luminescent tape. Forty minutes later in complete darkness, that rod went off again with a strike from an extremely powerful fish. A lady customer handled that rod; on the other end I just knew was a record salmon. Imagine my shock when a 9½ pound catfish appeared on the slider lure right next to a 19½ pound king salmon! My heart (Thede has a heart condition) can't take another episode like that."

Ken Coleman told me of catching whitefish from Lake Champlain in New York while downrigger trolling for lake trout. Denis Leger of Cornwall, Ontario, has actually fished for and caught carp and suckers in the St. Lawrence River with downriggers. Jim Rutkowski of Erie, Pennsylvania, related how his friends, Jim and Cliff Shelby, catch silver (white) bass in 70 feet of water in what is known as the First Trench in Lake Erie. They run downrigger weights to bottom, then release their thin spoons (Port Defiance spoons, Flutter Spoons and Southport Slammers) with a sharp snap of the wrist. As the lures flutter up, suspended silver bass nail them.

These Lake Erie fishermen compare white bass caught on small crankbaits fished with downriggers.

I heard other stories of fishermen catching crappies while trolling minnow rigs on downriggers and of bluegills hitting tiny jigs and spinners slow-trolled over their spawning nests. Just the other day, a Saginaw Bay (a shallow-water lobe of Michigan's Lake Huron) angler caught a 10-pound blue catfish on a downrigger. Huge blue catfish from Texas' Lake Texoma, already noted as among the premier striped bass lakes in the country, have set four world records in the past 18 months, and a fifth record is pending. Although no one has yet caught one of the 70-pound plus cats on a downrigger, sooner or later it will happen.

From catching bluegills to blue catfish, downriggers can not only do the job – they help to make it that much more fun.

Cooking

"Preserving and eating your own catch makes good sense for both nutritional and cost reasons."

A sharp, flexible knife is needed to fillet big fish like these king salmon.

Fish is good food. According to the Cooperative Extension Service, a 3½ oz. serving of raw Chinook salmon contains 19.1 grams protein and 310 units of vitamin A (the recommended daily allowance for an adult male is 1,000 units). Further, that same quantity will yield only 222 calories and 805 mg. of potassium, making it an excellent choice for dieters anxious to replace potassium lost through body liquid-reducing diets.

Other species of freshwater fish compare favorably. Not surprisingly, the smaller, warmwater species such as catfish, northern pike, yellow perch and bass contain even fewer calories. Yet they are reasonably high in complete, easily digestible protein; vitamins A, D and the B vitamins; as well as minerals.

And it seems as though good news about fish food-value appears all the time. A couple of years ago, a professor of medicine at the Oregon Health Sciences Center in Portland said that a diet high in salmon may well prevent, or even treat, coronary artery disease. Dr. Scott H. Goodnight said that salmon and other cold-water fish contain a special type of fat called "Omega 3 fatty acids," which may help keep blood vessels open and clear and prevent potentially dangerous, even fatal, clots from forming. Supposedly, these fatty acids are better even than the polyunsaturated vegetable oils of recent renown.

So fish is good for you, notwithstanding Grandma's maxims about its value as a brain food.

Cleaning

Proper cleaning of your catch is the key to fine eating – on the day caught or months later when retrieved from freezer or canning jar. Here's how: As quickly as possible after catching the fish, cut the entire length of its belly from vent to head, remove the viscera and gills, and sever the head above the collarbone. Break the backbone over the edge of a table or cutting board, then cut any tissue holding the head to the body. Remove the dorsal fin by cutting along each side and pulling the fin and attached bones out. Wash the fish sparingly in clean, cold-running water; then skin or scale.

Cooking

That is the correct method, according to a Cooperative Extension Service bulletin. When cleaning big fish, like salmon, however, I follow different steps. First, I like to slice lengthwise on both sides through the belly. Then, grasping the head firmly and holding the pectoral fin out of the way with the index finger of my left hand (I'm right-handed), I cut deeply to the bone behind the gillplate with a sharp, flexible knife and follow the ribline (with the knife tip sticking above the backbone) to the tail. A big fillet slab is the result. I repeat this procedure on the other side and then discard the carcass and insides.

Next, lay the fillet flesh-side up on a flat surface. Hold the skin tightly between fingers or with a pair of pliers (some anglers cut a finger-slit between the skin and flesh), and use your knife to skin the fillet. This is simply done by making a starting cut along the skin and then pulling the fillet toward you. The final step is trimming out any fat and bones (although if canning, the bones will be rendered harmless by the process) and then deciding how you want to prepare your catch for consumption. It is also a good idea to trim away dark flesh on the lateral line under the skin. This so-called "mud vein" is what gives fish its "fishy" flavor.

Incidentally, Cannon's *Fish-Bib*, a comfortable apron and shirt protector of heavy-duty vinyl, makes the chore of cleaning fish less messy. The Fish-Bib can be bought separately or in a kit which includes Cannon's popular 10-inch fillet knife (called the *Cannon-Cutter*), a knife sharpener, and protective mesh glove.

Some Great Lakes fish – salmon, lake trout and muskies in particular – have been known to contain slight amounts of contaminants. You can reduce health risk considerably on all fish, but especially the bigger ones (which, by virtue of their age and size are more prone to carrying contaminants), by cutting away all fat, particularly in the viscera.

Another important point to consider when dressing your catch is *bleeding*. According to the Sport Fishing Institute in Washington, D.C., bleeding freshly caught fish can greatly improve their table quality. Tests involving rainbow trout showed that cutting off the tails was the most effective means of bleeding the fish. Delaying the cutting until 20 minutes after capture greatly reduced bleeding efficiency. Fresh-bled fish look nicer, stay fresher longer, and taste better. In tests, unbled trout frozen for three months were slightly rancid, whereas bled trout took eight months of freezer storage to reach an equal level of decomposition.

Bob Kimble, a Cannon field tester and charter-boat captain from Whitehall, Michigan, always bleeds trout and salmon for his own table after subduing them. Kimble either cuts off the tail immediately or pierces the heart of the fish with a sharp knife. (The latter technique is suggested for anglers who wish to photograph their catch.) Back at the fish-cleaning house at the resort that Kimble operates on White Lake, he fillets his catch as described above. Then he cuts the fillets into thin, ¼-inch thick slices to be fried. I have never tasted Kimble's fried fish, but others say there is no finer eating on the planet. The ingredients are simple enough: flour, eggs, milk, salt and pepper, soda crackers and butter Crisco.

Kimble beats the eggs and milk together, then adds salt and pepper to taste. After rolling the fish strips in flour, he dips them in the egg-and-milk batter, then shakes them in a plastic bag of finely ground soda crackers. After heating a pan of butter Crisco to 400 degrees, he drops in the fish strips and fries them until crispy.

I'll have to try Kimble's recipe, though I confess to being a horrible cook. Then again, what can you expect of a fellow whose specialty is Rigid Rainbow Trout with Hash-blacked Potatoes? (You don't want to know that recipe.)

Others tell me the key to cooking fish with any recipe is not to overcook. Recently, I came across this little ditty in a Cooperative Extension pamphlet called "Fresh Fish." For poor cooks like me, it is worth remembering:

"What's the secret of cooking fish?
It's simple, yet easy to overlook;
When you hope for a splendid dish,
NEVER, NEVER OVERCOOK."

The pamphlet goes on to suggest that fish be cooked just enough so the flesh flakes easily when tested with a fork. Overcooking dries and toughens the naturally tender flesh.

Cooking

Freezing

Frozen fish will keep up to one year. One of the best ways to ensure that is to place a single layer of fish in a shallow pan. Cover with water and freeze solid, then remove the block of ice containing the fish, wrap it in freezer paper, and return it to your freezer. I have found that water frozen around fish is the best way to keep air out. Dry wrapping and freezing spoils fish much more quickly, even if you are careful to force out any air.

For best results, freeze at 0-degrees F. When you're ready to prepare the fish, allow about 18-24 hours thawing time in your refrigerator for a one-pound package. *Do not* thaw at room temperature or by holding the frozen fish under warm-running water (cold water is an acceptable substitute for slow thawing as long as the package containing the fish is waterproof).

Salting

Another good way to preserve fish (and one which requires no electricity) is to salt it. Properly salted fish that are stored in a cool, dry place can keep up to a year. Salting is an ancient procedure known to Europeans long before they set foot in North America. For nearly a hundred years, train carloads of salted whitefish and herring from Michigan's Lake Huron were shipped to coal miners in Appalachia. Salting is still practiced today. Just two years ago, while fishing a remote tundra stream in Alaska, I watched a native salt-down silver salmon for his winter food supply.

If you are salting less than 50 pounds of fish, you will need no special equipment, just a sharp knife and a medium-sized stone crock, wooden or food-grade plastic tub with a lid. Salt should be clean and pure and uniodized. Split small, dressed fish, such as herring, down the back so that they lie flat. Cut salmon and other large fish into two fillets, removing the backbone and gills but not the skin or collarbone (which will support the weight of the fish if it is to be later smoked). The pieces should be small enough to lie flat in a crock.

For good salt penetration, score the flesh of the thickest pieces lengthwise, about a half-inch deep and an inch or so apart. Do not pierce the skin. Soak the fish for a half-hour in a brine solution of one-half cup salt to one gallon of cold water. This will draw off all blood. Next, drain the pieces.

Then fill a dish pan or shallow box with dry salt. Sprinkle a thin layer of salt on the bottom of the brining container. Dredge each piece of fish in salt in the dish pan, then place skin-side down in the container, arranging them to make even layers. Overlap pieces as little as possible, taking care to place large pieces with the backbone toward the container wall and smaller pieces with the heads toward the wall. Keep the layers level and stagger them so that each fish rests on two fish in the layer below.

Scatter a thin coat of salt between each layer. For the top layer, place the pieces skin-side up. A general rule is one-part salt to three-parts fish. Use a wooden or china plate, and weight it with something heavy that is non-metal. Small fish will brine in two days; larger fish may take 10 days.

After brining, remove the pieces and scrub them in saturated brine (four cups of salt to one gallon of cold water), using a stiff brush. Then repack, scattering a thin layer of salt between layers. Fill the container with fresh, saturated salt brine and store in a cool, dark place until needed. After three months or at the first sign of fermentation, change the brine. You'll know if it is fermenting if the brine becomes cloudy.

Canning

The best method for long-term use is to can the fish. You'll need pint or quart jars and a pressure cooker. Only pessure processing will reach the necessary 240-degree temperature required to kill the spores of *Clostridium botulinum*. Here is how friends of mine can their fish: First, they dice the boned and trimmed fillets into one-inch chunks and pack them into quart mason jars. They add a tablespoon of salt and vinegar, which will soften any missed bones. A tablespoon of olive oil will keep the meat moist, and a tablespoon of catsup will color the meat a reddish-pink. Seal the jars (leave a one-inch air space for pints, two inches for quarts) and boil in a pressure cooker at 10 pounds pressure for 90 to 110 minutes.

When you are ready to use the canned fish, drain off the oil, then pat it away from the fish chunks with paper toweling. You can make fish patties, fish loaf or sandwiches with the canned fillets.

Pickling

You can pickle or smoke salted fish, although they will not last as long as in freezing or canning. To pickle, clean the pieces thoroughly and soak for one hour in a weak brine of one cup salt to a gallon of water. Then make a saturated brine of four cups of salt to one gallon of water and soak fish for about 12 hours at refrigerator temperature. Rinse in fresh water and cut into serving-sized pieces.

To pickle 10 pounds of fish, bring to a boil five cups of water (soft water is best), two quarts of white vinegar, ½ pound of sliced onions, and any spices, such as red and white pepper and garlic. Add fish and simmer 10 minutes or until fish can be pierced with a fork. Remove and spread fish in a single layer in a shallow pan; then refrigerate for rapid cooling. Pack cold fish loosely in clean glass jars. Add onion slices, bay leaves and lemon slices if desired.

Next, strain the vinegar solution, bring to a boil, and pour into jars to cover the fish. Seal immediately and store in a refrigerator. Use within a few weeks. This recipe will make six to eight quarts of pickled fish and is especially suitable for carp, herring, suckers and smelt.

Smoking

Smoked fish will keep in the refrigerator for about two weeks or in the freezer for up to a year. Nearly any species can be smoked with good results. My favorites, however, are lake trout, whitefish, salmon and herring. To smoke fish, cut fillets into one-by-four-inch strips, and soak in a salt brine as described for five or six hours. The weaker solution of one cup of salt to one gallon of water is about right, depending on your own taste. To the brine, however, may be added lemon, brown sugar, molasses or honey. Remove the fish after soaking and allow to dry.

Then heat the smoking unit to 150 to 200 degrees, and add chips to a pan to get the smoking started. Fruitwoods and maple, hickory, birch, beech and oak are commonly used. One friend of mine smokes fish with corncobs that he picks from farm fields, and I know of no one who prepares better-tasting smoked fish. Depending on piece size, the smoking may take several hours. Properly smoked meat will become firm and dark and will flake when scratched with a knife.

Preserving and eating your own catch makes good sense for both nutritional and cost reasons. When a nine-ounce can of tuna sells for over $1.50 and when fresh walleye, perch and lake trout fillets fetch $5 to $6 per pound over the counter, you know you're saving money. Besides, there is something special about sitting down to a meal of great-tasting fish that you caught yourself.

Canning your catch may provide good eating all year long.

Photographic Credits
Tony Caligiuri: *pages 130 and 131.*
Randy Carrels: *pages 12, 13, 14, 17, 19, 28, 31, 32, 40, 43, 44, 45, 47, 48 bottom, 51, 56, 57 middle, 57 bottom, 59 top, 62, 63 bottom, 64, 70, 75, 78, 80, 81, 89, 91, 92, 93, 109, 121, 125 and 134.*
Mark Hicks: *pages 48 bottom, 114, 115 and 133.*
Robert Jackson: *pages 15, 48 top and 53.*
Lowrance Electronics: *page 74.*
Mercury Marine: *page 124.*
George Richey: *page 90.*
Dick Swan: *pages 10, 82 and 104.*
All other photographs are by the author.